The London Midland & Scottish Railway
A century and a half of progress
LMS 150
Patrick Whitehouse & David St John Thomas

The London Midland & Scottish Railway
A century and a half of progress
LMS 150
Patrick Whitehouse & David St John Thomas

David & Charles

A DAVID & CHARLES BOOK

Hardback edition first published 1987
Reprinted 1991, 1998
Paperback edition published 2002

Distributed in North America
by F&W Publications, Inc.

ISBN 0 7153 1378 9

Printed in China by
Hong Kong Graphics & Printing Ltd
for David & Charles
Brunel House   Newton Abbot   Devon

Frontispiece: The classic LMS express of the 1930s. Royal Scot class 4-6-0 No 6130 The West Yorkshire Regiment *of Edge Hill shed climbs through the deep sandstone cutting and tunnels between Liverpool Lime Street and Edge Hill with a train for Euston in 1939.*

Title page: Cup Final Excursion. Excursions were more than just ex-public timetable trains. They were often the only means of transport to the seaside, London and for sporting occasions (cheaply at that) for the non-car owning public, those days the great majority. Patriot class 4-6-0 No 5532 Illustrious *of Bushbury shed passes Headstone Lane in 1938 with an up Cup Final excursion – football hooligans just did not exist in those bad old days.*

Above: The Welshman. One of the named trains of the 1930s this express joined Euston with the holiday resorts of the North Wales coast. Before the introduction of Stanier's new locomotives it was usually the preserve of an ex-LNWR Claughton – indeed one of the last regular trains for the class over this section. The engine is No 5968 John O'Groat *grimy and in black livery although the class would have been red up until 1928. Beyond the station a tall LNWR bracket signal is in its off position for a down fast train – Colwyn Bay was the beginning of a four track section to Llandudno Junction. Note the footpath alongside the track and the red-painted distant signal arms.*

CONTENTS

FOREWORD

This book is a close and affectionate look at one of the great railway companies of the past, the London Midland & Scottish Railway. As General Manager of the London Midland Region of British Railways I suppose that I come as close as anybody to being able to claim that inheritance today. But while there is an unbroken chain with the past, and railway managers today would claim to be just as forward looking in their outlook as their illustrious predecessors, I am aware that many readers would look back on the LMS as the golden era of steam railways.

The LMS was quite simply the most important railway of its day. It linked the capital city with the major connurbations and industrial heartlands of the West Midlands and the North West, and on to Scotland. These are key routes, the very core and foundation of the passenger and freight railways of the United Kingdom. The main line from Euston is still of central importance, mirroring the whole of Britain.

The Region still covers most of England west of the Pennines. It has a greater route mileage than any other part of the network. It is also extremely rich in engineering achievements of the highest quality. The determination and boldness of the early pioneers is truly admirable. Yet the return on capital was often elusive. Today the viaducts, tunnels, bridges, stations, and trackwork stand as monuments to men of vision who were at the leading edge of industrial and social progress in their day.

I joined the LMR in Liverpool shortly after nationalisation. Even then the loyalty to the LMS was qualified for many by personal identification with pre-grouping companies. This ability of railwaymen to identify with the past is a source of strength – and a possible weakness. It is a strength in that it is a focus of legitimate pride in genuine achievement. It is a weakness only if it blinds us to the reality of current issues and the need to identify tomorrow's opportunities as part of today's task.

The management task for the LMS was to create a corporate loyalty that transcended the constituent companies. The affection with which we now recall the LMS is a measure of the achievement. Today there are of course, still many reminders of achievements and which we see as part of our heritage. Sometimes it is revealed in elegant silverware, such as the cups that we award for first aid competitions or sporting events. Sometimes it comes to light as a fine logo, such as the one in the booking hall at Bangor. There are also many family connections: for example, one of our senior traction engineers is a 'Stanier' – a grandson of the famous locomotive engineer who gave us those wonderful 'Pacifics' which for many settled the issue of locomotive superiority for a generation.

This book inevitably recalls brave attempts to keep railways competitive through engineering achievement. Not all the ideas could succeed, but they were part of a conscious policy to compete and to operate profitably. Today the traffic patterns and the competitive climate have changed. We manage within a new style, yet within our structure of business management we have similar objectives to the LMS. We are seeking still innovation as a means of providing value for money to our customers, and creating profits for our commercial services.

Perhaps in reading this book you will think of those who created history in their quest to make the railway a business success. I do not believe railwaymen today are so very different in seeking that same fulfilment which comes from providing good customer service. This book too is a reminder that railways and its workforce can adapt and change. I rather hope, and secretly believe, that future generations will look back on today's railway with something of the same nostalgia that is still reserved for the LMS. But that will be another book. I hope it will be as interesting as this.

Cyril Bleasdale,
General Manager, London Midland Region, BR

1
INTRODUCTION

Operator of some of the world's most famous, fastest and certainly most comfortable express trains, of prestigious 'club trains' for the cream of Manchester's commuters, a miscellany of unconnected and different electric systems, each a pioneer effort, express goods trains (some carrying containers which marked the birth of what decades later has developed into the Freightliner business) making ever longer non-stop runs; but also of branch lines with a single daily service and whose last evening train completed its run only if sufficient passengers presented themselves (or enough fares were paid for), of a Highland line with so sparse a service that passengers were carried in goods guards' vans and of countless branches where time stood still it seemed throughout the Grouping years, commuter and excursion trains a few still using six-wheeled coaches whose interiors were so dirty that discriminating passengers sat on a cloth or newspaper, of London-bound coal trains that averaged barely 20mph and spent time queueing in the permissive block sections; provider of Britain's most luxurious holidays but also of the greatest number of bargain excursions to the seaside and sporting events; technical innovator in many fields yet giving its signalmen at its headquarters station, London Euston, nothing more than a blackboard and piece of chalk to tell which platforms were occupied, empty stock being loose shunted; builder of the finest express locomotives and passenger coaches but retainer of many inherited oddities and much out-dated equipment; the country's largest employer after the Post Office, sufficiently interested in training to create the first college for railwaymen yet not able to key up its executives so well that they could prevent imports from another system eventually dominating theirs after nationalisation.

The LMS. A system of enormous size and complexity – and everlasting paradoxes. The world's largest transport organisation, the Empire's largest commercial undertaking, it was not only by far the largest of Britain's four railways between 1923 and nationalisation at the end of 1947 but also the Empire's largest hotel chain, and had an involvement in every kind of industrial activity including of course land development and shipping, bus and air services.

The LMS. It was an essential part of Britain's fabric, the subject of music hall jokes and songs (especially about Crewe), and its traffic receipts were often regarded as the best yardstick of the state of the economy.

From Shoeburyness at the mouth of the Thames and Richmond higher up the river to Swansea and up many of the South Wales valleys,

Quotes of the Line

'I should like to think that the best Goods Agent in Derby would have something to learn from the best Goods Agent in Ross & Cromarty.'
Sir Josiah Stamp (as he then was) at the laying of the foundation stone of the School of Transport, Derby, 1937.

'Did you know that I've now got twins?'
Mr David Evans, stationmaster Manchester London road taking charge of both parts on the retirement of the LNE station master.

We flogged her so hard up the Peak that when we went into Dove Holes tunnel the water was out of sight below the bottom nut [of the gauge glass]. I could only pray that the crown of the firebox would be covered and we should get out of the tunnel without exploding.'
Locomotive inspector on the St Pancras–Manchester dynamometer car trial in April 1937, preceding that year's accelerations.

from the Midlands and through the industrial heartlands of the North including much of the West Riding to the slate villages and quarries of North Wales, from the industrial Cumberland coast and along the industrial and tourist Ayrshire coast to greater Glasgow and almost throughout the Lowlands, the LMS carried armies of people to and from their daily work. It is indeed always as a working and workmen's railway that the LMS will be chiefly remembered. Liverpool Street and Waterloo might be quoted as the stations with the largest morning inflows, but Fenchurch Street, Birmingham New Street, Manchester Victoria, and Glasgow Central were not merely taxed to the limit and beyond but exuded such crowds as to bring the streets outside to a virtual standstill – and moreover almost all with steam traction.

Many more travelled by the old workmen's tickets, ten or twelve seats to a compartment, than ever travelled on one of the famous expresses out of Euston or St Pancras. The names on the destination boards not merely remained just names to the vast majority who saw them, but there was no expectation or even wish to visit them. Bournemouth would not have seemed much handier or more relevant than New York to colliers of the West Riding, or Inverness to the commuters of Watford. And so, though much of the vast system was linked by prestigious expresses, passenger-wise the LMS was in reality more a series of different railways. Especially in the Midlands and North, it included numerous lines between two major towns provided with six to a dozen daily mainly all-stations trains, usually of non-corridor coaches. Though some passengers would transfer to another service, some indeed going on to London, Manchester or even the Lakes or Glasgow, nearly everywhere the strictly local demand dominated.

And here is one of the paradoxes. As we shall see, the LMS went in for standardisation; indeed standardisation almost became a religion. And by the end of the company's existence, there was indeed a great commonality; smell and sound would quickly have told even the blind railway-minded person that he was on LMS territory. Yet the LMS in the Highlands was quite different from that in the Lowlands; the extensive systems in South Wales might almost have been on a different continent from that along the North Wales coast; and there was strong individuality even in the muck of the Black Country, Workington and Dalmellington. Though the way in which stations were (or were not) maintained and trains operated became ever more standardised, regional individuality was helped by a more flexible approach to timetabling than for example used by the Great Western.

The train services indeed changed frequently, reflecting the seasons, state of the economy and prosperity of individual local industries, sometimes the shortness of coal, and in the war and postwar years which account for nearly a third of the LMS's life many other shortages too. Late night services for picture-goers, lunch-time extras from market towns on early closing days and mid-morning semi-fasts for shoppers to them, through trains to and from Blackpool and Llandudno, trains which started or terminated half or two thirds the way along a branch line . . . there was always something different, and the arrival of the new

Adaptation. The 4.15pm St Pancras to Manchester Central near Elstree hauled by LMS three-cylinder compound No 1059. The photograph was taken during the prolonged coal strike of 1926 and shows the locomotive fitted for oil firing. The load appears to be above that normally allowed for class 4 locomotives; the normal limit may have been relaxed as train services were curtailed during the strike.

The Byrom Cup was awarded annually, commencing in 1935, to the Division winning the Express Passenger Train Competition for the best punctuality record during the previous year. (The Central Division won the cup three years running in 1936, 1937 and 1938). Mr Byrom is seated on the left. The location appears to be the senior mess or one of the private offices on Euston station and not the shareholders meeting room, the usual venue. Lord Stamp presents the cup.

Native and newcomer. Inverness station c1935 with a double headed train about to leave for the south. The pilot is ex-HR Castle class LMS No 14690 Dalcross Castle while the train engine is a brand new Stanier Class 5 4-6-0. The leading van is ex-Highland with the second vehicle a former Pullman restaurant car purchased by the LMS in 1933 and repainted in maroon.

timetable invariably started discussion about new or reduced possibilities, in England, Wales, Scotland and on the LMS owned Northern Counties Committee in Ulster.

Though even in these pages it will be difficult to resist the temptation of highlighting the great express developments, most of the passenger business was pretty dull. The only break in monotony for most of its regular customers was a day or two by the sea. Compared with the other three main railways, the LMS had little English coastline and much of that was industrialised. It did however have the jewel in the crown: Blackpool. Advertised and non-advertised trains started at an incredible range of Lancashire, West Riding and other main and branch line stations. The trains themselves were for the most part the humdrum, largely non-corridor stock used on other days to take people to and from work. But there was nothing ordinary about the regulation of the traffic or the excitement on board as the engine whistled for the final signal into one of Blackpool's three great stations. Discomfort for those who had drunk too much when the return journey was delayed . . . yes, that was familiar enough and occasionally led to desperate situations and desperate remedies!

Though Blackpool was the most convenient choice for the largest concentration of population and its attractions, and cheap fares steadily drew people from further away, so that mixed with those going to work by the filthy two-coach non-corridor local from Dudley to Dudley Port (High Level) might be a handful lucky enough to have the day off. Morecambe also expanded on the back of the railway's ever more generous service. The Lakes and Cumbrian Coast normally attracted fewer and better-to-do visitors but on holiday weekends nearly a thousand souls were wafted for a few bob from almost anywhere between Rugby and Glasgow.

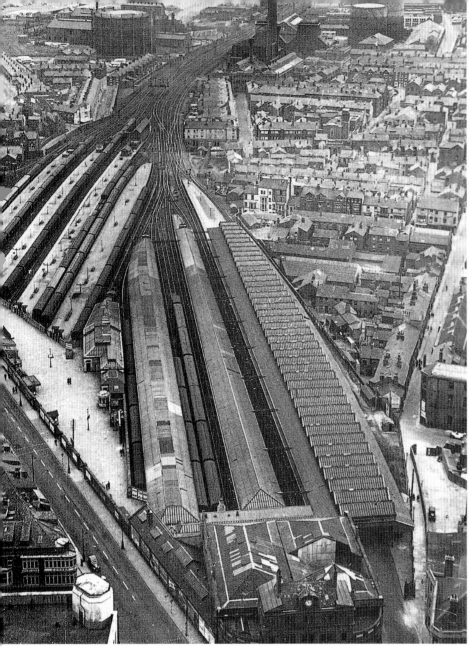

Excursionists paradise. Blackpool Central station seen from the Tower. The main station is in the centre of the picture and was used throughout the year; the eight excursion platforms are to the left. The station was closed on 2 November 1964 and now all this is swept away with a car park. The remaining rail traffic to Blackpool uses the North station apart from an hourly service of dmus from Kirkham to Blackpool South.

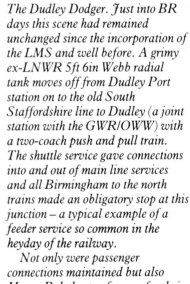

The Dudley Dodger. Just into BR days this scene had remained unchanged since the incorporation of the LMS and well before. A grimy ex-LNWR 5ft 6in Webb radial tank moves off from Dudley Port station on to the old South Staffordshire line to Dudley (a joint station with the GWR/OWW) with a two-coach push and pull train. The shuttle service gave connections into and out of main line services and all Birmingham to the north trains made an obligatory stop at this junction – a typical example of a feeder service so common in the heyday of the railway.

Not only were passenger connections maintained but also Messrs Palethorpe, famous for their sausages and pies sent most of their long distance traffic by rail using their own special insulated vans with a packet of sausages as their trade mark. Their vans were shunted by the Dudley Dodger in quiet periods and attached to main line services as required.

Private Train
Considerable interest has been aroused by the Prime Minister's journey from Dunrobin, the Duke of Sutherland's private railway station on the LMS to Inverness behind the private engine belonging to the Duke.

Under an old right dating from the promotion and construction of the railway, the Dukes of Sutherland are entitled to run a private train between Inverness and Wick, subject to the railway company's rules and regulations, and this privilege was exercised on the occasion of the Prime Minister's recent journey from Dunrobin Castle to London. The engine used belongs to the Duke. It is an 0-4-4T built by Sharp Stewart & Co's Atlas Works about 1895 and is the second private engine owned by the Dukes of Sutherland, the previous one, *Dunrobin* having been sold to the Highland Railway. It became No 118A on that line, and was broken up in 1923.

The present engine is stated to have been in steam only about three times during the past 15 years. The special train it hauled was run subject to a speed restriction of 30mph, the time allowed for the 86 miles from Dunrobin to Inverness being 3½ hours.

A tablet fixed in the cab of the engine bears the names of past distinguished passengers of the train.
Meccano Magazine, June 1938.

Llandudno was the LMS's second most important resort, again served by through trains to and from an incredibly wide range of Midland and Northern cities – and towns that the Welsh would not even have heard of. Rhyl and indeed the whole North Wales Coast, and even the Cambrian Coast by through train via Bangor and Afonwen, steadily became more popular under the LMS – and enjoyed a second explosion of business in the company's few postwar years.

Glasgow, like Birmingham, Manchester and Liverpool, offered regular and excursion trains to just about everywhere within 150 miles range, sometimes further, but while there was a steady increase in those basing themselves on Oban or taking a day trip south of the border, this was still the age of mass-carryings to the Clyde Coast and along it by steamer. Large though the LMS was, and distant though its control from London, no points were lost in the competitive business between the rival railway fleets and Glaswegians enjoyed some of the best tourist bargains in the land.

Among the thousands sailing to Rothesay there would have been few who had even begun to explore their own country, the tourist emphasis on the Highland line to Inverness being English gentry up for the sport. London to Inverness still seemed an awfully long journey and only a very few could afford it. But like the rest of the LMS, the former Highland routes were mainly concerned with indigenous local movements, journeys for shopping, education, family reunions or to take a job away (but not that far) from home. So the 'shorts' from Tain still brought as many passengers into Inverness as the through services from Wick.

Depot modernisation. The LMS embarked upon a programme of modernisation of engine sheds and their facilities in the 1930s, equipping many with mechanical coaling and ash disposal plants. This picture shows ashes, which had been removed from locomotives into the pit on the left, being tipped from a skip into a waiting wagon. Behind is a concrete mechanical coaling plant. The photograph was taken at Toton on 9 June 1932.

The interim years. A mid-1930s picture showing the beginnings of modernisation. The scene is Liverpool Edge Hill and the train London bound. It is headed by a three-cylinder Patriot (Baby Scot) class 4-6-0 No 5527 Southport of 8A (Edge Hill) shed and apart from the second and third coaches is made up of the new steel-sided corridor stock which was extremely modern and comfortable – seating only six in the third class with arm rests. The engine is a nominal rebuild of an LNWR Claughton but in truth a replacement; an interim measure before the coming of Stanier's revolution.

In the late 1930s there were only two LMS day-time services from Glasgow to London at ordinary fares. The majority of Scottish and north of England men who came to London in the twenties and thirties did so by excursion for a sporting event. Football and rugby excursions did appear to give the system more coherence, and with at least one northern team invariably in the Cup Final at Wembley, the LMS carried a substantial part of such business – along with again more regional services for the ever increasing flower and dog shows, band and other competitions.

Mail, parcels and goodswise, the system was altogether more integrated. There were still enormous tonnages of coal, steel and other minerals carried only a few miles to port, power station or other works, and Scotland and Wales were still substantially loyal to their own brews, but national brands of foods, soaps and toiletries were already universally used. And as every schoolboy was taught, the goods traffic was more important, more profitable than the passenger. Goods and mineral trains were everywhere. Almost any hill you climbed would show you at least one engine shunting away during working hours; on most journeys you saw as many goods as passenger trains, albeit many of them were at a standstill waiting signals, taking water, changing crews, or about to shunt. The pall of smoke was almost continuous over the large marshalling yards of Carlisle or the major collieries of the East Midlands or the shipyards of Barrow – as it was over locomotive depots and works, depressing property values around. But then memories of catching LMS trains at St Albans or Rochdale, Chesterfield or Bedford, inevitably include fog, which the railway both helped create and suffered from, especially from the point of view of safety. Britain still had a coal economy and the LMS was a king pin in it.

The collieries' private-owner wagons were marshalled in their thousands; industrialists and even private householders still ordered their fuel by name, so that the average distances covered were much

Saving Water

When a pick-up scoop plunged through the water in a trough, the water level built up at the sides and was lowered in the middle. The result was spillage over the sides of the trough and reduced depth from which to collect. LMS engineers overcame the difficulty by designing a simple vane attachment which was lowered with the scoop. Two vertical vanes placed 1ft 4in in front of the scoop projected down into the water and were angled to throw water inwards so that it heaped up at the centre of the trough while the level at the sides was lowered. Not only did this type of deflector reduce wastage, but it increased the amount of water picked up. If the scoop was kept down for the whole length of the trough about 400gal of water was saved at each operation. It was estimated that fitting the deflector to all locomotives with pick-up scoops would reduce the quantity of water supplied to troughs by 20 per cent.

greater than in our enlightened age when coal is just coal. Much of the LMS's best talent was indeed devoted to buying the best and most appropriate coal for itself, as much of its research effort was devoted to burning the stuff more economically in the locomotive firebox. The company consumed six and a half million tons annually, giving it was said employment to 26,500 miners.

The substantial disappearance of the coal and other heavy mineral traffic is undoubtedly what one notices most when retracing boyhood ground. The Midland line up from St Pancras will always seem uncannily quiet without the constant passage of coal trains up and empties down drawn by a kaleidoscope of locomotives including until the end pre-Grouping machines and of course the not particularly successful Garratt articulateds. Likewise the long detour round the Cumbrian Coast seems like Hamlet without the ghost now that the coal and ore trains have gone. But even more is this true of substantial parts of the Lancashire system, where today's diesel multiple-unit endlessly passes abandoned yards, colliery sidings, narrowed formations and the stubs of countless routes that have disappeared along with their mineral traffic.

Pride of the Line. In its prestigious blue and silver livery the Coronation Scot storms up Shap in the summer of 1939. The locomotive is No 6222 Queen Mary, *one of the new Stanier streamlined Pacifics and the stock a specially produced set for this crack train, the rival to the LNER's* Coronation *which also used blue as its theme colour. This evocative scene has come from the camera of the then Rev (later Bishop) Eric Treacy, one of the finest ever recorders of the LMS.*

A system of enormous size and complexity, involved in every aspect of transport and commerce . . . in sheer size the world's greatest and never slow to boast of its importance and achievements. 'The finest permanent way in the world,' shouted the LMS posters like their LNW predecessors. 'The LMS anticipates the needs of modern industry even before such needs arise,' stated an advertisement in the centenary issue of *The Times*. Says another: 'Year in, year out, day in, day out, LMS Express Trains provide a superb service of communication to all parts of Great Britain . . . Aboard these graceful shining hotels on wheels, passengers recline and read in cosy comfort, eat unhurriedly, sleep peacefully, or move about the spacious corridors . . . The menus are attractive and varied, and the meals served with celerity and efficiency.' Again: 'Today the LMS is not merely a railway company, it is a comprehensive transport system in itself; it employs every form of transport in its endeavour to provide efficient service. The history of the last hundred years is inevitably bound up with the railways now forming part of this great group; but it is equally certain that when the history of our times comes to be written the LMS will earn an important place in the story.'

And so it does. Here, as the LMS made its centenary out of the opening of the first trunk railway, from London to Birmingham, we celebrate not merely 150 years of inter-city out of the capital but everything that went into the making, shaping and ultimate achievements (tempered with a few surprising failures) of Britain's most important railway. Inevitably the task is somewhat harder, or at least less well defined, than it was for GWR 150, but that makes it the more challenging.

For the uninitiated, while the Great Western retained its identity in the amalgamations that created the Big Four of the Grouping era from 1923 until nationalisation, the others were new creations made up at least to some extent of former rivals. The LMS was by far the largest and geographically most widely flung, with systems plural across the Irish Sea as well as in England, Scotland and Wales, and its early days were beset with the problems of bringing the former rivals under one management. In England that especially meant making the former London & North Western and Midland railways, their staffs and operating practices, live together. In the North the Lancashire & Yorkshire with its closely-woven network of short and medium distance routes mainly cutting east-west across the country and the highly independent North Staffordshire and the Furness were among those that had to be digested, although the LNW and L&Y had already amalgamated twelve months before the Grouping. In Scotland the arch rivals, the Caledonian and the Glasgow & South Western, were flung together, and men of that colourful institution the Highland Railway found themselves suddenly governed from Glasgow or even London instead of Inverness.

Some critics allege that the LMS never totally succeeded in putting it all together, and certainly at the time of the centenary some of the publicity seemed as much directed to giving the company self confidence as attracting new business. 'The Railway Service has to work through thousands of servants touching the millions of the travelling and com-

Boat Trains at St Pancras

Having been absorbed by the Midland in 1912, the system of the former London, Tilbury & Southend Railway came into the LMS Group. Up to 1963 commuters at St Pancras saw Tilbury boat trains in the platforms and postcards of ocean liners on sale at the bookstall. Some sailings were to the Far East and Australia, others to Scandinavia, and for a short time there was a service to Dunkerque with connecting trains on the Continent. This service was short-lived but at its peak in 1931 four trains awaited the boat from Tilbury. They were: to Basle via Hirson, Metz and Strasbourg with through coach to Lucerne (in 1930 there had been an Interlaken coach); to Paris, non-stop after Dunkerque Ville, with through coach to Paris–Lyon for passengers to PLM stations; to Lille and principal stations to Basle, through coach to Brussels; and to Paris, semi-fast, calling at Lille, Arras and other important intermediate towns. The Tilbury–Dunkerque service was announced in the LMS timetable for May 1927 as 'New Route to the Continent – Night Boat Service by the steamers of the Angleterre–Lorraine–Alsace'. The timetable showed a boat train with restaurant car leaving St Pancras at 10.30pm and conveying through carriages from Manchester and Glasgow. Operations at Tilbury Marine were brisk, for the boat train arrived – behind a tank locomotive – at 11.15pm and the ship was scheduled to sail at 11.30. The service was withdrawn in the early 1930s.

The Soap & Towel Brigade

A vital adjunct of LMS passenger traffic was the Hotels & Catering Service, controlled on behalf of the LMS management by Arthur Towle, distinguished grandson of the innovator of MR catering services from 1871, Sir William Towle. In 1938 the LMS activity comprised nearly 30 hotels, over 200 dining and kitchen cars (the modern version of the latter being able to serve over 200 main meals at a sitting), and providing over four million meals annually, mostly on the well-known Midland basis of 'eating at your seat'. The LMS always showed a book surplus from the hotels and refreshments activity, which just prior to World War II employed 8,000 people (including an entertainments manager) and grossed over £3 million receipts per annum, from 50 million customers.

Grouping brought about a considerable extension of restaurant cars, new building enabling older kitchen-dining cars of both LNWR and MR designs to be released elsewhere, though a 42-tons ex LNWR diner tended to look a bit odd when marshalled into a six-coach train over the Somerset & Dorset Joint!

Not least among the numerous functionaries who looked after the welfare of LMS passengers were the divisional soap and towel inspectors (they also looked after toilet paper, tactfully omitted from their job specification). They were the front-line troops of the divisional superintendents of operation at Derby, Crewe etc in ensuring adequacy of supply and distribution, while at the same time checking on economical issue. A general instruction issued from Derby in 1935 sternly required the 'instant withdrawal' of any towels currently in use in inspectors' and foremens' offices, signal-boxes and even platelayers' cabins.

mercial public at hundreds of different points,' wrote Lord Stamp, the company's chairman with an emphasis quite different from that of the other systems. 'It has to preserve uniformity of treatment and yet keep individuality, spontaneity and resourcefulness . . . with a staff so scattered geographically and so diversified in function, organisation . . . has to achieve cohesion and *esprit de corps*.'

Organisation was a word ever used by the LMS lingo, and not surprisingly so. Sir William Wood, later to become head man, once realistically let slip that the LMS was too large for effective management. It had no precedent, least of all in Britain. There had indeed been considerable doubt about its creation, alternative plans including a Big Six instead of four, Scotland having its own railway and another being created basically out of an amalgamation of the Midland and Great Central in a wedge between the LMS and LNER. There were two objections to this: the railways were planned to pay their way and serve their shareholders and there had to be doubts about the success of an all-Scotland railway; and yet the railways were still supposed to compete between themselves, so penetrating lines such as the LMS into South Wales were seen as a good thing, and there would have been genuine fears that Scotland's economy would have suffered deprived of railway competition. Another difficulty was the transfer of assets from one private company to another.

So an improbable if not impossible animal was born, a system of about 7,000 miles or 19,000 single-track miles with around a quarter of a million employees serving every industrial region of the United Kingdom except the North East and including joint lines and running powers reaching every coastline of all four countries. It penetrated 32 of England's 40 counties. Geographically it made no sense at all. It embraced three of the four trans-Pennine routes, an isolated North Western inheritance as well as the busiest system and joint ownership of the largest narrow-gauge one across the Irish Sea, three rival hotels in Liverpool, and an incredibly dense network of Lancashire lines. In South Wales there were the separate North Western and Midland routes deep into Great Western territory to integrate into some kind of entity, while despite the enormity of the system there were few major cities without competition from one of the other Big Four.

Inter-city routes, locomotive works, docks, marshalling yards, hotels . . . they were all put together as an arbitrary act of merger following their previous owners' varying policies of aggression, idiosyncrasy and merger. The hotel chain was as numerous as that operated by the whole of British Rail before privatisation and ranged from the best resort and provincial city centre hotels, world renowned as the ads claimed, to the humble playthings of smaller companies. Many had the telegraphic

Opposite
Air Raid damage. Manchester Exchange station on 22 December 1940 showing damage to the structure, platform No 1 and the refreshment rooms – a sad and dismal approach to Christmas. The LMS along with the other companies suffered major damage from German marauders but the system kept the trains rolling.

'Stop-Over' Facilities
The London Midland and Scottish Railway has arranged a comprehensive programme of 'Stop-over' facilities. American passengers, when travelling between Liverpool and London (Euston) or between Windermere (Lake District) and London (Euston), may break their journey at the following places: – Chester, Leamington for Warwick and Stratford-on-Avon, Northampton for the Washington Country, and Bletchley for Oxford and Cambridge.

Holders of Through Tickets between Liverpool and London (St. Pancras) may break their journey at Matlock or Matlock Bath; Bakewell or Rowsley for Haddon Hall and Chatsworth; Miller's Dale for Eyam, Buxton, Tideswell, and the Derbyshire Dales, and certain other stations including Manchester and Derby.

Holders of Through Tickets between Glasgow (St Enoch) and London (St Pancras) – 'The Burns Route' – are allowed to stop over at any station in Scotland on the direct route via Carlisle, Appleby (for Penrith and the Lake District) and certain other stations.

STAY AT LMS HOTELS	
LONDON	Euston Hotel
BIRMINGHAM	Queen's Hotel
BRADFORD	Midland Hotel
CREWE	Crewe Arms Hotel
DERBY	Midland Hotel
FURNESS ABBEY	Furness Abbey Hotel
HOLYHEAD	Station Hotel
LEEDS	Queen's Hotel
LIVERPOOL	Adelphi Hotel
	Exchange Hotel
MANCHESTER	Midland Hotel
MORECAMBE	Midland Hotel
PRESTON	Park Hotel
STOKE-ON-TRENT	North Stafford Hotel
STRATFORD-UPON-AVON	Welcombe Hotel
AYR	Station Hotel
DORNOCH (a)	Dornoch Hotel
DUMFRIES	Station Hotel
EDINBURGH	Caledonian Hotel
GLASGOW	Central Hotel
	St. Enoch Hotel
GLENEAGLES (b)	Gleneagles Hotel
INVERNESS	Station Hotel
KYLE OF LOCHALSH	Lochalsh Hotel
STRATHPEFFER (a)	Highland Hotel
TURNBERRY	Turnberry Hotel
BELFAST	Midland Station Hotel
LARNE (c)	Laharna Hotel
PORTRUSH	Northern Counties Hotel
GREENORE	Greenore Hotel (With G.N. (I) Co.)

(a) Open May to September   (b) Open Easter to November   (c) Open June to September

Map of LMS hotels.

17

Last LMS Stranraer Road Winter

The snowstorm of Wednesday, 12 March 1947, came on with great suddenness. At 5pm there were but wandering flakes of snow, but by 7 o'clock the little station of Glenwhilly, in North Wigtownshire, was cowering beneath a blizzard that was to make history. In the five railwaymen's cottages which form the little outpost away in the heart of the great moor there were anxious hearts as the gale shrieked and the drifts mounted up. At 7.53pm out of the smother to the North came the 5.10pm express from Glasgow. '5X' 4-6-0 No 5728 *Defiance* had a load of four corridor coaches only, but its Stranraer crew, Driver George Hannay and Fireman Henry Lightbody, had had a grim struggle getting her over the dreaded Chirmorie summit. And now they could not get any further, for the section ahead was occupied by the north-bound freight for Glasgow, which had long since left New Luce, and which was still battling away in the blizzard. An hour the 5.10 lay there in the drive of the storm, waiting for the freight to arrive; 70 minutes, 80; then came word from New Luce that the freight was back there. It had failed to get through the drifts, and now a snow-plough was essential before the 5.10 could attempt the passage. Snow-ploughs were at a premium, for Scotland had lent generously to Northern England. It was 11 o'clock before a plough got south to Glenwhilly and drove on into the New Luce section; at two minutes to midnight New Luce gave out-of-section for the plough. At 12.3am the 5.10 resumed its journey.

Anxiously the Glenwhilly signalman watched his clock. Eight minutes should have taken her down the 4½ miles to New Luce, but eight minutes went by, 15, half-an-hour, three-quarters,

continued opposite

address of BESTOTEL. Stations and engine sheds of the former rivals sometimes faced each other literally across the street, yet even had there been the desire there was no way in which they could (to use a word happily not then known) be rationalised.

The thing would have been an act of near madness even without taking into account a series of depressing factors. The railways had taken a serious battering through heavy usage and little maintainance during the First World War and its immediate aftermath, labour relations were low, and road competition was rising dramatically. True, all the Big Four suffered, but clearly the company facing the greatest administrative upheaval was going to be knocked hardest. Then there was the emnity between the constituents to settle . . . and in practice that is what dissipated much of the initial energy and enthusiasm.

The public had no immediate respect for the LMS. Why should it? There was not the attraction of state ownership that nationalisation offered, yet some of the old companies now lost had been much loved. Staff loyal to their old employers liked the newcomer even less, fearing change and even loss of job, though it was perhaps one of the LMS's less successful features that it achieved little to increase productivity in manpower as opposed to machinery.

Though as different as chalk from cheese, the North Western and the Midland each had loyal bands of staff, customers and even railway enthusiasts. The North Western was the 'premier line' running heavy trains such as the 'Corridor' for Scotland and serving North Wales, Manchester, Liverpool and many other places from Euston. It of course included Stephenson's magnificent London & Birmingham, of a quality matching Brunel's Great Western to Bristol. The West Coast main line and associated routes had pioneered water troughs, exchanging mail at speed, and much more. They were also early in the field with corridor trains. Proud of its history and making full use of its excellent routes, the North Western was ever commercially aggressive and remarkably it reached every major English and Welsh industrial region – even to Tyneside. It was both autocratic and gentlemanly in a patriarchal manner; its staff were expected to obey, but that especially meant being good mannered – and going to war to serve your country. That the Midland element substantially dominated the emergent LMS was due perhaps in part that fewer of its executives and staff had seen military service. The Midland was altogether harsher, more self-motivated, even selfish, but of course had some endearing characteristics, notably the comfort of its express passenger rolling stock. In locomotive matters it was exactly the opposite of the North Western. The Midland was for frequent, light-weight trains, double-headed at a touch of a hat.

After amalgamation, Midland men dominated especially in locomotive matters. Many are the stories of arguments and upsets with North Western stalwarts, especially when they were instructed to double head trains that one of *their* machines was perfectly capable of handling on its own. Railways have always stirred passions, and many a career and heart was broken by earlier amalgamation and change of practice. But the agony caused by the creation of the LMS was of a totally new order – and

18

Semi-fast from London. Watford Junction station from the north footbridge (removed before electrification in 1964) with ex LNWR Prince of Wales class 4-6-0 No 25752 entering with a Euston to Bletchley limited stop train on 12 September 1946. Stafford and Bletchley sheds were the last homes for the Princes with 25752 surviving until 1949. At that time Bletchley had nine of the class used for these semi fasts and over the Oxford branch. An interesting sign of the times and soon to disappear are the private owner wagons on the far left. The now collectable advertisements include Camp and Virol, while the latter malt extract for children is also advertised on enamel signs alongside Palethorpes sausages, most of which were delivered by rail at this time from the factory at Dudley Port.

possibly could be said to have spelt the beginning of the end for those who wished to take pride in the railway way of life. People were bound to be hurt on the grand scale as traditions and resources were cast aside as we have seen happen on a larger scale under nationalisation. Control seemed impossibly remote, and increasingly groups of men looked inward as they grumbled among themselves and lacked a real voice.

Things were worse in Scotland. The pride of the Highland, strong though it had been, became visibly cracked once Inverness men had the new black LMS livery cast upon them. The Caledonian and Glasgow & South Western fared little better, because the vast new business instinctively brought in an English way. There was of course a head man in Scotland and Wales had some local control, but the emphasis was strongly on centralisation and standardisation. The smaller the company, in a sense the more it had to lose. Great was the grief on that small but busy little system, the Furness Railway. Some kind of merger was perhaps inevitable, but to become so lost in such a vast machine . . . and with only a single director on the new board.

In many ways there was little change either at the start or throughout the LMS era. A substantial proportion of withdrawals of passenger services in the Grouping era was on the LMS, and had it not been for the 1939–45 war there would undoubtedly have been at least a mini-Beeching. But in comparison to the total system, the losses were small, and the number of people inconvenienced minute. Little rationalisation was attempted, only a handful of stations being closed through the diversion of trains into that of a former rival. Practically the most significant advantage from the amalgamation was the freedom to reroute Anglo-Scottish traffic from the saturated North Western Shap line to the Midland's 'long drag' of the Settle & Carlisle, which now handled several

continued
and still no sign of her. It was just on 1am when a burly, snow-shrouded figure plunged in out of the storm. It was Guard John Wright, of Stranraer. The 5.10 was stuck fast in a drift half-a-mile south of Glenwhilly.

That was bad, but Guard Wright reported the train well-heated and lighted, and in his van a consignment of foodstuffs for the NAAFI canteens. Authority was given to issue these to the passengers, and Big Jock tramped resolutely back to his charge. Rations were doled out and the 57 passengers settled down in reasonable comfort in their snowy prison. All night the driver and fireman remained on the engine and kept the heating going.

Dawn broke on a Thursday of screaming gale and snow which never ceased to whirl and drift. Stationmaster R. Blackwood of Glenwhilly had mobilised his limited forces and at 7am a supply of hot tea was carried perilously up to the half-buried train. Thrice during the day these devoted car-
continued overleaf

continued

riers made their terrible journey, and with one such party Fireman Lightbody returned to the station with his tablet, collapsing before he got there and having to be carried to the signalbox. By noon came a cruel moment when the engine water supply gave out. The fire had to be thrown out and the steam heating was finished. Towards night a new peril developed, when the train windows began to crack with the pressure of the snow. One caved in, and two passengers were cut rather badly. Thursday night closed grimly in. The train was deathly cold; the lights had gone out. Away to the North a relief plough was 10 miles off, stuck fast between Pinwherry and Barrhill, while to the South the plough had not even reached New Luce.

With Friday came an easing, the storm ceased, and even a spark of sun came out. No time was lost. Fires were built up in Glenwhilly stationmaster's house, in the booking office, waiting room, and in a surfaceman's hut. Then the 57 passengers were escorted down to the station, where, in shelter and warmth, the big-hearted folks of Glenwhilly tended and fed them. But Thursday is ration day, no supplies had arrived, and their own larders were getting empty. Fuel was short, too, and a sledge expedition had to be made to No 5728's tender for replenishment.

About 5 o'clock on Friday afternoon came the first contact with the outer world. A Stranraer guard, Harry Rice, walked in from the South and reported that a plough and a train of workers had won through to New Luce and that it was possible for fit persons to make their way down. Thirty-two passengers and the three trainmen volunteered to return with him, and Guard Rice led his Pilgrim Band down through the wilderness. A sore

continued opposite

dozen daily goods and mineral trains each way; likewise the G&SW route via Dumfries could be used as a practical alternative to the Caledonian's line over Beattock summit. In passing, the LMS inherited nearly all of the most famous main-line banks, and the provision of banking engines and their depots and in some cases settlements in the isolated places housing the enginemen and their families remained a costly item.

What simply did not happen was the closure of routes to avoid wasteful competition, or even to remove some of that mileage especially in the centre of England that resulted from the second railway mania and probably never justified itself economically throughout its life. The LMS indeed had little idea, even little interest, in what paid and what did not; sophisticated traffic accountancy had to wait until after nationalisation. Except for the glaringly wasteful or unnecessary (such as the narrow-gauge Leek & Manifold), most of the system not merely continued to be operated as though there was some God-given instruction to do so, but along little changed lines. Even when wages became a more significant element in costs, most signalboxes continued to be manned often almost within shouting distance of each other; just a few non-junction boxes were replaced with intermediate block signals. On numerous secondary and branch lines, porters regularly attended trains doing no business. Herein indeed was the tradition that led to the London Midland Region of British Railways for many years forbidding the introduction of unstaffed halts, especially in England, though they had been successfully used on other lines decades before.

Almost all the change was concentrated in two areas: the way the railway managed itself, and its locomotives and rolling stock.

From the start it was decided to go for central management, by function, rather than a divisional devolution. Here the LMS differed from the other two great new companies, though in fairness the make up of both the LNER and Southern systems more readily allowed devolution. Against which, there were feelings that the LMS had not got it right and hints that had it not been nationalised it might have imported a touch of the devolution the LNER successfully used. Indeed, at nationalisation that made it possible to start with separate Eastern and North Eastern Regions a division between London Midland and North Western Regions was also considered but it would have meant such radical change from the LMS pattern that the cost was deemed too great.

While centralisation and standardisation were the key objectives, infighting between the former rivals, especially over locomotive matters, clearly hindered progress. Moreover there was a chronic shortage of express motive power to match the desire for heavier and faster trains. In its supremacy, Euston had also made some silly decisions such as stationing the newly-appointed advertising and publicity officer (of course ex-Midland) in Derby, ideally placed for printers but where in pre-telex days he must have found it as difficult communicating with those operating the former 'premier line' as with the London Press.

But while acknowledging that something had to be done to drive the vast machine more effectively, the railway world was astonished when in 1926 it was announced that in future the LMS was to have not a general manager but an American-style president; and still more astonished that the president-elect was not a railwayman but an economist, an expert on taxation and a director of a large industrial concern. Sir Josiah Charles Stamp, twelve years later to become Baron Stamp of Shortlands, was a very unusual figure in the transport industry. A lifelong teetotaller and non-smoker, a Nonconformist lay preacher, author of economic text-books, he had risen through the ranks of the Inland Revenue to reach City board rooms.

'He was silver-tongued: he could appear before a Royal Commission and put his case magnificently . . . he could go to Parliament . . . he could go where he liked . . . he was an adviser to the government in all sorts of ways,' was how someone who knew him well summed him up.

Not merely was he president but a year later became chairman, the only top railwayman of his age to report to himself. But he brought unequalled power and prestige in the railway world. The detailed job of running the railway was given to the three vice-presidents to whom he gave great scope provided they could express themselves clearly and convincingly when the executive committee met under Stamp's presidency. He could – and did – ask the most penetrating questions. Why, he demanded soon after his arrival at Euston, were so many of the LMS heavy trains double headed while on other lines a single locomotive normally sufficed. He did not like the reply, either.

Not that even he was always far-sighted enough. Once he engaged in a classic row with Frederick Smith, the chief transport executive of the Unilever group who was urging that the railways should concentrate on trainload business between major railheads, with road distribution to outposts. Briefed by orthodox LMS goods managers, Stamp entered an acrimonious debate, on the wrong side. But a railway was ever a railway whose official line was hard to budge.

Euston became steadily stronger, the unrivalled power base. To be sure the company's first general meeting had been held in the Great Hall, the grandest but least-functional room ever bestowed on a British railway station. But now it was taken for granted that publicity and public relations would be conducted from there.

Later general meetings were also held at Euston, though not in the Great Hall. At one of them Stamp demonstrated his instant command of statistics. Answering a shareholder who felt his £15,000 salary was a trifle steep, he said it represented only the cost of one ham sandwich for each shareholder. 'I'm sure that you will not grudge me my ham sandwich.'

Inevitably Stamp imported many business ideas from outside. Some worked well, others less so. The so-called Executive Research Office, intended to reduce administrative costs by reviewing paperwork, rationalising the design of files, and so on, gave the LMS the most wretched quality of paper for correspondence that ever disgraced the image of a great business. That, coupled with the fact that letters were invariably signed in the name of the head of department, made the LMS seem even more aloof. Incidentally departments could be huge and conduct arguments between themselves, both sides of the case being signed in the same head's name.

continued

floundering it must have been, but they got to the relief train before dark, and to Stranraer that night.

On Saturday all hands mustered in a final rescue party. A squad of police, led by the chief constable and a large company of German prisoners, helped the plough and train to within two miles of the block, then walked up to Glenwhilly. The remaining passengers were brought down to the train, German prisoners with stretchers carrying the older passengers over the worst drifts. All had reached Stranraer by afternoon.

Still the ploughing and digging went on. On Sunday the party from the South broke through at last to the snowed-up train. From the North another force was working hard, but in a charge on a hard-packed drift the plough broke, the engine (a Caledonian 0-6-0) became derailed, and, pushed vigorously by a Mogul, travelled some distance off the road. Then the digging out of 5728 and her train was a long and difficult task; it was Thursday, 20 March, before the road was fully open again.

Stranraer had been completely cut off by rail and road for a week. The Glasgow trainmen, stranded in Stranraer, had to return home by *steamer* via Gourock!
David L. Smith, *Stephenson Locomotive Society Journal*, January 1948.

But back to standardisation. Wrote Stamp at the time of the centenary in 1938: 'Organisation for a standard performance is one thing – organisation to absorb, control and utilise a constant stream of change, both human and technical, is far more difficult and important . . . Modernised methods have evolved largely through the medium of an engineering outlook on non-engineering problems . . . During the past five years such methods have been applied for three ends – namely, to reduce costs, to diminish fatigue, and to increasing operating efficiency and service . . . The policy of the company is to overhaul every operation fundamentally in the light of modern engineering and even psychological changes and possibilities.'

Which, he said, brought him to the locomotive. Now LMS critics pointed to the lack of physical change on the ground, other than at locomotive depots where new coaling and other procedures were steadily introduced. Stations, they said were allowed to run down. There was certainly little building or even major overhaul for the size of the operation. There was no grand electrification design that even the Great Western had toyed with, no major progress with signalling. True, just before nationalisation an automatic train control system similar to that later adopted by BR was being experimented with on the Tilbury line, and out of Euston distant semaphores were replaced by colour lights. But with few exceptions everything remained manual, and at many boxes the signalman could still pull off the starting signal to allow a

Track of the future. The LNWR had dubbed itself the Premier Line and certainly its track was some of the finest in the land. The LMS sought to maintain this tradition over all its main lines as shown by this print from a Derby *negative dated 21 December 1936 showing an early investment in flat bottom track at Cricklewood.*

second train into a section before a first had been cleared on the block instrument. Though the death toll on the railways was minor compared to the carnage on busier roads in the thirties and in the black-out during the war, the LMS share of disasters was high and caused much bad publicity. Lessons were slow to be learnt, some of BR's worst accidents including Harrow & Wealdstone were but a continuation of the performances on the LMS lines it inherited.

But productivity at the great locomotive and other works was dramatically improved, ever greater use being made of standard components. As already stated, there was a chronic shortage of express motive power in the 1920s. So desperate was the position that the Great Western was asked if it could hurriedly build fifty Castles, a request not seriously considered by Paddington and Swindon. But it was partly Swindon influence with the appointment of William Stanier from Swindon in 1932 that helped turn the LMS locomotive position round.

In 1938 Stamp was thus able to say: 'The policy of standardisation, coupled with the construction of more powerful types, has been followed, and it has enabled the number of locomotives since the amalgamation to be reduced from 10,396 to 7,688 at the end of 1937 to perform no less work, while the reduction in the number of types has been from 404 to 162, and on the completion of work now authorised the stock will be 7,458 of 132 types, and of course the end is not yet.

'In coming to decisions about the right types on which to concentrate new capital expenditure, the most elaborate and detailed methods of individual working costs have been adopted. A much greater practical use of a given number of locomotives has been obtained by various methods; improvements in repair methods in the shops and interavailability of standardised parts have released them more quickly; improvements in the motive power sheds and stimulation of the worker's interest have recently increased the average number of miles between "breakdowns" to a most remarkable extent.'

Locomotive designs no longer suffered from the company's personality problems; even the Royal Scots of the late 1920s had been largely designed by an outside company, the North British Locomotive in Springburn, Glasgow. Backed by what was probably the Empire's largest engineering capacity in single ownership, Stanier quickly introduced a whole range of new classes: the express-duty Coronation Pacifics, the mixed-traffic Class 5, arguably the best all-round locomotive in the country, the 2-6-4 tanks for suburban work (often recorded at over 80mph on the longer non-stop sprints into Euston or St Pancras), and the heavy-freight 2-8-0 (which at last provided a reliable bulk-mover, enabling many diminutive 0-6-0s to go to a belated valhalla).

But many people remember the LMS most fondly for the vast improvement it wrought in passenger comfort. Its mass-produced standard corridor coaches with their then novel picture windows and small opening top lights and even more novel three-a-side seating with intermediate armrests even in third class made great impact. Some corridor coaches included an odd half compartment, with just one row of seats, and great use was also made of open coaches, the third class mostly

William Stanier

When Sir Harold Hartley invited William Stanier to lunch in October 1931, the need for a new cme was pressing. Under LMS auspices over 2,000 new locomotives had been built, yet less than 400 of them were satisfactorily geared to the needs of the times.

Stanier, at 55, had had many years on the GW to absorb and be conditioned to Swindon lore. His long experience in senior managerial appointments both in the works and in the London district on the running side, had given him total confidence in the rightness of Swindon practice in all its aspects. It had proved its superiority over its rivals for the previous 25 years. So it was not surprising that, as part of his dowry, he should have brought with him a large box of Swindon drawings of its salient features which were handed out to his Euston development team.

That team, with E. S. Cox in charge of design development, R. A. Riddles as locomotive assistant, and others, was living proof of Stanier's judgment of men. After the Crewe–Derby infighting of the previous decade, he could motivate them to work enthusiastically towards a new and sharply-defined objective. He oversaw the rise to eminence of Tom Coleman, who was brought first to take charge of the Crewe drawing office at a particularly busy time and then to Derby as chief draughtsman. Roland Bond, too, was one of those whose career was carefully fostered. As Cox later wrote: 'Stanier was big in stature and in mind, and we quickly realised that he was no doctrinaire . . . he did not immediately or blindly graft Swindon practice as a whole on to his new charge. His other outstanding characteristic was that when he found he had made a mistake . . . he would never seek to cover up bad engineering by worse, but *continued overleaf*

continued

would change direction quickly and completely.'

One would be hard pressed to sum up Stanier more succinctly. He would stroll through the machine and erecting shops of one of his works with a keen eye, interested in any of a wide range of problems and ready with entirely practical advice born of long experience. How horrified must have been the faces at Crewe when, to cure what looked like becoming a recurrent problem of hot trailing truck axleboxes on the first Princess, they were instructed to attach strips of the finest emery cloth to the oil pads and run the engine up to Carlisle and back to get a decent surface finish on the journals; but it worked, and they respected him for it. No humming and hawing, only quick but considered decisions. When the streamlined Pacifics were at an early design stage and looking uncomfortably like a Princess at the front end, Coleman laid a superior scheme for the layout of cylinders and motion on his desk. Stanier immediately recognised its merit and gave it his blessing.

Mistakes he undoubtedly made in the design field; some of them at least sprang from a failure to appreciate the full consequences of LMS organisation which separated the Motive Power Department from the CME, and the looser training and supervision of footplate crews which resulted. But once design mistakes were recognised, they were corrected with all speed, sometimes to the discomfort of the accountants whose number-crunching suffered.

First class dining car breakfast and luncheon menu, 9 February 1938.

having tables for four or in a few cases for four and two for dining, just as in today's first class. First and third class open coaches were normally marshalled either side of a kitchen car or kitchen/diner, and passengers were encouraged to telephone stations for informal (no charge) reservations and to keep their place through the serving of successive meals and light refreshments. The Midland influence was obviously welcome in rolling stock and dining matters. Catering was of a high standard with emphasis on seasonal change. One famous publicity photograph showed the Royal Scot's chefs holding Christmas puddings out of the kitchen car windows on Christmas Day itself, when those without close family connections must have found the service especially congenial.

On suburban lines, though much less comfortable stock of earlier vintage was by no means eliminated, there was a massive introduction of standard non-corridor stock, and here again passengers benefitted from more space. There was an extra foot between compartment divisions compared, for example, with Gresley's suburban stock at neighbouring King's Cross. And LMS seats genuinely related to the human body. Nothing had ever been done like this before.

While the real achievement lay in improved productivity on freight, mineral, parcels and humdrum passenger trains, publicity was naturally concentrated on the new express designs, ultimately the Coronation Scot

---

Breakfast • Luncheon

3/6

Tea - Coffee - Cocoa

Horlicks

•

Grape Fruit

or

Porridge and Cream

•

Fried Small Plaice

or

Kippers

•

Bacon and Eggs

or

Grilled Mushrooms and Bacon

Tomatoes

or

Cold Ham

•

Honey - Jam - Marmalade

•

PLAIN BREAKFAST, 2/6

3/6

Crème Solferino

•

Fried Fillet of Cod

Remoulade Sauce

•

Roast Mutton, Red Currant Jelly

Savoy

Baked and Boiled Potatoes

or

Sauté of Veal Napolitain

•

Manchester Pudding

or

Vanilla Ice

•

Cheese - Salad

•

Coffee, per Cup, 4d

FIRST CLASS   9-2-38

Railway Air Services. Three of the four main line railways were involved in commercial air transport from 1933/4. One route opened on 7 May 1934, was from Plymouth to Liverpool via Haldon (for Torquay), Cardiff and Birmingham. The picture shows the arrival of the first flight from Plymouth at Speke airport, Liverpool.

The official party outnumber the passengers! Second from the right is Ashton Davies, Chief Commercial Manager of the LMS.

of 1937. The streamlined locomotives hauled a highly luxurious nine-coach train from Euston to Glasgow in six and a half hours. It was a triumph, helping to give the whole LMS credibility and perhaps for the first time enabling a majority of the company's servants to take pride in their employer. How economic it was in itself nobody would have bothered to calculate or even care about; it gave the whole company a new-found confidence and vindicated its overall policies.

For the record, it carried only 232 passengers, in first class only two abreast, third class three, in a mixture of open and compartment seating. First and third class each had their own complete kitchen car. These were the days when only a small minority of people could even think about a journey (at least on a non-excursion train) between London and Scotland, and a large proportion of those who did took the cost of morning coffee, lunch and afternoon tea in their stride. Following a successful American tour by the Royal Scot, a whole Coronation Scot set, locomotive and nine coaches, was shipped across the Atlantic and made a big hit.

It was still in America when the war started. So badly needed was the locomotive that in 1942 it was brought back, into Cardiff, despite high shipping losses. But the coaches had to wait until the end of hostilities meanwhile having served as an American forces leave centre. By then things were very different. One German bomb killed Stamp and his wife and son, in 1941. There was much unfinished business . . .

A railway that should never have been born had taken time to get to grips with itself, and in some ways achieved major success, though for half the 1930s there was no dividend for ordinary shareholders. At the start there had not only been the political and organisational problems, but strike and deep depression. Even in the days when few would have gone by road from Scotland to London, some Euston and St Pancras expresses had carried merely handfuls of passengers, the restaurant car chief steward imploring those that there were to come for lunch or

Junction realignment

An ambitious scheme was installed at Trent Valley Junction, Stafford, in the summer of 1938 (nearly a year after the introduction of the high-speed Coronation Scot). The main Trent Valley route approached the original Grand Junction route from Birmingham by the 25-chain radius Queensville curve; this curvature and the junction turn-outs imposed a 30mph restriction for nearly ¾ mile. To raise the permitted speed to 55mph the junctions were relaid with two level chairs and switch diamonds installed. The less important Grand Junction route was sacrificially realigned, though the permitted speed remained 30mph. Queensville curve itself was slewed by up to 11ft 7in and given additional cant; if a train were stopped on the curve there was a distinct tendency to become more intimate with one's neighbour! The extensive scheme cost about £8,000 for track and £2,000 for signalling alterations.

Coleraine and Portrush

Coleraine is quite a busy station at times. There are five through trains from Belfast to Derry, leaving York Road at 7.15 and 9.45am, 12 noon, and 3.45 and 6.15pm, and each of these, in addition to conveying a Portrush coach, has a connection from Portrush to Derry at Coleraine; similar operations take place in the reverse direction, and with re-marshalling of stock and interchanging of passengers the station is often a scene of great animation, to which the presence of a main-road level crossing immediately north of the platforms adds not a little. The two through roads are signalled for running in either direction, and the non-stopping Portrush expresses take what would be the up line in an ordinary double-tracked station. Although situated on a curve, this road is well-aligned, and the 80min flyers usually go through at 55 to 60mph in either direction. The engine shed at Coleraine is interesting as housing two of the oldest NCC passenger engines still in service, the Malcolm 2-4-0s Nos 23 and 46, built in 1876.

Leaving Coleraine, the Derry line swings away westwards and the Portrush branch climbs away from the River Bann to gain the high ground behind the Portstewart cliffs. The station here lies about 1¾ miles inland, and the NCC used to operate a steam tramway between it and the town. It is not until within two miles of the terminus that the sea comes in view, but then it is to reveal as glorious a seascape as can be seen from a train anywhere in the British Isles.

Portrush station is second only in size to York Road, Belfast; it has three platform roads and considerable siding accommodation alongside, which is very necessary in view of the large amount of excursion traffic. The exterior of the station has a very bright and

continued opposite

dinner. Coal and mineral traffic, though still largely a railway monopoly, had been seriously hit. Road competition especially damaged the business of distributing more valuable manufactured goods that carried a higher tariff – and took away many local passengers, particularly from the thousands of badly-sited stations with sparse services. The revenue losses could not be matched by savings in expense – at least not while the railway believed implicitly that its nearly 3,000 goods stations were all needed and no fundamental traffic reorganisation was even discussed.

As early as August 1927, Stamp sent a personal note to his quarter of a million employees (in fact quite a few thousand more than when the company came into being) warning of the threat from road competition. Early in 1928 he followed it up with a plea ('it is confidently expected that the whole of our employees will unite in a firm determination to make good in every legitimate way all avoidable inroads into the industry on which we are all dependent for our daily bread') and enclosed a copy of the case lobbying government for fairer treatment. But it was not to be. On the freight side the rules continued to make it all too easy for lorry owners to extract the most lucrative traffic. Passengerwise, the LMS in common with the other railways had built up a substantial network of its own bus services by the end of the 1920s, but from 1930 was prohibited from running its own buses. Since it was however allowed a substantial shareholding in the newly-protected 'territorial' bus companies, there could now be neither sensible co-operation or competition. Exactly the same scenario was repeated in Ulster where the LMS Northern Counties Committee lost direct control of the buses with which it had sensibly replaced several narrow-gauge and branch-line services. Even in the compact Six Counties, integration was impossible.

Stamp, as we have seen, had a reputation for being heard by government, and often found himself effective spokesman for the whole industry. But government was still obsessed by the view that the railways might become too powerful; and though there was much sympathy for the later Square Deal campaign to free them from some of their shackles – like having to publish and stick to their tariffs so that road operators knew exactly by how little they had to undercut – virtually no progress was made. The industry was not even allowed to raise its charges without higher approval. The Railways Act of 1921, that which brought the Big Four into being, laid down 'standard revenues'. For the LMS, the standard was fixed at a profit of £20.6 million, or a return of 4.8 per cent on the investment. Stated a piece of lobbying at the time of the centenary: 'The actual net revenue of the company in 1937 was £14.4 million, or a deficiency compared with the standard of £6.2 million. In fact the LMS has not yet succeeded in securing its standard because the Rates Tribunal have been unable to adjust the charges to make this possible. The securing of this modest standard revenue is in the interests of the community as a whole, because it lies at the root of all progress in railway transport (with its comprehensive national service).' Stamp might have been the most effective spokesman, but he must have felt bitter disappointment at the lack of response, and one wonders how much more effective he might have made nationalisation. He was certainly badly missed during and immediately after the war, though his successor, Sir William Wood, also enjoyed a powerful reputation.

Undoubtedly the railway's real success was its express passenger service: the locomotives, the rolling stock, the timetable and the way that services were marketed. The groundwork was laid for today's Inter-City as London and the larger industrial towns in particular started to be brought effectively closer together. But once the railway had got its act together and traffic grew in the more buoyant economy of the thirties, almost every route enjoyed a better service, especially in summer, the timetables for the last seasons making entertaining reading. Especially note the seasonal express workings to resorts missing out the junctions and largest places en route traditionally calling places for all trains, and the introduction of more short workings (as between Llandudno Junction and Bettws-y-Coed). Through services were now at their peak. One Birmingham–Walsall stopper began its journey as an express from Bournemouth. Merthyr had its daily through train to Manchester, and two miles out along the branch line even Cefn Coed Halt was served by a peak season through train from Blackpool. But the railway was clearly right to give greater prominence to the main long-distance expresses; nobody could have foreseen that half a century later they would remain the railway's principal mainstay, but even now their contribution was increasing.

And, again, it was the expresses that achieved the publicity and made the whole enterprise more credible, something incidentally as true on the Northern Counties Committee system across the Irish Sea as it was in Britain.'"This is your way Sir" in England, Scotland, Ireland, Wales,' said one poster. Though never on the same scale as the Great Western's publishing operation, the publicity department poured forth holiday guides and leaflets. As with the excellent posters, the emphasis was on what today we would call discretional pleasure travel. The LMS was portrayed as serving a very pleasant, varied land, and many more indeed went touring by rail – and counted their journeys as a highlight of the holiday. Many saved through the LMS shilling stamps and ten-shilling vouchers offering generous interest.

The war prevented Stamp and everyone else knowing what the outcome might have been. The LMS just hove to, carrying mightily increased traffic with diminishing resources. It was badly mauled in air raids, with particularly heavy losses of passenger coaches, played a vital role in evacuations from big cities and the dispersal of troops from Dunkerque, and saw much of its own manufacturing capacity switched to armaments. Who else would the War Office indeed turn to in preference to the railways, and of them the LMS, not merely the largest but now most mechanised and scientific, inevitably played a major role, often co-ordinating the contributions of outside companies as well. Even while the Coronation Scot was being launched, the War Office asked the LMS to design a medium tank. Mass production of tanks during the war at both Crewe and Horwich works was just one piece of the LMS contribution.

But the real wartime challenge was the sheer pressure of freight and

continued

pleasing appearance; it is finished in black and white half-timbered style, and has the added distinction of a tall clock tower. Just outside the station is the terminus of the electric tramway that runs to Bushmills and the Giant's Causeway. The branch is single line throughout, with a passing loop at Portstewart, but it carries a surprising volume of traffic; with excursions from both Belfast and Derry there may be up to 30 trains a day in each direction during the winter months alone. The quickest of the Belfast excursions usually runs to the same timing as the Portrush Flyer, making its first stop at Portstewart in 73min from Belfast, and reaching Portrush in 80min. No less creditable from the running point of view are the Derry excursions which do the journey in an hour, calling at Castlerock and, of course, at Coleraine to reverse direction.

The star train of the Portrush service is the North Atlantic Express. This leaves at 8.10am and returns from Belfast at 5.15pm, calling only at Ballymena. When the service was inaugurated a three-coach formation was run, including a buffet car, but it has proved so popular that the normal load is now five, and often six, cars. The Portrush Flyer, which leaves Belfast at 9.20am, is an 80min train only in the down direction, for the 7.15pm up makes calls at Ballymoney and Ballymena in addition to Portstewart, and is allowed 90min. On Saturdays during the summer there is another 80min down train at 1.15pm; The Golfer's Express, which calls at Ballymoney, gives the fastest service of the day between Belfast and Ballycastle, namely 1¾hr. A special narrow-gauge train leaves Ballymoney at 2.20pm, non-stop to Ballycastle in 40min.

O. S. Nock on the NCC in *The Railway Magazine*, 1936.

Paddle Steamer. The LMS was involved in Clyde Steamer services through a wholly owned subsidiary company, the Caledonian Steam Packet Co Ltd. Its fleet consisted of both screw and paddle steamers and here PS Jupiter *built by Fairfield Shipbuilding & Engineering Co Ltd in 1937 is seen approaching Gourock Pier in 1938 or 1939.* Jupiter *was requisitioned during the war and converted to a mine sweeper named HMS Scawfell. It was returned to the CSP fleet in 1946 and sold for scrap in 1961.*

passenger traffic on routes that inevitably became run down. 'Remember, the RAILWAYS are ESSENTIAL IN PEACE, VITAL IN WAR. Their financial position is grave,' was a message no longer immediately needed. There was now no shortage of business, a virtual absence of competition. For the first time the LMS was really profitable, but the excess of course went straight to the government.

The short postwar years before nationalisation were distinctly unhappy. Overcrowding was bad everywhere, but passengers approached the large LMS stations which had not been given any priority of investment even before 1939 with grim apprehension of uncomfortable waits and excruciating journeys. The average train now carried 140 per cent of its pre-war load; passenger miles were up 70 per cent, train miles down 30. Coal quality got worse and, after some restoration of normality in 1946, the LMS went out of existence with a mean timetable, more overcrowded and later running largely as the result of coal shortages.

For what does one remember the LMS? For those of us not yet of retirement age, if we are old enough to remember it at all, it will be of the days of poor steaming, engines so dirty that for identification numbers often had to be chalked up, and terrible overcrowding. 'The LMS – a Hell of a Mess.' There were those everlasting delays at Crewe comically communicated during the war since the BBC's variety department was evacuated to Bangor. Re-reading boyhood diaries emphasises that the LMS really was in a worse state than most and seemed unaccountably chaotic and disagreeable to those brought up in gentler Great Western territory. One recalls everlasting delays at New Street in whose dirt survival rather than respectability was the order of the day, and how from Rugby to London the choice was often the LNER because the theoretically superior LMS service was less reliable. And on branch lines whose stations seemed to have been neglected since the last war but one, the arrival of non-descript 0-6-0s disguised in dirt, whose train windows were so covered in soot and grime that you had to open the door to see if there were spare seats – and how young school boys would follow you into the compartment and swing their satchels against the seats to send up a cloud of soot and dust into the air.

One also recalls the utter matter-of-factness of the LMS. The GWR seemed to make the starting of every train something of an occasion; the LMS perhaps did it so often in such unglamorous surroundings that it just happened. But the larger stations, filthy and noisy though they were, had awe-inspiring grandeur missing from the South and West. Preston, Carlisle, Glasgow Central, Manchester Central and Victoria, even Liverpool Exchange with its frequent electrics . . . your stature was increased merely by inspecting them. Here and there pre-war holiday posters (for which the LMS was distinguished) survived along with wartime posters issued jointly by the Big Four; and on an important service you might be able to spot an occasional brand new coach and if there was a lull in the overcrowding even enjoy the three-a-side third class seating and appreciate the Empire veneers with which the carriage internals were nicely finished. And one special memory of a rapid transit across the Midlands when things went right in a spotless half compartment at the carriage end.

We all knew that the LMS was not merely the largest (20,000 passenger vehicles, 10,000 locomotives, 30,000 road vehicles, over 70 steamers before wartime deprivations), but different in using outside talent to generate innovation. Those of us who had read about American dieselisation were sure that if it happened in Britain, it would be the LMS setting the lead, as indeed it did if only experimentally; while the rapidly-spreading system of centralised control seemed set to take away the signalman's importance though at that stage not threatening his job. In its last years the company indeed spent considerable sums advertising how central control and many other things were being used to try and get things back to normal. And we all knew that that meant a return to the pride, the speed, the splendid inter-city comfort and the endless variety of through coaches of the thirties. Had he been still alive, it is unlikely that even Stamp could have foreseen what then actually happened.

Wrong Way

In LMS days, down expresses not stopping at Rugby were signalled by special block bell codes, depending on whether they were taking the Trent Valley or Birmingham routes. The driver would give the appropriate whistle code at Weedon, the bobby there phoned the route to his colleague at Hillmorton box, and from there the train was offered right through to Rugby No 7, where the routes diverged, as 4-4-4 for Trent Valley trains and 4-4-4-2 for Birmingham.

One afternoon in 1939, soon after the colour lights were brought into use (by which time switch diamonds had been laid in for the down fast Trent Valley/up Birmingham crossing) the down side signalman at No 7 was offered, and accepted, 4-4-4-2. Odd, because he was expecting 4-4-4 for the Mid-day Scot, with the Birmingham following. He set the Birmingham road and then made enquiries whether the trains were out of course. Nobody knew. Thus, as the train came into view, he studied it closely and recognised a Princess on a long train with roof headboards all the way; undoubtedly the Mid-day.

Panic! He threw back the signals, and, despite what the rule book might have said about not changing points within the clearing point, started to reset the road in front of the train, approaching to take the 45mph diversion to the Trent Valley. It was quite a road to set, what with the switch diamonds and several 'trap' routes to avoid potential conflict, and before he had got very far into the operation a glance told him that he could not complete it in time. So he hastily abandoned the move and feverishly reset the road as it had been – just as the Princess thundered past, only then beginning to brake. It stopped ½ a mile towards Birmingham. So much for drivers' route knowledge.

2
THE TREE OF GROWTH

InterCity Emblem. The London & Birmingham Railway armorial device being the shields of the City of London, and of Birmingham. This is from the old arms of Birmingham before being created a city and county borough in 1889. The colours of the four quarters are reversed from the later arms, which also has a band of ermine across the shield. On this emblem quarters 1 and 4 have lozenges on a gules ground and 2 and 3 the right hand sides are azure.

Birmingham was destined to be the crossroads of trunk railways in England. Just 150 years ago, in 1837, the north-south legs of this cross opened as important links in the as-yet infant network. To the south ran the London & Birmingham Railway, though as yet incomplete as a through railway; thanks to delays in the completion of Kilsby Tunnel, the middle section between Denbigh Hall and Rugby remained the preserve of stage coaches until the following year. Northwards, the Grand Junction Railway opened as far as Warrington and a link to the Liverpool & Manchester Railway. All three railways became founder components of the mighty LONDON & NORTH WESTERN RAILWAY at its incorporation in 1846, by which time the north main line had reached Preston, had thrown off sundry branches and was busily building the Trent Valley cut-off enabling trains to avoid Birmingham altogether.

The east-west leg of the cross was not far behind. The Birmingham & Derby Junction Railway opened in 1839, though its title was initially misleading in that it made connection with the London & Birmingham at Hampton-in-Arden, nearly ten miles away. To the south west, the Birmingham & Gloucester Railway opened in 1840, linking to the Bristol & Gloucester Railway to give a trunk route extending from the Avon to York and beyond.

The MIDLAND RAILWAY, on its formation in 1844, concentrated on the eastern and northern constituents, not bringing in the Bristol route companies until two years later. The acquisition of the broad gauge Bristol & Gloucester in the teeth of the Great Western's broad-gauge aspirations was an inspired move. Midland tentacles were steadily extended as the century progressed until by the First World War they stretched from London to Carlisle and from Shoeburyness to Swansea.

Meeting the LNWR's Grand Junction line at Norton Bridge, the NORTH STAFFORDSHIRE RAILWAY opened to Stoke in the spring of 1848 and by the following year had reached Macclesfield to the north and another junction with the LNWR at Colwich. It formed part of a valuable London–Manchester through route, with North Staffordshire engines working LNWR expresses between Manchester and Stoke.

The LANCASHIRE & YORKSHIRE RAILWAY came into being as a new title for the Manchester & Leeds Railway in 1847. It spread subsequently by takeovers and new construction until there were few parts of the counties of its name which its lines did not reach. Particularly in its later years it tended to work closely with the LNWR.

On the southern fringe of Lakeland, the FURNESS RAILWAY

opened in 1846 as a detached local line serving the Barrow area. Its later link to the LNWR at Carnforth and Whitehaven turned it into a useful if roundabout secondary route.

Across the Border to Scotland, the CALEDONIAN RAILWAY formed the natural West Coast route to Glasgow (and to a lesser extent to Edinburgh). Its line from Carlisle up Annandale to Glasgow, completed by the takeover of minor Lanarkshire railways, opened early in 1848. Thereafter it expanded steadily, usually in fierce competition with the North British on the eastern side and in the Central Lowlands, to reach as far north as Aberdeen. But another important company arose in the west to dispute Caledonian plans; the GLASGOW & SOUTH WESTERN RAILWAY was formed in 1850 by amalgamation of the Glasgow, Paisley, Kilmarnock & Ayr and the Glasgow, Dumfries & Carlisle to provide an alternative main line from Glasgow to the Border which in later years carried through services operated jointly with the Midland. The Sou'-West was ever a bitter rival of the Caledonian in their common territory.

Further north, railway development was inevitably later. The HIGHLAND RAILWAY was born out of amalgamation of lesser concerns in 1865, giving it a spine stretching from Stanley Junction (north of Perth) past Inverness as far as Invergordon. In time it penetrated even less hospitable terrain to reach Wick, Thurso and Kyle.

All these concerns were brought together in the LONDON, MIDLAND & SCOTTISH RAILWAY by the Railways Act of 1921. The nominal date of the union was 1 January 1923, but in practice the process was less clean-cut, since the LNWR had absorbed the Lancashire & Yorkshire a year earlier and the Caledonian and the North Staffordshire did not come into the fold until July 1923. In the stilted Parliamentary language of the Act it looked to have some logic in its favour. In practice, the welding into a homogeneous body of such a disparate collection of assets, with contrasting environments, traditions, financial strengths and weaknesses, organisational structures and, above all, personalities was to prove a formidable and lengthy process.

The Jet Set in 1838
The Birmingham Railway at length is finished and opened for the public – the longest line and greatest work yet completed for a railway. A continued railway communication is now existing between the Metropolis and the important towns of Liverpool and Manchester, and in about a month it will extend to Preston by the opening of the Northern Union . . . The opening journey on the 17th was performed, including stoppages, in 4 hours 39 minutes to Birmingham. On this day a friend of ours breakfasted in London, dined at Birmingham and returned to town after; the first time such a feat was ever performed, though we do anticipate breakfasting in London, dining at Liverpool and supping at Edinburgh the same day before many years are elapsed.
Herapath's Railway Magazine, October 1838.

The Construction. A print dated 10 June 1837 taken from J. C. Bourne's book of engravings depicting the construction of the London & Birmingham Railway: work is in progress near Berkhampstead, Herts.

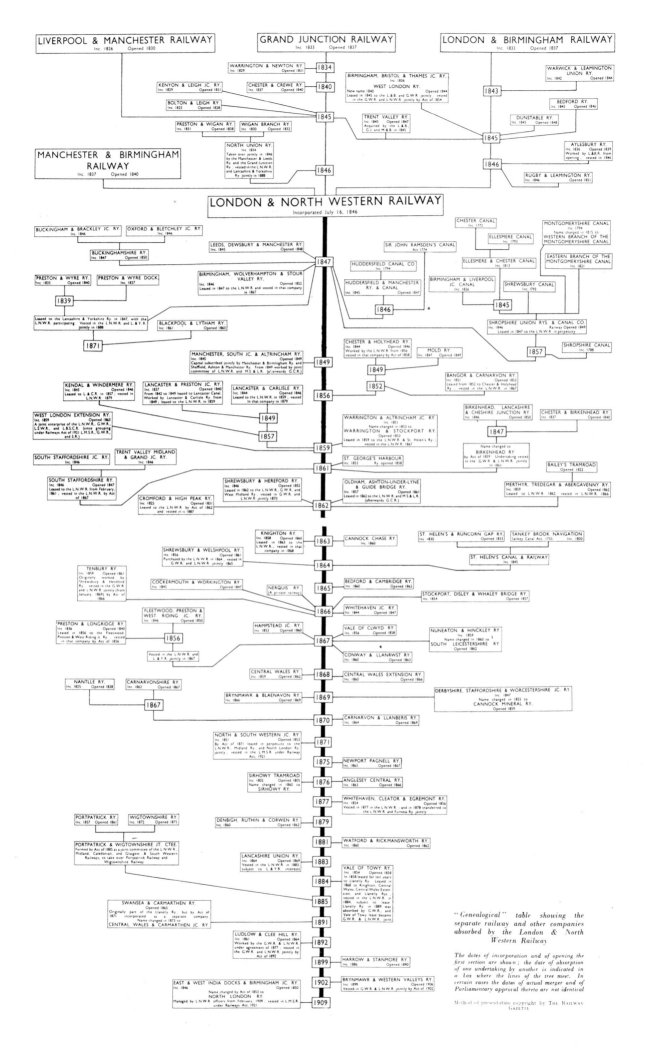

LIVERPOOL & MANCHESTER RAILWAY
Inc. 1826   Opened 1830

GRAND JUNCTION RAILWAY
Inc 1833   Opened 1837

LONDON & BIRMINGHAM RAILWAY
Inc. 1833   Opened 1837

WARRINGTON & NEWTON RY.
Inc. 1829   Opened 1831

1834

WARWICK & LEAMINGTON UNION RY.
Inc. 1842   Opened 1844

KENYON & LEIGH JC. RY.
Inc. 1829   Opened 1831

CHESTER & CREWE RY.
Inc. 1837   Opened 1840

1840

BIRMINGHAM, BRISTOL & THAMES JC. RY.
Inc. 1836
New name 1840   WEST LONDON RY.   Opened 1844
Leased in 1845 to the L.&B. and G.W.R. jointly ; vested
in the G.W.R. and L.N.W.R. jointly by Act of 1854

1843

BOLTON & LEIGH RY.
Inc. 1825   Opened 1828

BEDFORD RY.
Inc. 1845   Opened 1846

1845

PRESTON & WIGAN RY.
Inc. 1831   Opened 1838

WIGAN BRANCH RY.
Inc. 1830   Opened 1832

TRENT VALLEY RY.
Inc 1845   Opened 1847
Acquired by the L.&B.,
G.J. and M.&B. in 1845.

DUNSTABLE RY.
Inc. 1845   Opened 1848

1845

MANCHESTER & BIRMINGHAM RAILWAY
Inc. 1837   Opened 1840

NORTH UNION RY.
Inc 1834
Taken over jointly in 1846
by the Manchester & Leeds
Ry. and the Grand Junction
Ry. ; vested in the L.N.W.R.
and Lancashire & Yorkshire
Ry. jointly in 1888

1846

AYLESBURY RY.
Inc. 1836   Opened 1839
Worked by L.&B.R. from
opening ; vested in 1846

1846

RUGBY & LEAMINGTON RY.
Inc. 1846   Opened 1851

LONDON & NORTH WESTERN RAILWAY
Incorporated July 16, 1846

BUCKINGHAM & BRACKLEY JC. RY.
Inc. 1846

OXFORD & BLETCHLEY JC. RY.
Inc. 1846

LEEDS, DEWSBURY & MANCHESTER RY.
Inc. 1845   Opened 1848

CHESTER CANAL
Inc. 1772

ELLESMERE CANAL
Inc. 1793

MONTGOMERYSHIRE CANAL
Inc. 1794
Name changed in 1815 to
WESTERN BRANCH OF THE
MONTGOMERYSHIRE CANAL

BUCKINGHAMSHIRE RY.
Inc. 1847   Opened 1850

1847

SIR JOHN RAMSDEN'S CANAL
Acc 1774

ELLESMERE & CHESTER CANAL
Inc 1813

EASTERN BRANCH OF THE
MONTGOMERYSHIRE CANAL
Inc. 1821

PRESTON & WYRE RY.
Inc. 1835   Opened 1840

PRESTON & WYRE DOCK
Inc. 1837

BIRMINGHAM, WOLVERHAMPTON & STOUR
VALLEY RY.
Inc. 1846   Opened 1852
Leased in 1847 to the L.N.W.R. and vested in that company
in 1867

HUDDERSFIELD CANAL CO
Inc. 1794

BIRMINGHAM & LIVERPOOL
JC. CANAL
Inc. 1826

SHREWSBURY CANAL
Inc. 1793

1839

HUDDERSFIELD & MANCHESTER
RY. & CANAL
Inc. 1845   Opened 1847

1846

1845

Leased to the Lancashire & Yorkshire Ry. in 1847, with the
L.N.W.R. participating. Vested in the L.N.W.R. and L.A.Y.R.
jointly in 1888

BLACKPOOL & LYTHAM RY.
Inc. 1861   Opened 1863

SHROPSHIRE UNION RYS. & CANAL CO.
Inc 1846   Railway Opened 1849
Leased in 1847 to the L.N.W.R. in perpetuity

1871

CHESTER & HOLYHEAD RY.
Inc. 1844   Opened 1846
Worked by the L.N.W.R. from 1856 ;
vested in that company by Act of 1858

MOLD RY.
Inc. 1847   Opened 1849

1857

SHROPSHIRE CANAL
Inc. 1788

MANCHESTER, SOUTH JC. & ALTRINCHAM RY.
Inc. 1845   Opened 1849
Capital subscribed jointly by Manchester & Birmingham Ry. and
Sheffield, Ashton & Manchester Ry. From 1849 worked by joint
committee of L.N.W.R. and M.S.& L.R. (afterwards G.C.R.)

1849

1849

KENDAL & WINDERMERE RY.
Inc. 1845   Opened 1846
Leased to L.&C.R. in 1857 ; vested in
L.N.W.R. in 1879

LANCASTER & PRESTON JC. RY.
Inc. 1837   Opened 1840
From 1842 to 1849 leased to Lancaster Canal.
Worked by Lancaster & Carlisle Ry. from
1849 ; leased to the L.N.W.R. in 1859

LANCASTER & CARLISLE RY.
Inc. 1844   Opened 1846
Leased to the L.N.W.R. in 1859 ; vested
in that company in 1879

1856

BANGOR & CARNARVON RY.
Inc. 1851   Opened 1852
Leased from 1852 to Chester & Holyhead
Ry. ; vested in the L.N.W.R. in 1867

1852

WEST LONDON EXTENSION RY.
Inc. 1859   Opened 1863
A joint enterprise of the L.N.W.R., G.W.R.,
L.S.W.R., and L.B.S.C.R. (since grouping
under Railways Act of 1921 L.M.S.R., G.W.R.,
and S.R.)

1849

1857

WARRINGTON & ALTRINCHAM JC. RY.
Inc. 1851
Name changed in 1853 to
WARRINGTON & STOCKPORT RY.
Opened 1853
Leased in 1859 to the L.N.W.R. & St. Helen's Ry. ;
vested in the L.N.W.R. in 1867

BIRKENHEAD, LANCASHIRE
& CHESHIRE JUNCTION RY.
Inc. 1846   Opened 1850

CHESTER & BIRKENHEAD RY.
Inc. 1837   Opened 1840

1847

SOUTH STAFFORDSHIRE JC. RY.
Inc. 1846

TRENT VALLEY MIDLAND
& GRAND JC. RY.
Inc. 1846

1859

ST. GEORGE'S HARBOUR
Inc 1853   Ry. opened 1858

1861

Name changed to
BIRKENHEAD RY
by Act of 1859. Undertaking vested
in the G.W.R. & L.N.W.R. jointly
in 1861

BAILEY'S TRAMROAD
Opened 1822

SOUTH STAFFORDSHIRE RY.
Inc. 1846   Opened 1847
Leased to the L.N.W.R. from February,
1861 ; vested in the L.N.W.R. by Act
of 1867

CROMFORD & HIGH PEAK RY.
Inc 1825   Opened 1831
Leased to the L.N.W.R. by Act of 1862
and vested in 1887

SHREWSBURY & HEREFORD RY.
Inc. 1846   Opened 1852
Leased in 1862 to the L.N.W.R., G.W.R., and
West Midland Ry. ; vested in G.W.R. and
L.N.W.R. jointly 1870

OLDHAM, ASHTON-UNDER-LYNE
& GUIDE BRIDGE RY.
Inc. 1857   Opened 1861
Leased in 1862 to the L.N.W.R. and M.S.& L.R.
(afterwards G.C.R.)

1862

MERTHYR, TREDEGAR & ABERGAVENNY RY.
Inc. 1859   Opened 1862
Leased to L.N.W.R. 1862 ; vested in L.N.W.R. 1866

KNIGHTON RY.
Inc. 1858   Opened 1860
Leased in 1863 to the
L.N.W.R., vested in that
company in 1868

CANNOCK CHASE RY.
Inc. 1860

1863

ST. HELEN'S & RUNCORN GAP RY.
Inc. 1830   Opened 1833

SANKEY BROOK NAVIGATION
Sankey Canal Act, 1755   Inc. 1830

SHREWSBURY & WELSHPOOL RY.
Inc. 1860   Opened 1861
Purchased by the L.N.W.R. in 1864 ; vested in
G.W.R. and L.N.W.R. jointly 1865

1864

ST. HELEN'S CANAL & RAILWAY
Inc. 1845

TENBURY RY.
Inc. 1859   Opened 1861
Originally worked by
Shrewsbury & Hereford
Ry. ; vested in the G.W.R.
and L.N.W.R. jointly (from
January, 1869) by Act of
1866

COCKERMOUTH & WORKINGTON RY.
Inc. 1845   Opened 1847

NERQUIS RY.
(A private railway)

1865

BEDFORD & CAMBRIDGE RY.
Inc. 1860   Opened 1862

1866

WHITEHAVEN JC. RY.
Inc. 1844   Opened 1847

STOCKPORT, DISLEY & WHALEY BRIDGE RY.
Inc. 1854   Opened 1857

FLEETWOOD, PRESTON &
WEST RIDING JC. RY.
Inc. 1846   Opened 1850

HAMPSTEAD JC. RY.
Inc. 1853   Opened 1860

VALE OF CLWYD RY.
Inc. 1856   Opened 1858

NUNEATON & HINCKLEY RY.
Inc. 1859
Name changed in 1860 to
SOUTH LEICESTERSHIRE RY.
Opened 1862

PRESTON & LONGRIDGE RY.
Inc. 1836   Opened 1840
Leased in 1856 to the Fleetwood,
Preston & West Riding Jc. Ry. ; vested
in that company by Act of 1856

1856

1867

CONWAY & LLANRWST RY.
Inc. 1860   Opened 1863

Vested in the L.N.W.R. and
L.&Y.R. jointly in 1867

CENTRAL WALES RY.
Inc. 1859   Opened 1862

1868

CENTRAL WALES EXTENSION RY.
Inc. 1860   Opened 1866

NANTLLE RY.
Inc. 1825   Opened 1828

CARNARVONSHIRE RY.
Inc. 1862   Opened 1867

BRYNMAWR & BLAENAVON RY.
Inc. 1866   Opened 1869

1869

DERBYSHIRE, STAFFORDSHIRE & WORCESTERSHIRE JC. RY.
Inc. 1847
Name changed in 1855 to
CANNOCK MINERAL RY.
Opened 1859

1867

CARNARVON & LLANBERIS RY.
Inc. 1864   Opened 1869

1870

NORTH & SOUTH WESTERN JC. RY.
Inc. 1851   Opened 1853
By Act of 1871 leased in perpetuity to the
L.N.W.R., Midland Ry. and North London Ry.
jointly ; vested in the L.M.S.R. under Railway
Act, 1921

1871

1875

NEWPORT PAGNELL RY.
Inc. 1863   Opened 1867

SIRHOWY TRAMROAD
Inc. 1802   Opened 1805
Name changed in 1860 to
SIRHOWY RY.

1876

ANGLESEY CENTRAL RY.
Inc. 1863   Opened 1866

1877

WHITEHAVEN, CLEATOR & EGREMONT RY.
Inc. 1854   Opened 1856
Vested in 1877 in the L.N.W.R. ; and in 1878 transferred to
the L.N.W.R. and Furness Ry. jointly

PORTPATRICK RY.
Inc. 1857   Opened 1861

WIGTOWNSHIRE RY.
Inc. 1872   Opened 1875

DENBIGH, RUTHIN & CORWEN RY.
Inc. 1860   Opened 1862

1879

PORTPATRICK & WIGTOWNSHIRE JT. CTEE.
Formed by Act of 1885 as a joint committee of the L.N.W.R.,
Midland, Caledonian, and Glasgow & South Western
Railways, to take over Portpatrick Railway and
Wigtownshire Railway

1881

WATFORD & RICKMANSWORTH RY.
Inc. 1860   Opened 1862

LANCASHIRE UNION RY.
Inc. 1864   Opened 1869
Vested in the L.N.W.R. in 1883
subject to L.&Y.R. interests

1883

1884

VALE OF TOWY RY.
Inc. 1854   Opened 1858
In 1858 leased for ten years
to Llanelly Ry. Leased in
1868 to Knighton, Central
Wales, Central Wales Extension, and Llanelly Rys. ;
vested in the L.N.W.R. in
1884 subject to lease.
Llanelly Ry in 1889 was
absorbed by the G.W.R., and
Vale of Towy lease became
G.W.R & L.N.W.R. joint

1885

SWANSEA & CARMARTHEN RY.
Opened 1865
Originally part of the Llanelly Ry. but by Act of
1871 incorporated as a separate company.
Name changed in 1873 to
CENTRAL WALES & CARMARTHEN JC. RY.

1891

LUDLOW & CLEE HILL RY.
Inc. 1861   Opened 1864
Worked by the G.W.R. & L.N.W.R.
under agreement of 1877 ; vested in
the G.W.R. and L.N.W.R. jointly by
Act of 1892.

1892

HARROW & STANMORE RY
Inc. 1886   Opened 1890

1899

EAST & WEST INDIA DOCKS & BIRMINGHAM JC. RY.
Inc. 1846   Opened 1850
Name changed by Act of 1853 to
NORTH LONDON RY.
Managed by L.N.W.R. officers from February, 1909 ; vested in L.M.S.R.
under Railways Act, 1921

1902

BRYNMAWR & WESTERN VALLEYS RY.
Inc. 1899   Opened 1906
Vested in G.W.R. & L.N.W.R. jointly by Act of 1902

1909

"*Genealogical*" table showing the
separate railway and other companies
absorbed by the London & North
Western Railway

*The dates of incorporation and of opening the
first section are shown ; the date of absorption
of one undertaking by another is indicated in
a box where the lines of the tree meet. In
certain cases the dates of actual merger and of
Parliamentary approval thereto are not identical*

Method of presentation copyright by THE RAILWAY
GAZETTE

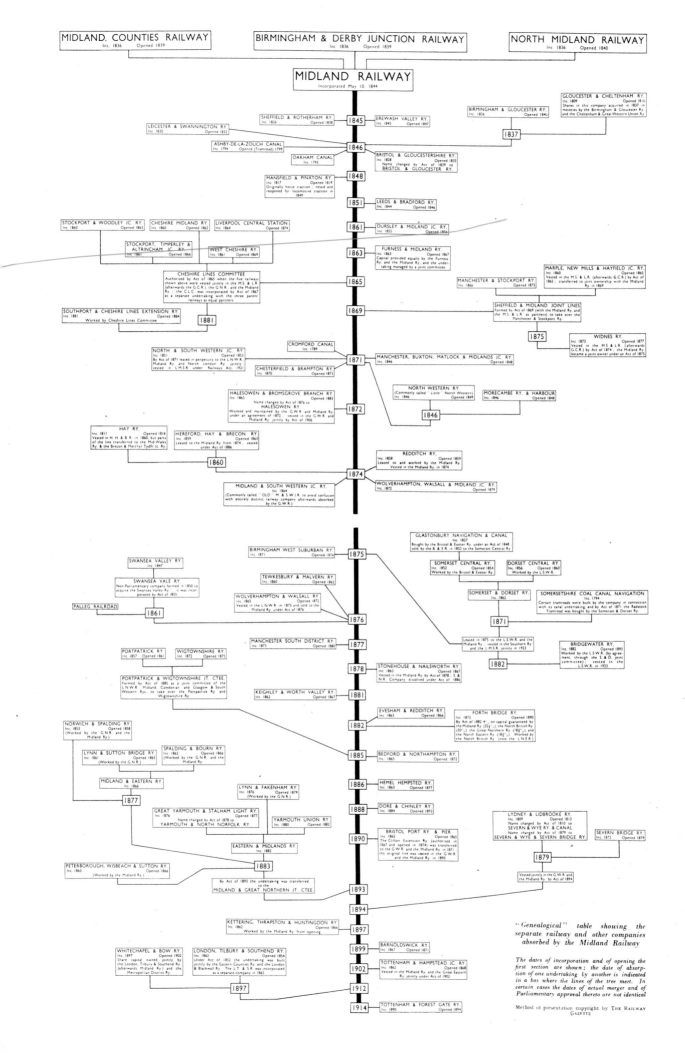

"Genealogical" table showing the separate railway and other companies absorbed by the Midland Railway

The dates of incorporation and of opening the first section are shown; the date of absorption of one undertaking by another is indicated in a box where the lines of the tree meet. In certain cases the dates of actual merger and of Parliamentary approval thereto are not identical

Method of presentation copyright by THE RAILWAY GAZETTE

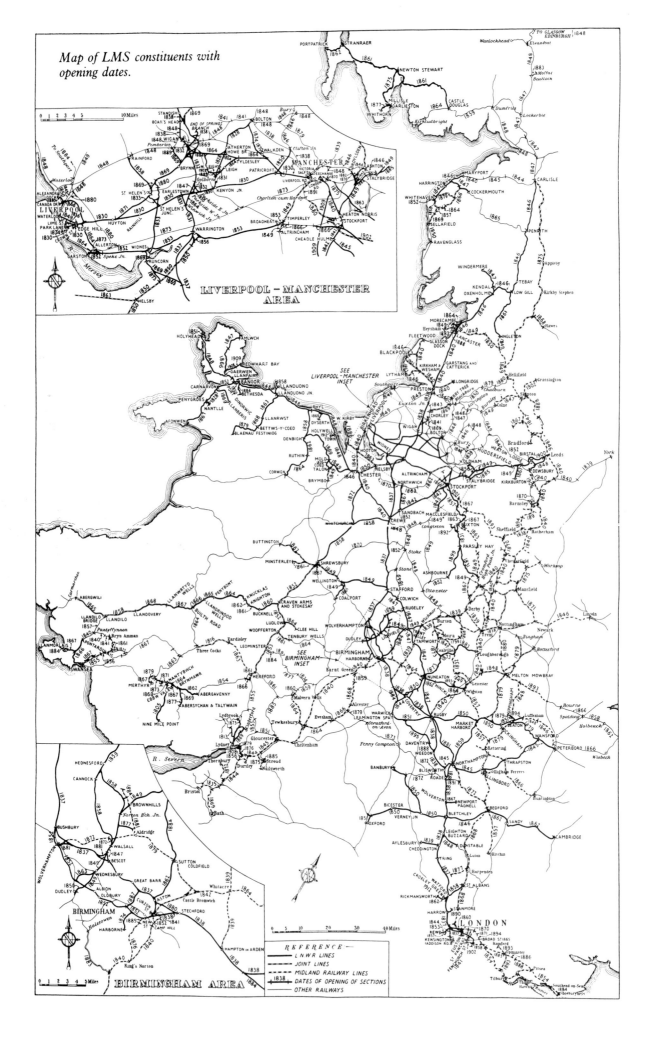

Map of LMS constituents with opening dates.

LIVERPOOL — MANCHESTER AREA

BIRMINGHAM AREA

REFERENCE
L N W R LINES
JOINT LINES
MIDLAND RAILWAY LINES
DATES OF OPENING OF SECTIONS
OTHER RAILWAYS

3
BIG MEN FOR
A BIG BUSINESS

The LMS was unquestionably the biggest of Britain's railways; whether it *was* greatest in achievement and national esteem was – and still is – a matter of debate. Inevitably in the early years of its corporate life, some of its officers and servants were sadly disappointed with their personal situations under the new regime. But if the first decade or so of Grouping formed the Years of Conflict, the second decade of the LMS between 1930–39 represented the Years of Progress and Achievement, which only World War II cut short, and in which a new spirit of corporate pride began to emerge within the company's staff of some 233,000. Initially a railway company with many 'characters', it developed into an undertaking with a character of its own.

In 1919, with World War I just over and a powerful new Ministry of Transport formed under Sir Eric Geddes (himself an ex-railway manager), the railway companies were physically exhausted by the stresses, strains and losses of the past six years. Those which were to become the two largest components of the LMS, the London & North Western Railway and the Midland Railway, had released to the armed forces a combined total of 53,555 staff, representing 34 per cent of the total LNWR staff and 29 per cent of the Midland; over 10,000 had died. The railways had suffered too, from inadequate financial compensation for their burden of extra work while under government control, particularly because the government had awarded wage increases and had conceded the eight hour day, without increasing, prior to 1920, a rate of compensation based on the companies' net revenues of 1913.

As early as 1916, in the middle of World War I, the government had been considering the national role of the railways after the end of hostilities. In 1918 a Select Committee reported that 'unification of the railway system is desirable under suitable safeguards . . .' so the preparation of an acceptable scheme became an early task. Sir Eric produced a White Paper proposing that 123 railways should be reorganised into seven groups. There was a good deal of lobbying in and out of Westminster before the Railways Act 1921 became law on 19 August of that year. Under that Act, four groups were formed 'with a view to the reorganisation and more efficient and economical working of the railway system of Great Britain'. The largest was the North Western Group, under the title of London Midland & Scottish Railway Company. Merger arrangements had to be completed '*on or before* the first day of January 1923', which meant that subject to the approval of the Amalgamation Tribunal established under the Act, any two railway companies designated as being within the same group could voluntarily amalgamate earlier. Within the

Sir William Valentine Wood. President of the LMS from 1941 until 1947. He was born in 1883 joining the Belfast & Northern Counties Railway in 1898 and coming to the LMS in 1924 via the Ministry of Transport. He became a vice president in 1930 succeeding to the highest post on the death of Lord Stamp who was killed in an air raid in April 1941.

35

Tall and Short
To clothe its employees, the LMSR use 750 miles of British-manufactured cloth which, if stretched in a single line, would extend further than from London to Wick. The requirements are of a varied character, and include garments for station and yard staff, enginemen, permanent way men, guards, signalmen, messengers, carters, police, hotel and restaurant car staff and the crews of steamers. The height of the tallest man in the service of the Company is 6ft 8in, and that of the smallest 4ft 3in. Engine drivers possess the finest physique, with an average chest measurement of 50in, but honours for height are carried off by the passenger guards.
Meccano Magazine, June 1936

LMS group, the LNWR and the Lancashire & Yorkshire amalgamated under the former title on 1 January 1922.

This merger, previously the subject of abortive discussions, had been foreshadowed by the appointment of (Sir) Arthur Watson, General Manager of the L&Y, to be GM of both companies as from 1 January 1921. A substantial pattern of running powers and working agreements already existed between the two companies, particularly in Lancashire; the amalgamation now put under one management the hitherto joint lines from Euxton Junction through Preston to Blackpool and Fleetwood, gave the combined undertaking two trunk routes across the Pennines, and afforded the LNWR access to the developing South Yorkshire coalfield and to the East Coast at Goole and Hull.

On 1 January 1923, Britain's biggest railway, the LMS, officially came into being with an initial capital, in round figures, of £400 million. A second stage incorporation of the LMS company took place on 1 July 1923, to give formal effect to the inclusion of those companies which had not concluded terms of amalgamation by 1 January.

The Act provided that the LMS should comprise 8 constituent and 27 subsidiary companies: the constituents were the LNWR, the L&Y, the Midland, the North Staffordshire, the Furness, and in Scotland the Caledonian, the Glasgow & South Western, and the Highland Railway companies. The subsidiaries comprised mostly railways worked by one or more of the constituents, but including some of Britain's well-known smaller lines such as the Maryport & Carlisle, the North London, the Stratford-upon-Avon & Midland Junction, and the Wirral railways.

Railways apart, what the LMS described as its 'ancillary activities' imparted the character of a vast industrial conglomerate. By absorbing a number of railway-owned or leased canals (notably the Shropshire Union and the Trent & Mersey) it controlled the largest group of such waterways in the country. It took over some 27 hotels, important docks including Garston, Fleetwood, Barrow-in-Furness and Heysham, and either owned or had a joint interest in fleets of steamers totalling over 100 vessels, plying variously between the West Coast and Ireland, the East Coast and the Continent, on the English lakes and Scottish lochs, and even a Thames ferry.

Clearly the management task in taking over this vast array of assets and its army of people was both complex and formidable; some of its consequences and complications were still detectable a decade later. Fully a decade after Grouping, an observer at Carlisle on the arrival of the Royal Scot non-stop from Euston, recalled an ex-Caledonian Railway official checking with his ongoing Polmadie driver that the Camden crew had brought coal forward, cleared the footplate, etc, and being satisfied that all was well to proceed, pronouncing 'get the English off the engine and ye're awa' noo'. Paramount among the problems of the first formative stage were the differences of organisation between the major constituents, and the variations in the philosophy of running a safe and successful railway. Perhaps such differences were most marked in the slightly more aristocratic bearing of some senior LNWR officers compared with their new colleagues from the Midlands and North, while the draconian tenets of Sir Richard Moon ('never let me see that man again') and G. P. Neele could still be heard at Euston.

Differences of philosophy were especially in evidence between Euston and the Midland management at Derby, where some matters were viewed with a distinctly provincial bias. The LMS directors who took office in 1923 comprised six each from the LNWR, the former L&Y, and the MR, plus one each nominated by the three Scottish constituents (two more from the Caledonian a little later) the Furness and the North Staffordshire. The chairman was the Hon Charles Napier Lawrence (later Lord Lawrence of Kingsgate), and the joint deputy chairmen, E. B. Fielden (L&Y) and Sir W. Guy Granet (Midland). The last-named had a remarkable career: a barrister who had succeeded Sir Henry Oakley as secretary of the Railway Companies Association in 1900, and from assistant general manager of the MR in 1905, rose to become chairman in 1922. Another member of the first LMS board was Sir Thomas Williams, who had been the last general manager of the LNWR, 1919–20, before the amalgamation with the L&Y; confronted with two former GMs on the new board of which he was not himself a member, (Sir) Arthur Watson, the first GM of the new LMS, must have faced a few problems . . .

The first tasks of the new management were to inform staff, customers and relevant public bodies of the new organisation and contacts; and to meet the requirements of the Railways Act 1921 in such matters as a new rates classification and the setting up of the Railway Rates Tribunal, machinery for staff relations and other matters. The general manager was fortified with assistants for these purposes (including Parliamentary), and in the interim organisation, three LMS divisions were set up: Midland (with HQ at Derby), Western (with HQ at Manchester), and Northern (with HQ at Glasgow). The Western Division was notable for bringing to the fore two ex-L&Y men, Ashton Davies as superintendent, and T. W. Royle as assistant, both of whom were destined to become vice-presidents of the LMS; they were typical of the pragmatic, no-nonsense yet usually approachable executives produced by the L&Y.

The interim organisation greatly enhanced the status and strength of Derby in LMS management. Under the authority of the chief general superintendent (J. H. Follows, who had succeeded (Sir) Cecil Paget, the architect of the Midland train control system) was placed the central direction of all train operation, motive power, and even commercial passenger matters; hence, in the absence as yet of acceptable alternative designs for bigger engines, the initial proliferation of Midland 4-4-0 designs which the new locomotive running regime considered would be suitable even for loads of 400 tons or more over the long steep grades of Shap and Beattock.

One factor which contributed to the expansion of Derby was the shortage of office accommodation at Euston, the company's official headquarters. The splendid Central Offices, reached through Hardwick's Great Hall and up the staircase leading to the Shareholders' Meeting Room, accommodated the general management, secretariat, directors' rooms, and so on. (The central staircase from the Great Hall was entered

T. W. Royle, chief operating manager LMS from 1938 until 1944 when he was appointed a vice president becoming deputy chief regional officer, London Midland Region on nationalisation, retiring later in 1948. He came to the LMS from the Lancashire & Yorkshire Railway and held various posts in the operating and commercial departments before succeeding C. R. Byrom as chief operating manager.

The Last President

Sir William Valentine Wood ('Willie Wood' to colleagues on the railway, 'Val' to family and close friends) had never anticipated becoming president. When Stamp was killed on that dreadful night of 16 April 1941, Wood was shattered. He broke the news to the Railway Executive Committee with an emotion very strange to his quiet nature. He must have felt daunted by the need to follow such an outstanding figure.

Wood was smallish, clean-shaven, with strong glasses that gave him a slightly owlish expression, though he had a quiet, rather quizzical smile. You never saw him – or hardly ever – without a cigarette in his mouth. This combined with a very low voice, rapid speech and a strong Ulster brogue to make communication rather difficult, unless you knew him well and could guess in which way his quicksilver mind was working.

He had started on the Midland's NCC as an accountant, at which work he was supreme. But he was also interested, and rapidly became knowledgeable, in almost every aspect of railway work. He once told of a slight collision in which an NCC locomotive had been involved – 'actually', he said with that delightful twinkle, 'I was driving the engine'.

In the 1914–18 war he was involved in Government work and when Sir Eric Geddes' Ministry of Transport was created in 1919 he became its first director of finance. There he began a long friendship with Sir Cyril Hurcomb, later the first chairman of the British Transport Commission, who had the highest regard for him. He returned to the railway to rise through the accountancy side of the LMS and eventually became vice president (finance and services). Here he made a wonderful two-man team with Stamp, dealing with all the *continued opposite*

by two short flights of curved stairs, it being alleged (not always jokingly) that the flight on the left was for North Western officers, and that on the right for Midland). There was hence a great overflow into later office blocks in Drummond Street and other streets around the station and towards Camden Town; one of the older of these satellites contained a huge general office with high desks topped by brass rails, on which the clerks of an earlier generation could place their top hats. As another echo of the past, accommodation existed on the west side of the station for the horse-drawn carriages which once bore some senior officers to work and home again.

As the new grouping era progressed, the staffs of smaller departments expanded into four rows of terraced houses in Euston Square and Euston Grove which lay between Euston Road and gardens and the station. Even the two porters' lodges fronting on to Euston Road, one on each side of the station approach (as they are today – the last vestiges of old Euston) were pressed into use as offices.

Nevertheless, in the early days of the LMS, numbers of ex-LNWR staff from Euston, and some ex-L&Y men from Manchester, belonging mostly to the traffic departments, had to move to Derby while things were being sorted out; one senior assistant from Euston recalled sharing a small room with his opposite numbers from the Midland and the L&Y, and perforce writing memoranda to each other via a central typing bureau, the signed memos being delivered by messenger to the official at the next desk.

Meanwhile, there were major changes at Euston. Sir Arthur Watson resigned in 1924 due to ill-health, and was succeeded by a man with a remarkable career, the Rt Hon H. G. Burgess. He had served the LNWR successively as its representative in Scotland, and then for twenty years as its general manager for Ireland. During World War I he was a director of Irish Transportation on behalf of the government, retaining that position until he became the second general manager of the LMS railway – and the last to hold that title. He was known affectionately among senior staff as 'the Right Honourable Gentleman', deriving from his honour as a privy councillor and a senator of the Irish Free State.

In the same year (1924) Sir Guy Granet succeeded Lord Lawrence as chairman, while a year later George Hughes, who had been the last CME of the L&Y and LNW, and the first of the LMS, retired, leaving the way clear for his former pupil and assistant at Horwich, by now Sir Henry Fowler, to assume the top job and so incidentally to strengthen still further the Derby influence. Fowler (despite his substantial physique, reputed a 'great man for getting into boilers') had succeeded R. M. Deeley as CME of the Midland in 1909.

Meanwhile under Granet's chairmanship the directors had been reviewing current and future problems of organisation and management, and had decided on radical change: the establishment of a small control group of chief officers under the leadership of what today would be called a chief executive. The upshot was the appointment as from 1 January 1926 of Sir Josiah (later Lord) Stamp as president of the

Executive. Burgess stayed on to hold the fort as GM while the new broom was looking round and planning his organisation, but at the end of 1926 both he and Matheson, the former Caledonian GM who since grouping had been deputy GM for Scotland, retired.

The pattern of top management which began work on 1 January 1927 (in which year Stamp became Chairman of the company as well) was to continue unchanged except for people, for the remaining twenty-one years of the company's life. Stamp presided over an executive committee of usually four members, overseeing respectively railway traffic operating and commercial (two members), finance, and works and ancillary undertakings except hotels.

Probing and planning by Stamp and his new team quickly led into a two-pronged attack: analysis leading to standardisation of equipment and practices; direct savings from amalgamation of offices or jobs; and how to finance the new equipment and methods which would not only

continued
economic and financial aspects of the railway. He wrote 90 per cent of the short volume *Railways*, officially a joint work with Stamp.

His speed at juggling with numbers was legendary. Quote almost any figure to him and he would whip out an old-fashioned calculating machine from the top drawer of his desk and rapidly convert it into something else – a price per ton of engine weight, a weight per mile of fishplates . . .

His points in discussion could be difficult to ascertain because of his speed and inaudibility – but on paper he was formidable. Everyone on the LMS respected Willie Wood – those who knew him personally were deeply attached to him. He should have retired at nationalisation, instead of accepting Hurcomb's pressing invitation to soldier on: his last five years were an anti-climax after a long and happy life on the railway.

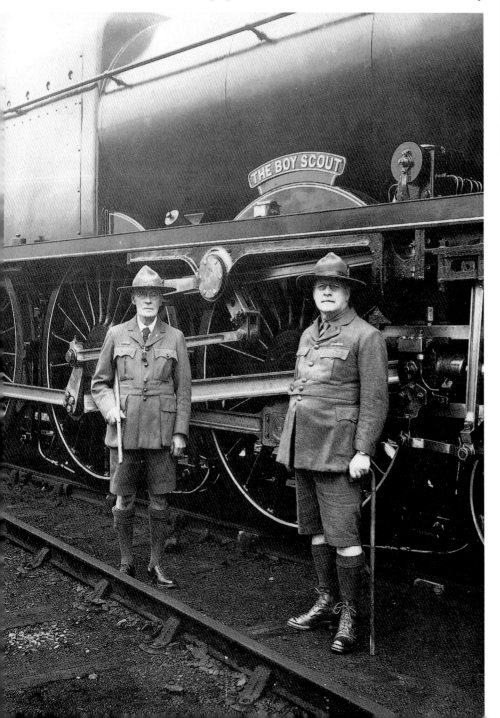

Good Scouts. Dr H. H. Bemrose, scout commissioner for Derbyshire, and Sir Henry Fowler, chief mechanical engineer LMS (also a former district scout commissioner) alongside Royal Scot class locomotive No 6169 The Boy Scout *on 25 October 1930. This was the last of a batch of 20 Royal Scots built at Derby in 1930. It was officially named by Lord Baden-Powell at Euston on 9 December 1930 when the Scouts' Fleur-de-Lys badge was also fixed to the splasher.*

Princess class Pacific No 6201
Princess Elizabeth *heads the down*
Royal Scot express on its way from
Euston to Glasgow and takes its first
dip into the water troughs at Bushey.
This class had charge of the prestige
services on the West Coast route from
their introduction in 1933 until the
Coronation class joined them in
1937. On the right a Euston-
Watford electric train is being
overtaken.

Sleeper, Please
A little authority could take you
(sometimes) a long way on the
LMS. Two rising sparks in the
management once had a night out
in the West End of London,
accompanied by two lively nurses
from a big hospital. Midnight
passed and the quartet had nowhere to stay. No problem; they
descended on Euston, pulled rank
with the night relief stationmaster
and ordered out a first-class sleeping car from the sidings, in which
the rest of the night was passed.
Early morning tea was ordered
from the refreshment room. Not
the sort of escapade that would
have amused Lord Stamp!

Overleaf.
Map of the LMS system.

enable the LMS to overtake the lost years of World War I but also lift it
into the 1930s and beyond. All this had to be accomplished against a
background of recurrent trade depression, and in face of the steadily
growing competition of a rapidly expanding and largely unfettered road
haulage industry.

Hence there appeared some externally-recruited experts 'to help' (or
so it was put) the company's officers. Most powerful was the executive
research office (ERO), which took over the control and ordering of all
stationery and printing, somewhat to the lowering of its quality; a
Colonel Ord came to advise on the modernisation of goods stations; and
two experts from the world of marketing and sales. Journalists, advertising men and film makers were to come later. Those recruits who were
taken on the staff, as distinct from being consultants, imposed something of a strain on the machinery of the staff departments, who were
expert in the classification of graded employees but somewhat unfamiliar
with the outside world; a staff inspector who had to report on a request
for an article of special office equipment plaintively reported that 'Mr X
does not supervise any clerks.'

The LMS vice-presidents were all professional railwaymen until 1930,
when there arrived as vice-president, and in the new job of director of
scientific research, the distinguished scientist, Sir Harold Hartley. This
led to the establishment at Derby of a new research laboratory where
products of every kind were tested, including (to the delight of the
publicity people) a device called 'the mechanical bottom' which for many
hours thumped up and down on a carriage seat, happily testing it and its
upholstery to destruction. Later, in 1934, when Railway Air Services
was formed, Sir Harold became its chairman; in that year also, RAS
began operations with services between London and Glasgow via
Birmingham, Stoke-on-Trent and Liverpool; and Liverpool–Belfast–
Glasgow.

In 1929 the railway companies had been relieved of the obligation to
pay duty on fares in excess of one old penny per mile, on condition that
the capitalised value up to 90 per cent was used for development. In the
same year, in order to relieve unemployment during the recession, the
Development (Loans, Guarantees & Grants) Act helped the railways
with interest payments on approved projects. By these means and its
own capital financing, the LMS was able to carry out quite extensive
programmes of new rolling stock, modernisation of marshalling yards
and motive power depots, its first installation of automatic warning
control and two electrifications. These were the Manchester South
Junction & Altrincham (MSJ&A) (eight miles, joint with LNER) which
was converted in 1931 at 1500V dc with overhead collection, and the
LMS Wirral lines (16 miles), converted in 1938 at 650V dc with third rail
collection, necessary for the physical connection with the Mersey
Railway. Somewhat curiously, perhaps, the LMS did not seem particularly interested in main line electrification.

With the railway companies having successfully obtained Parliamentary powers to participate in both road and air transport in 1928 and 1929
respectively, the LMS needed to bring more staff up to London, which

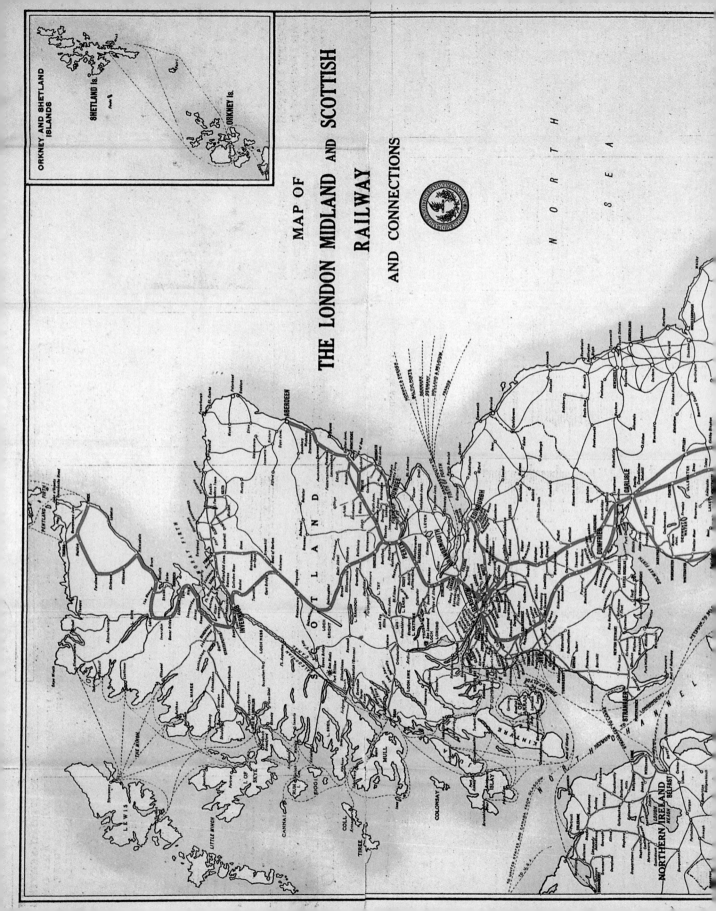

MAP OF
**THE LONDON MIDLAND AND SCOTTISH
RAILWAY**
AND CONNECTIONS

ORKNEY AND SHETLAND
ISLANDS

SHETLAND Is.

ORKNEY Is.

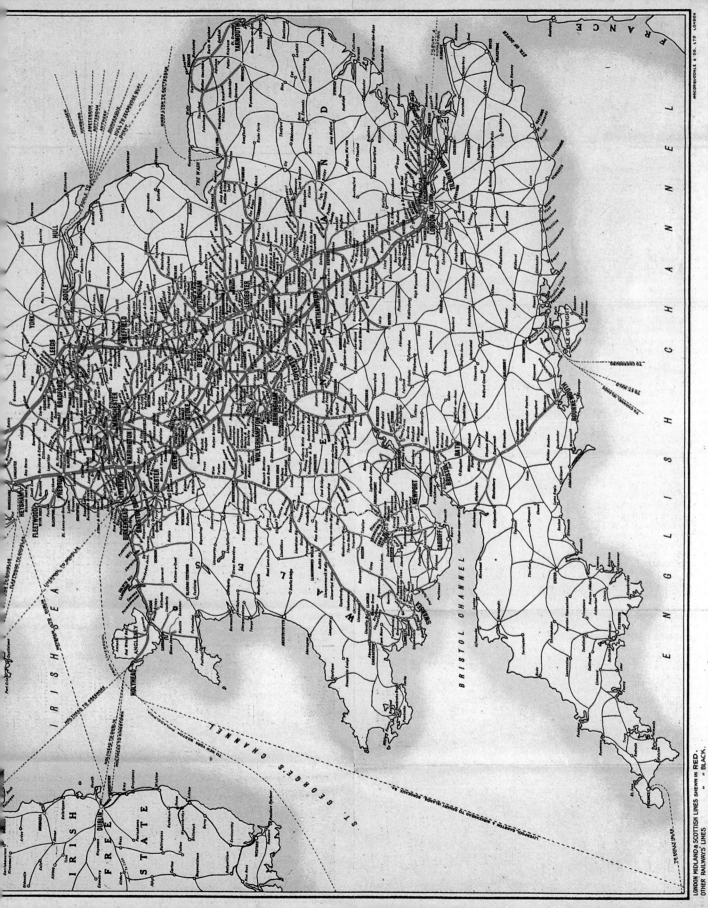

LONDON MIDLAND & SCOTTISH LINES SHEWN IN RED.
OTHER RAILWAYS' LINES " " BLACK.
STEAMER ROUTES. COACH ROUTES

Stamp had from his arrival always envisaged as the company's rightful power-base to deal with ministries, industrial and public bodies at national level. So, with the arrival at Euston of the general superintendent (passenger commercial), Ashton Davies, and initially a nucleus staff much concerned with the road and air powers, the interim concept of three managing divisions began to diminish into four operating (including motive power) divisional superintendents of operation at Crewe, Derby, Manchester and Glasgow; that at Manchester controlled mainly the old L&Y lines, and was named the Central Division. The concentration of HQ staff at Euston was not fully accomplished, however, until 1934, with the opening of Euston House close to the station.

1930 ushered in a decade of growing progress and prestige but of falling profits. The LMS executive committee saw new stars rising in the managerial firmament; first (Sir) W. V. Wood, who became the statistically-minded Stamp's right-hand man as vice-president (finance) and, after Stamp's untimely death in 1941, became president (but not chairman) until the eve of nationalisation.

In 1938, the LMS staged a splendid exhibition at Euston to commemorate the centenary of the opening of the London & Birmingham Railway. But by this time the railways, through the Railway Companies Association, were deep in political battling and publicity for the 'Square Deal' campaign against the inequalities of road versus rail. Well they might, for the company's ordinary stock had fallen from a price of 101.25 at 1 January 1925 to 30 in 1938, and was to drop to 13½ a year later. Ordinary stock dividend had been £2 per cent for the year 1930, but was to be nil in 1938; a bad year for all Britain's railways.

As 1939 dawned, the railways were once again committed to large programmes of work devoted to national defence, as the shadows of aggression closed in on Europe. Organisationally and in the strength of morale, the LMS had overcome traumas and tests of initial reorganisation in the 1920s such as the complacent GWR had never had to suffer. Today, old Euston has been swept away in the electrification of the 1960s; the grass grows green and young trees burgeon where once stood the powerful Hunts Bank headquarters of the L&Y; although Derby is still an important place with its locomotive works and its Railway Technical Centre, some of its red brick offices facing Midland Road are empty, while of the great central operating control MR building known as 'Paget's Palace', only the blank wall facing No 1 platform remains; behind it, a car park!

On Shed. Shed scene at Bletchley in June 1938 showing the dirt associated with disposal – mounds of ash everywhere. In the background is a typical LNWR water tower-cum-coaling shed – the tank on top with coal wagons unloading onto a platform below – the coal then being hand shovelled into the tender. In the foreground are two generations of LNWR freight locomotives – a Super D 0-8-0 and a Webb 18in 0-6-0 still carrying its original LMS number 8592. It shows signs of being thrashed and air leaking through the smokebox door.

Midland Division Freight. A scene very much reminiscent of LMS days though taken in August 1954, the only real difference being the engine number – BR 44143 – instead of LMS 4143. The long partially fitted freight (probably only one or two of the vans at the front with vacuum brakes) is passing Kettering South Junction with Midland Railway signals and signalbox still intact. In LMS days it was a picture so commonplace that few would notice it.

4
LOCOMOTIVE DEVELOPMENT

Sir William Stanier FRS. Chief mechanical engineer of the LMS from 1932 until 1944. Stanier commenced his career on the GWR in May 1892 (the same month that the last remaining sections of broad gauge track were abolished) and rose to become principal assistant to C. B. Collett. He was persuaded to change his allegiance at the request of the LMS who needed a new broom to bring order out of chaos in the LMS cme's department. He was knighted in 1943 for his services to the Ministry of Production and died aged 89 in 1965.

Carlisle station, on a cold night in February 1923. At the end of the main southbound platform, easily overlooked in the gloom, stand a couple of men in overcoats and bowler hats. They take a knowledgeable interest in the Scottish locomotives arriving on the overnight expresses, and in the Midland and LNWR engines taking over from them. They note punctuality, assess train weights, talk to the enginemen, look at the coal on the tenders, and between times spend a little while in the cab of a waiting Claughton in the middle road. Unrecognised by the station staff, they are important men who will shape the locomotive strategy of the newly-formed LMS Railway for years to come: they are George Hughes, chief mechanical engineer, and J. E. Anderson, superintendent of motive power, responsible to the chief general superintendent. In the small hours as the flow abates, Hughes goes off on the footplate of a crimson lake 990 class 4-4-0 heading for Leeds and piloted to Hawes Junction by a Johnson 2-4-0. Anderson, Midland-bred, takes up a breezy position in the cab of another Claughton 4-6-0, spurning assistance to climb to the 915ft of Shap Summit and descend to the Lune crossing at Lancaster.

Railwaymen, sometimes disappointed with the present, are particularly prone to consider 'might-have-beens'. So far as is known, this little episode never took place. Had it done so, however, history might have been rather different. For the inherited problems of the LMS in the locomotive field were not difficult to see.

Visualise, if you will, Carlisle Citadel for two hours from 11.30pm. A procession of up trains arrives; off come the Scottish engines (the old company frontiers held firm until the late 1920s) though few had come much more than 100 miles, through coaches are added, wheels tapped, brakes tested, whistles blown, and off go the trains into the darkness to fight their way over the Cumbrian fells and the Pennines. Trains from the Caledonian predominate, from Glasgow, Edinburgh, Perth and Aberdeen, arriving mostly behind gleaming blue 4-4-0 Dunalastairs and their derivatives, though a Pickersgill 60 class 4-6-0 could well put in an appearance. From the Nithsdale line, the G&SW's St Pancras sleeper comes in behind one of Manson's pretty little saturated 4-6-0s, shiny in its dark green livery. The assistant engines that helped these trains to clamber out of the Clyde valley to the Southern Uplands have long since been detached. The Port Road 'Paddy' arrives behind a pair of Manson 4-4-0s, necessary to get its steamer passengers from Larne over the long 1 in 80 Galloway gradients.

Onward to Shap the big blackberry-black Claughtons usually go forward alone, getting no assistance to the summit until the load tops 420 tons. Even the George V 4-4-0s and the 4-6-0 Princes take 370 tons without argument. But on the Midland route to Ais Gill there is nothing bigger than Deeley's 4-4-0 compounds and 990s; weight for weight very similar to the Georges, they are rigidly limited to 240 tons, and so double-heading is rife. There is an utter dichotomy of thought between the major LMS partners at Derby and Crewe, which D. W. Sanford aptly summed up:

At Derby the nice little engines were made pets of. They were housed in nice clean sheds and were very lightly loaded. There must have been a Royal Society for the Prevention of Cruelty to Engines in existence . . . At Crewe they just didn't care so long as their engines could roar and rattle along with a good paying load, which they usually did.

In a land which had dissipated much of its wealth in a great and bloody war, could it continue?

The LMS inherited over 10,300 steam locomotives, nearly two thirds of them of Crewe and Derby parentage. Many were elderly, and some were positively antediluvian. Fewer than 1,900 were superheated, and when the rough-and-ready Midland power classification was applied to them, only about a third warranted anything higher than Class 2. Most companies had built or bought locomotives for use system-wide, rather than producing horses for courses. A notable exception with its larger engines was the Caledonian; it only possessed 65 4-6-0s, but they were of 10 different classes!

Almost all the railways which had attempted the transition from successful 4-4-0 to more powerful 4-6-0 for express passenger work came more-or-less unstuck; the Midland had seen no reason to go down that road at all. On the LNWR the outstanding performer was undoubtedly the 60-ton superheated George the Fifth 4-4-0 which was expected to take 400-ton expresses south of Preston as a matter of course. They did it brilliantly, thanks to a boiler and front end designed to produce horse-power at speed, but their frames were light and whippy and more than one went into Crewe Works for overhaul fractured from horn gap to top edge. The superheated 4-6-0s, Princes and 4-cylinder Claughtons, could hardly outperform them except on a greasy rail. The Prince's shallow grate was tricky to fire, while the Claughton had been strangled at birth by an undersized boiler barrel thanks to weight restrictions. Hughes' first venture into the 4-6-0 arrangement at Horwich had been an unmitigated disaster, but total rebuilding and superheating had given a creditable but hardly outstanding machine which could work turn-and-turn about with the Claughtons. Economical they were not, however, and a cost conscious management could work up little enthusiasm for them. The Scottish engines were a generally indifferent lot, with the possible exception of the six Highland River class, and offered no prospects south of Hadrian's Wall.

On the freight side the provision of more powerful engines had proved

Fast 'Old Scrap'

The late Colonel Cantlie well known as a railway engineering consultant, especially for his work in the design of the famous 4-8-4KF class for China was trained as a premium apprentice at Crewe under C. J. Bowen-Cooke. He used to tell the story of how he once went to Euston with the great man – as usual in the saloon behind the famous 8ft 6in diameter single wheeler *Cornwall*. On arrival Bowen-Cooke found that he did not have some papers he needed so Cantlie was detailed to take the special back to Crewe and get them back for late afternoon. So they set off and at Rugby were held by the bobby alongside the box. On enquiring why the driver was told that he could be holding up the 'Corridor': somewhat naturally the crew and Cantlie were not happy with this knowing the wrath which could ensue if their task was not undertaken to time; they said so in no uncertain terms indicating that there would be no trouble in showing the LNW's crack train a clean pair of heels.

'What with that load of old scrap', said the signalman. But they made further loud noises and were given permission via control to proceed. Cantlie said that apart from the wobble of the short saloon it was an uneventful trip with the old engine clocking up speeds well in excess of 80mph. But as he watched through the window, the piston only moved (because of that huge single wheel) as though they were doing 50.

Southbound from Carlisle. During the early days the LMS was chronically short of 'big' motive power and until the coming of the Royal Scots in 1927 the heavy Scottish expresses needed to be double headed, particularly over the steep banks north of Preston. With the amalgamation ex-L&Y 'Dreadnought' 4-6-0s were drafted into this work but they certainly failed to outshine the Claughtons. Ex-LNWR George Whale unsuperheated Precursor No 5263 Oceanic pilots an unknown member of the Hughes class probably in the mid to late 1920s. Note the coal piled high on the tenders and the approximate date confirmed by the lack of an LMS type shed plate on the smokebox of the Precursor plus the newly marked LMS on the LNWR van to the right of the picture.

Small Engine Inheritance. 'M stands for Midland with engines galore, two on each train and asking for more'. So ran the jibe of its competitors. This policy was continued by an ex-Derby dominated locomotive department in the early years of the LMS with the building of a large number of Class 2P 4-4-0s and three-cylinder Compounds. The principle is well illustrated here by a Class 1P 2-4-0 No 237 piloting an unknown 4-4-0 Compound on an up Manchester Central to St Pancras express near Chapel-en-le-Frith. The first and third coaches are ex-LNWR while the second is a comfortable MR twelve-wheel diner: all are wooden bodied.

easier, since speed was unimportant and sheer boiler power was seldom demanded. The LNWR and L&YR had adopted the 0-8-0 in the last decade of the nineteenth century, and on both railways progressive development had provided highly competent machines. Indeed, the G2s of the LNWR almost monopolised the main line freight into the 1930s, and were still well in evidence in the 1960s, having lasted longer than their LMS derivatives. The Caledonian, alone north of the border, dabbled with an ungainly 0-8-0 design, but elsewhere the 0-6-0 reigned supreme. Some were positively ancient – over 400 Midland double-framed engines were already 50–60 years old in 1923; the LNWR contributed nearly 90 DX class, the earliest of which was the 399th locomotive built at Crewe, in 1858! The most modern were the Midland Class 4Fs, practically all built since 1917, but they were certainly no masterpieces and had to be used in pairs on the bread-and-butter coal trains from Toton to Brent. Only for the jointly owned Somerset & Dorset had Derby produced 2-8-0s.

So our Carlisle subcommittee of two might have recognised three gaping voids in the new LMS fleet. First was the need for a big passenger engine, capable of dealing single-handed with heavy trains over the northern hills. With the possible exception of the Hughes Dreadnought there was no existing engine of proved worth with the potential for development and reproduction. Secondly, a versatile mixed traffic engine, equally at home on much freight and all but the fastest passenger trains, was becoming a clear requirement; the outside cylindered 2-6-0 was by now well established on other railways in the South. Finally, there was a yawning gap in heavy freight power, particularly for the Midland's lucrative coal traffic to London and the South of England, ánd also as a replacement for ageing 0-8-0s. It was a daunting picture.

Nor were the problems confined to overall design concepts. Detailed mechanical design often left a great deal to be desired and resulted in inflated maintenance costs, and loss of availability. Frequent hot axle-boxes tended to be regarded as one of the facts of life; for many years the use of two inside cylinders, the crank axle usually encumbered by the four eccentrics of Stephenson valve gear, had resulted in undersized and overloaded journals. Axlebox design and provision for lubrication often compounded the problem, so that shed wheeldrops or sheerlegs were seldom idle. Boiler and firebox design, too, left ample scope for improvement, particularly when small boilers were pushed to high evaporation rates; tubes and tubeplates suffered.

The new organisation set up by the LMS now had a profound effect on the locomotive fleet. The Midland star was in the ascendant within the operating function, and the majority practice of the CME managing the locomotive running activity was overturned in favour of a superintendent of motive power answerable to the chief general superintendent, J. H. Follows. This brought to the fore a strong Midland character – J. E. Anderson – who held the motive power reins until his retirement in 1932.

Looking at the elderly fleet and its weaknesses, a 'scrap-and-build' policy was inevitable. The LNER, severely handicapped financially,

Pickersgill bogie. An eleven coach train of mixed Caledonian and LNWR stock between Aberdeen and Ferryhill around 1924/5. The engine is No 14452 still with smokebox wing plates, Caledonian style, but LMS cast iron smokebox numberplate, crest on cabside and large numerals on the eight-wheeled tender. The coaches in the background have already been painted in the new livery but those on the train appear to be in their pre-grouping colours.

LNWR as LMS. George V class 4-4-0 No 5337 T. J. Hare *heads an up express on Whitmore troughs in the early 1930s. The locomotive was built at Crewe in 1910 and withdrawn from service in 1936. It is seen here in black livery. The coaches are all LNWR, the first and last 50ft arc roof corridor brake composites, the remainder 57ft elliptical roof corridors.*

Interim Express Power. Rebuilt Claughton Class 5XP 4-6-0 No 5946 Duke of Connaught *hauling the 11.50am from Euston to Liverpool and Manchester on Whitmore troughs in the early 1930s. The locomotive was rebuilt to the form shown in 1928 with larger boiler and Caprotti valve gear and was withdrawn in 1941.*

The stock is either LNWR or early LMS and there is a 12-wheel dining car sixth from the engine.

could find material which was worth rebuilding or even putting into further production; not so the LMS. There was some limited rationalisation, by fitting Caledonian standard boilers to suitable Highland classes, but otherwise rebuilding was largely confined to two attempts to rescue the Claughtons from the slough. E. S. Cox has given details of the daily availability of 23 of them on the Midland Division (where, it must be admitted, they were regarded with little sympathy). During two months in 1930–31, an average of 29 per cent of their days were spent under repair either in main works or at sheds, with a further 13 per cent under shed examination, and they averaged no more than 91 miles a day! The rebuilding failed to achieve a major improvement.

The powerful Midland influence saw Midland locomotive designs, with minor changes to reflect conditions elsewhere on the system, as the immediate answer to most problems. The Derby drawing office was set to work updating three classes, mainly by conversion to left hand drive and some cutting-down of height to meet Scottish gauge restrictions. They were the 4-4-0 Deeley/Fowler compound, the Class 4F 0-6-0 and the Johnson Class 3F 0-6-0 shunting tank; later the Fowler Class 2P 4-4-0 rebuild was added, on which some further work to improve the unsatisfactory front end was also done. From the 1924 building programme until the end of 1932 these four classes were built to a total of 1,265 locomotives. They may have been the apples of Anderson's eye, but they were obsolescent from the time they appeared.

The operating impact of these engines and associated Midland load limits on the West Coast main line was immediate. LNWR engines which had walked away with prodigious loads were now expected to take a pilot engine. It did not always happen, of course, for an independent spirit dies hard. T. Lovatt Williams told of a George the Fifth at Euston under the new era at the head of a 15 coach train including two 12-wheel diners totalling well over 400 tons. The driver, leaning over the cab side

Before the delivery of the Royal Scot class 4-6-0s the Royal Scot express between London and Glasgow was entrusted south of Carlisle to selected LNWR locomotives chosen for their mechanical condition and marked with 'S' at the top of the cabside. Here the 15-coach up train double headed by Precursor class 4-4-0 No 5295 and small-boilered Claughton 4-6-0 No 6009 pass Hatch End in 1928, then still a green fields area but today very much part of the North West London suburbs.

Delivery of a Giant. The first LMS Beyer Garratt, No 4997, en route from Beyer Peacock's works at Gorton, Manchester to Derby in April 1927. (To traffic 6 April 1927). This was an only partly successful attempt to solve the problem of doubleheading coal trains on the Midland main line. The first cost of these locomotives was £10,000 each, money sadly wasted as instead of letting the experienced manufacturers get on with the job, the LMS authorities at Derby insisted on their own modifications, for example standard Class 4F 0-6-0 axleboxes, causing ever onward problems of running hot.

in quiet contemplation of the platform scene, was challenged by a Midland-reared official 'Good morning, driver, where's your pilot engine?' The driver removed his pipe from his mouth and remarked, more in pity than in anger 'In the shed, where she ought to be. Who do you think we are, the b . . . . . Midland?' The compounds could cope with the Euston–Birmingham two-hour expresses, which were of moderate weight, but not the Anglo-Scottish trains. A temporary compromise led to selected LNW engines in first class condition getting dispensation to exceed laid-down loadings – the 'S' scheme – but it was only a temporary palliative. The futility of the whole policy became woefully apparent in the summer of 1927 with the introduction of the new prestige Royal Scot; its 15-coach formation of about 420 tons had to be worked by a Claughton assisted by a George or Precursor south of Carnforth, and by a *pair* of new compounds over Shap.

The mixed traffic deficiency was tackled head-on; at the end of 1923 Hughes was asked to produce a design for a new 2-6-0 with wide route availability. The design went through numerous permutations, and a degree of Midlandisation – including the anachronistic tender – before emerging in 1926. It showed Horwich practice at its most enlightened in a robust, free running and economical engine which set new standards for the infant LMS.

1925 saw the problem of the Toton–Brent coal train workings tackled, though the method of approach was well nigh incredible. Hughes, as CME, after much study of proposals for a 2-8-2 freight engine, concluded that a Beyer–Garratt might well be the answer, and went to Beyer, Peacock in Manchester with his ideas. The firm recommended a 2-6-2+2-6-2 to their normal excellent standards, but with Hughes' departure it was not pursued. Meanwhile, *quite independently*, Anderson

as superintendent of motive power had approached Beyer, Peacock in the very same month to work up a scheme for a 2-6-0+0-6-2, using the S&DJ 2-8-0 design as the basis for the cylinders and motion, Midland undersized axleboxes, and even the 8ft 0in + 8ft 6in coupled wheelbase which was Derby's universal trademark. Perhaps more remarkably, it was Anderson, and not the CME, who initialled the contract with the firm for this inferior machine. It could handle trains of up to 1,400 tons, but coal and water consumptions were high and mechanically it proved totally unsatisfactory. One can now only wish wistfully that the builder's own proposal had been adopted instead.

Having cleared its desks of most of the redesign work on the four Midland classes, Derby was now charged with designing a new suburban tank engine. That such an engine was badly needed may be gleaned from the fact that the intensive and difficult service on the London, Tilbury & Southend was being operated by nothing bigger than saturated 4-4-2 tanks, the last batch of which was built as late as 1930! The 2-6-4 wheel arrangement was wisely selected. By the greatest good fortune a late but vital change in the design was made; Fowler came back from the reading of an Institution of Locomotive Engineers paper by one of his junior staff and ordered the redesign of the Walschaerts valve gear for long lap and long travel. The resultant engine was an outstanding success, and it was by no means uncommon for the 5ft 9in diameter wheels to turn at well over 80mph – even 90mph on occasions – on London suburban trains.

Meanwhile, the problem of a heavy express passenger locomotive would not go away. Hughes had outlined a Pacific design based on pre-amalgamation work at Horwich, but Anderson would not touch it. Fowler's people in 1925 had had thoughts of a three-cylinder compound 4-6-0, but in the following year interest was switched to a four-cylinder

> **Coal Garratts**
> New schedules for coal trains from the Nottinghamshire area, which may consist of as many as 87 wagons, and weigh, with load, approximately 1,400 tons, have been put into operation, so that the fastest will now cover the 127 miles from Toton Sidings to London in 6 hours 40 minutes at an average speed of over 19mph. This speed is a comparatively high one for a long and heavy coal train with which great care has to be exercised in starting and stopping, and is made possible by the use of Garratt locomotives, of which the LMS has 33 in service . . . To feed them with fuel, mechanical coaling plants have been installed at Cricklewood, Wellingborough and Toton.
> *LMS Magazine*, January 1933.

St Pancras Suburban Power. The development of suburban tanks (all fitted with condensing apparatus for working over the partly underground Metropolitan Widened Lines to Moorgate) from Kirtley through Johnson on the MR to Fowler on the LMS. The engines are outside framed 0-4-4WT No 1220, 0-4-4T No 1377 and (early numbering) 2-6-2T No 15530.

Silver Jubilee Exhibition. Euston station during the exhibition of locomotives and rolling stock to mark 25 years of the King's reign with locomotives No 5348 Coronation *and 5552* Silver Jubilee *on display 2 May 1935. These two locomotives represented development during King George V's reign, No 5348 (The 5000th locomotive built at Crewe) was completed in his coronation year, 1911, and finally withdrawn in June 1940.* Silver Jubilee *built at Crewe in 1935 was specially painted in glossy black with raised chromium-plated letters and figures.*

compound Pacific. Again it was killed off; the users were convinced that a 4-6-0 was capable of doing all that was necessary. To prove the point, the GWR's *Launceston Castle* was borrowed in September 1926 for trials between Euston and Carlisle. The outline design of a big three-cylinder 4-6-0, patronisingly dubbed an 'Improved Castle' at the time, was put in hand with great urgency, and Fowler was told to get the new engines designed and *enough built* to take over the Anglo-Scottish service in the 1927 summer timetable. The story of their birth is now well known; North British Locomotive Co in Glasgow got the contract in December 1926 to design and build 50 locomotives, and the first Royal Scot was

delivered seven months later, a remarkable achievement. It proved to be basically a most successful design, taking 420 ton trains unaided over Shap and Beattock as part of long through workings between Euston and Carlisle (299 miles), and Crewe and Perth (292 miles). Yet had Fowler not asserted himself over the 2-6-4 tank valve gear, it was by no means certain that the Scot would have had similar valve events and thus proved the success it did. Weaknesses did appear with increasing mileage – coupled axleboxes, springing and bogie control (modified after the Weaver Junction derailment in 1930), frame fractures, and piston valve leakage, but apart from frames were overcome by modifications.

While the Claughton rebuilding failed to produce a machine giving overall satisfaction, at least the larger boiler was a success. Its combination with what was essentially a Royal Scot chassis produced the first Baby Scots as 'rebuilds' of Claughtons in 1930. These were an instant success, and from 1932 further examples appeared to a total of 52 engines; the Claughton content of the 'rebuilds' was negligible.

However, if a new halo of enlightenment pervaded the Derby drawing office, there were periods when it wilted for lack of a firm directing hand. This weakness showed up badly in two new designs. The class 7F 0-8-0s, an update of the LNWR G2, was given a good front end and proved highly efficient, but the axleboxes were totally inadequate, and they went to the wall before the G2s from which they were derived. The 2-6-2 tanks were quite inadequate for their power classification 3, with small boiler (due to weight restriction) and a short travel Walschaerts gear – this after the trail-blazing 2-6-4 tanks.

Record Breaker. Stanier's early Pacific No 6201 Princess Elizabeth *as originally built with domeless boiler and small straight-sided tender at Crewe in the early 1930s. Note the footbridge from the station to the works.*

55

Stanier's Stalwart. Probably the best mixed traffic 4-6-0 on Britain's railway system the Black Five was popular with both running and mechanical departments. No 5440 of Bath shed (22C) and very much off its beaten track, leaves Penrith southbound in 1947. On the right is a Webb LNWR 0-6-2 'Watford' tank – almost certainly No 6883 which was stationed at Carlisle Upperby (12B) at the time.

So the first phase of LMS locomotive development closed. By the end of 1930 the fleet had been reduced by a thousand, and the withdrawal of pre-Grouping designs was in full flood. The holocaust continued during E. J. H. Lemon's brief spell as CME in 1931. But the design vacillation and lack of firm direction by Fowler in the face of formidable pressure from Anderson left a fleet which as a whole was hardly capable of meeting the pressures which the severe recession of the 1930s would impose. With the dawn of 1932 Lemon was moved upstairs to a vice presidency to make room for William Stanier as CME, brought in from Swindon and with long and enviable experience of the Great Western mystique. Later that year Anderson retired, to be replaced by D. C. Urie. But now the balance between the two posts had swung the other way, with Stanier the dominant partner.

Stanier brought a strong sense of the superiority of Swindon practice. Henceforward, new engines would feature taper boilers with Swindon-style Belpaire fireboxes, low superheat and top feed; circular smokebox on a saddle; cylinders with large valves, straight steam ports and direct exhaust passages to a jumper blastpipe; large axle journals with Swindon-style axleboxes; side bolster bogies and pony trucks; and a comfortable cab with better grouping of controls. Looking over the stock of 9,032 locomotives for which he assumed responsibility, it was not difficult to recognise that there were only four classes which were sound

56

enough to develop using these design features. A massive effort by the three principal drawing offices produced new versions of three of these classes, the 2-6-0 in 1933, and the three-cylinder Jubilee 4-6-0 and three-cylinder 2-6-4 tank in 1934. The latter engine was a special purpose one with reduced hammerblow to meet the special requirements of the Tilbury line. In 1935 a two-cylinder 2-6-4 tank emerged for general duty, together with a 2-6-2 tank which was no great improvement on its Fowler predecessor, again due to boiler limitations.

Three unsatisfied requirements occupied his In tray on arrival. The most urgent was a larger West Coast express passenger engine, but nearly as important were a new 4-6-0 general purpose engine and a new heavy freight engine – all deficiencies recognised years before but not adequately met. The passenger requirement was for an engine to handle 500 ton trains between Euston and Glasgow, 400 miles without change or assistance, and offering scope for acceleration. This was beyond 4-6-0 capability, and Stanier set about producing a Pacific; how Hughes and Fowler must have squirmed at this development! Stanier looked back to his association with Swindon's only 4-6-2, and visualised an amalgam of *The Great Bear* and the more modern King 4-6-0. In the event this was largely what emerged as *Princess Royal* in 1933. The new mixed traffic engine appeared the following year, with GWR Hall influence stamped all over it, and the heavy freight engine came in 1935 as the long-awaited modern 2-8-0. The numbers built (842 4-6-0s and 852 2-8-0s) were living proof of their value. In these locomotives all the Stanier features, save two only, stood the test of time; the low superheat feature lasted no more than two years, and Stanier admitted later that it had been a mistake. The jumper blastpipe was also under suspicion by this time, and by 1936 it had been abandoned.

Stanier's early years also saw the start of a brave experiment and the winding up of another. In conjunction with Metropolitan-Vickers (now part of GEC) he produced a remarkable locomotive in 1935 which was essentially a Princess Pacific but with geared drive from two non-condensing turbines. 'Turbomotive' ran nearly 450,000 miles before withdrawal in 1950; it produced some impressive performances but mechanically had a rather chequered career, spending long periods in Crewe works with gear train failures and lubrication problems. The same year saw the emergence of *British Legion*, essentially a Royal Scot with tapered boiler and using parts of the experimental white elephant *Fury*, an ultra-high pressure 4-6-0 with three-stage Schmidt-Henschel boiler. The 'Legion' acted as a test-bed for the later rebuilding of the Royal Scots.

The Princess Pacifics, when fitted with large superheaters, were showing themselves most capable engines, but on the toughest workings such as the accelerated Midday Scot from 1936, which loaded at weekends to well over 500 tons, they were on their limit. To undertake new high-speed work and the heaviest duties, Stanier's magnum opus (with which the name of Tom Coleman, recently appointed chief locomotive draughtsman, must forever be associated), appeared in 1937, the Duchess or Coronation Pacifics. Most were built with streamlined

---

Hammer of the Scot

It was one of those tenderfuls that you quite often got at Camden, heavily laced with enormous slabs of hard – and that *does* mean *hard* – Yorkshire, lovely hot, clean coal but tough on the fireman because it was all coal hammer work to break up the jams behind the tender coal doors. It was a time just after the war when the engine tool supply was pretty desperate; the storeman was outwardly sympathetic, but when living hand-to-mouth for coal hammers the better ones were put aside for the home team. The Edge Hill crew on the rebuilt Scot were given one with a shaft which had seen some hard knocks.

All went well until after Linslade Tunnel; then a gaping void developed at the shovelling plate, with a particularly large slab wedged and blocking the smaller stuff feeding down. The fireman resignedly picked up the coal hammer again and started to attack the offender with the pick end. It meant hitting upwards where the point of impact could not be seen. He dare not open the coal doors, or the whole cab would be knee deep. Then one swing failed to contact coal, the shaft hit the underside of the doors and broke, the hammer head skittering across under the cab doors and out into the blue.

Calamity! The fireman prodded and levered with the shovel, but the slab stayed put. Fortunately, he had a heavy fire on, so the driver eased the regulator and pulled the reverser right up to 10 per cent to keep the train moving with a minimum of steam. By Roade the express was going more like a freight, the pressure gauge distinctly tired, but the fall to Blisworth got them rolling again.

Meantime the driver had foraged in his bag, torn the centre sheet from his Fortnightly Notice, and pencilled in large letters 'Coal Hammer at Rugby'. Looking over *continued overleaf*

continued

what bit of coal the fireman was getting, he selected a suitable nugget, wrapped his message tightly round it and waited for Banbury Lane Box to appear on the curve on the down side. Approaching the box, he leaned out, waving his package to attract the bobby's attention and judged how to lob it on to the landing outside the signalbox door. Just at the critical moment, the engine gave . . . not a real kick but enough to spoil his aim. The wrapped coal flew high, glanced off the door post and through the window in a shower of glass.

There was a cleaner waiting on Rugby platform with a replacement hammer all right, so after being overtime rebuilding the neglected fire they made Liverpool not much late. They were rostered for the same job two days later, and discussed whether to deliver an apology by the same means, but decided not. So passing Banbury Lane the driver stood in the cab doorway, his hands together, raised as in prayer and his eyes briefly closed in humility – and to hide the twinkle in them.

casing, but this was removed in 1946/9, leaving a most imposing engine. The boiler and firebox were enlarged to the very limit of the loading gauge, and the front end improved with removal of the inside valve gears, the inside valves being worked by rocking levers from the outside valve gear. The Duchesses proved their breeding by producing the highest horsepower on test of any steam locomotive on British rails.

This range of locomotive designs satisfied traffic needs, and the only significant step during the rest of Stanier's incumbency came in 1942, when two three-cylinder Jubilees were rebuilt with the larger 2A boiler developed from that used on *British Legion* and fitted with double blast-pipe and chimney. This increased their power classification to that of the Royal Scots, and the same features were used in rebuilding the Scots themselves.

The third phase of LMS locomotive development began with Stanier's departure to a government appointment in 1942, and under C. E. Fairburn and H. G. Ivatt became one of consolidation and refinement. Fairburn was not a steam locomotive man, having come from English Electric Co in 1934 to be chief electrical engineer, but was notable in his short reign for a short wheelbase version of the Stanier 2-6-4 tank which was built in quantity. He also actively encouraged development of design features to reduce shed servicing and increase shopping mileages to cope with difficult conditions of wartime operation.

With Fairburn's untimely death H. G. Ivatt became CME late in

Turbomotive. In 1935 the LMS constructed a non-condensing turbine locomotive on a standard Princess class chassis and numbered 6202. It is seen here at Rugby probably heading the 8.30am Euston to Liverpool and Manchester, a favourite turn. There were separate forward and reverse turbines and the photograph is of the forward turbine on the left hand side of the locomotive.

6202 was moderately successful and ran a total of 438,772 miles between 1935 and 1952. It was rebuilt as a four-cylinder reciprocating locomotive No 46202 Princess Anne in 1952 but was destroyed beyond repair in the Harrow disaster of 8 October 1952.

1945. With the war over the delayed scrapping of a host of over-age small locomotives restarted, leaving a need for new small engines for secondary services. Ivatt therefore introduced three new mixed traffic classes, incorporating all the new servicing aids built into their larger sisters. The Class 2 2-6-0s and 2-6-2 tanks emerged in 1946, to be followed in 1947 by a Class 4 2-6-0 the last new design of the LMS, to replace the obsolete Class 4F 0-6-0. One last fling saw the rebuilding of some of the parallel boiler Patriots with the same 2A boiler used on the two rebuilt Jubilees of 1942; unfortunately this work, started in 1946, was never completed under BR auspices.

Steam traction was inevitably the prime traffic mover throughout the life of the LMS, for electrification proposals were shelved for lack of capital or inadequate financial return. But the 1930s saw interested eyes turned towards diesel power for yard shunting. In 1932 a cautious toe was dipped into the water; an ex-Midland 0-6-0 shunting tank was rebuilt as a diesel-hydraulic shunter with jackshaft drive. It was not a success mechanically, and was soon laid aside. At the same time orders were placed with private builders for eight diesel-mechanical shunters of their standard designs, in the 150–180hp range, for evaluation. They proved unsuitable for general yard shunting duties. Another order placed in that year, however, was of far greater significance; Armstrong Whitworth was contracted to supply an 0-6-0 diesel-electric shunter with 250hp engine and single-motor jackshaft drive. Delivered in 1934, it was followed within months by an English Electric demonstrator with 300hp engine and two nose-suspended motors.

Flying Pig. The progenitor of Ivatt's post war 2-6-0 No 3000 when new in 1947. Built at Horwich the engine has all the looks of a modern utility locomotive, double chimney, high running plate, comfortable cab, tender back plate and top feed. Classified 4F No 3000 is painted in 1946/47 black with straw lettering and numbering.

From top to bottom. LMS version of the Midland three-cylinder Compound 4-4-0 built as a stop gap express engine prior to the introduction of the Royal Scots. Horwich built 'Crab' 2-6-0 based on a Hughes design, mainstay of many excursions and mixed traffic services until the coming of the Stanier Black Five. This illustration shows the locomotive in works grey with LMS crest and Midland style numbering on the tender. Standard Fowler design 2-6-4 tank for suburban services: forerunner of the Stanier and Fairburn taper boiler 2-6-4T. No 6100 Royal Scot as seen just after its trip to Canada and the USA in 1933 carrying amended nameplates, bell and headlamp. Hurriedly introduced in 1927 as the first LMS main line express locomotive of quality, designed and built by outside contractors to LMS requirements. The locomotive (in taper boiler form) is now preserved at Bressingham.

These two locomotives proved the answer to all prayers. They were available 24 hours a day and carried enough fuel for a week's work. The Armstrong Whitworth machine, manned round the clock by three drivers (an agreement with the unions for single manning having been negotiated in 1933) in Brent yard (Willesden) shifted loads of up to 1,000 tons at low speeds, using 60 gallons of fuel a day. No further proof of diesel potential was needed: late in 1934 orders were placed with the same builder for 20 more, with increased engine horsepower. With experience of all these locomotives, a specification was drawn up under Fairburn's guiding hand for a standard diesel-electric 0-6-0 shunter, using the 350hp English Electric 6KT engine, and providing a cab with duplicated controls, 600 gallon fuel tank and a maximum speed of 20mph. An interesting feature was a supplementary speedometer with 0–3mph scale for close control of speed when humping. Building started in 1939; by the end of 1947 50 were in service. But LMS diesel aspirations were not confined to shunting applications; there was full recognition of what other countries, notably the USA, were doing in the main line field. Following the desperate coal shortage of the 1946–7 winter, it was announced that three diesel-electric main line locomotives were to be built for evaluation. Two were to be Derby-built Co-Cos with 1,600hp English Electric engines, able to work in multiple on the heaviest Anglo-Scottish trains, while the third was to be a Bo-Bo from North British Locomotive Co with 800hp Paxman engine for secondary services. The first Co-Co, No 10000, was completed under pressure just in time to carry the raised LMS letters on her flank, but her sister was always a BR engine. They proved reasonably satisfactory prototypes, from which a lineage can be traced to today's Class 40s, 50s, 56s and 58s. The Bo-Bo did not appear until 1950, but was underpowered and had only a short life.

So the 25 years' existence of the LMS saw the locomotive stock reduced, thanks to improved breeding and greater availability, from 10,316 in 1923 to 8,084 steam and 54 diesel locomotives by the end of 1947. From a start which was hesitant and essentially backward-looking it came to take a strong lead in both steam and diesel development. It was to stand British Railways in good stead.

Locomotive Stock at 31 December 1947

4-6-2 (50) Princess Royal Class 7P: 6200/1/3–12 (12). Turbomotive Class 7P: 6202 (1). Duchess Class 7P: 6220–56 (37) (Nos 6226/9/43 streamlined).
4-6-0 (1104) Standard Class 5MT: 4758–5499 (742) (Nos 4826/7/9/30/44 oil-burning). Patriot Class 5XP: 5500–13/5–20/2–5/7/32–9/41–51 (44). Patriot rebuilt Class 6P: 5514/21/6/8–31/40 (8). Jubilee Class 5XP: 5552–5734/7–42 (189). Jubilee rebuilt Class 6P: 5735/6 (2). Royal Scot Class 6P: 6100/2/5–7/10/3/23/30/4/6/7/40–3/8/51/3/5/6/8/62–5/7 (27). Royal Scot rebuilt Class 6P: 6101/3/4/8/9/11/2/4–22/4–9/31–3/5/8/9/44–7/9/50/2/4/7/9–61/6/8–70 (44). LNWR Claughton rebuilt Class 5XP: 6004 (1). LNWR 19in Goods Class 4F: 8801/24/34 (3). L&YR Hughes Class 5P: 10412/23/9/32/42/8/55 (7) (Nos 10442/8/55 built LMS). CR 60 Class 4P: 14630/1/4–54 (23) (14630/1/4 built LMS). HR Clan Class 4P: 14764/7 (2). HR Cumming Goods Class 4P: 17950/1/3–6 (6). LNWR Prince of Wales Class 4P: 25648/73, 25722/52/87, 25827 (6).

4-4-0 (651) S&DJR Class 2P: 322–6 (5). MR 6ft 6in saturated Class 2P: 383/5/91 (3). MR 7ft superheated rebuild Class 2P: 332/7/51/3/6/9/62/4/70/7/94/7, 400–27/30/2–4/6–9/43/4/6–8/50/2–6/8/9/61–4/6/8/70–2/7–80/2–99, 500–62 (157). Standard Class 2P: 563–90/2–9, 600–38/40–99, 700 (136) (Nos 633–5 were S&DJR). MR Class 3P: 711/5/20/6–9/31/4–6/9–41/3/5/7/8/56–8/62 (22). Standard Compound Class 4P: 900–39, 1045–1199 (195). MR Compound Class 4P: 1000–44 (45). CR Dunalastair IV Class 2P: 14363 (1). HR Loch Class 2P: 14379/85 (2). HR Ben Class 2P: 14397–9, 14401/3/4/9/10/5/6 (10). CR Dunalastair III superheated Class 3P: 14434 (1). CR Dunalastair IV superheated Class 3P: 14438–41/3–60 (22). CR Pickersgill Class 3P: 14461–14508 (48). LNWR Precursor superheated Class 3P: 25297 (1). LNWR George V Class 3P: 25321/50/73 (3).
2-8-0 (567) Standard Class 8F: 8000–11/7/24/6/7/9/33/5–7/50/3–7/60/2–5/7/9/70/3–6/8–85/8–90/2/3/5–9, 8100–

99, 8200–25/64–85/93, 8301–99, 8400–79/90–5, 8500–59, 8600–8704 (556) (Nos 8064/79, 8191, 8269/73, 8370/85/6, 8606/53/96 oil-burning). S&DJR Class 7F: 13800–10 (11).
2-6-0 (308) Hughes Class 4P5F: 2700–2944 (245). Stanier taper boiler Class 4P5F: 2945–84 (40). Standard Class 4F: 3000–2 (3). Standard Class 2F: 6400–19 (20).
2-4-0 (3) MR Johnson Class 1P: 20155/85, 20216 (3).
0-10-0 (1) MR Lickey Banker: 22290 (1).
0-8-0 (706) LNWR G1 Class 6F: 8892/4, 8902/4/6/8/10–3/8/24/9/31/5/9/62, 9011–3/5/7/30/2/8/40/3/52–4/6/8–60/7/71/5/6/83/5/9/91/2/5/8, 9100/2/3/7/24/8/31/3/5/6/40/51/2/6/9/62/5/6/71/5/9/83/4/7/90/3–5/7, 9201/4/8/13/21/2/5/31–3/6/41/8/50/1/5/9/61/3/9/72–4/9/83/5/6/95/7, 9303/5/9/20/4/6/32/4/7/8/46/9/53/9/62/4/70/1/83/4 (123). LNWR G2 and G2A Class 7F: 8893/5–9, 8901/3/5/7/9/14/5/7/20–2/5–7/30/2–4/6/40–5/8/50–4/64/6, 9002–10/4/6/8–29/31/3–7/9/41/2/4–51/5/7/61–6/8–70/2–4/7–82/4/6–8/90/3/4/6/7/9, 9101/4–6/8–17/9–23/5–7/9/30/2/4/7–9/

41–50/3–5/7/8/60/1/3/4/7–70/2–4/6–8/80/1/5/6/8/9/91/2/
6/8/9, 9200/2/3/5/7/9–12/4/5–20/3/4/6–30/4/5/7–40/2–7/
9/52–4/6–8/60/2/4–8/70/1/5–8/80–2/4/7–94/6/8/9, 9302/
4/6–8/10–9/21–3/5/7–31/3/5/9–45/7/8/50–2/4–8/60/1/3/
5–9/81/2/5–99, 9400–54 (379). Standard Class 7F:
9500–9674 (175) (Nos 9511/33, 9613/42/70 oil-burning). L&YR Class 6F: 12727/82, 12806/21/2/5/7/8/31/
4/7/9 (12). L&YR Class 7F: 12841/56/7/70/3/7/86,
12906/10/3/6/35/45/52/6/62/71 (17).

0-6-0 (2180) MR double-framed Class 2F: 22630, 22846/
53/63 (4). MR 4ft 11in Class 2F: 22900–2/4/7/11–3/5/8/
20/1/4/6/9/31–5/40/4–7/50/1/3–5/8/9/63/5/7–71/4–8/82–
4, 2987–90/2–9, 23000–3/5–14/6/8 (75). MR 5ft 3in
Class 2F: 3021/3/7/31/5/7–9/42/4/5/7–52/4/8/61/2/4/6/
71/3/4/8/84/90/4–6/8/9, 3101/3/8/9/13/8/9/23/7 (43).
MR 4ft 11in Class 2F: 3130/4/8/40/4/9–51/3/4/6/7/61/4/
6/8/71/3/5–7 (21). MR 4ft 11in Class 3F: 3137/74/8/80/
1/3/5–9 (11). S&DJR 5ft 3in Class 3F: 3194, 3201/4/11/
6/8/28/48/60 (9). MR 5ft 3in Class 2F: 3190/5/6, 3229/
62/4/70, 3311/60/72/7/85, 3420/3–5/37/45/51/66/73/7/9/
85/9/92/3, 3503/8/11/2/6/7/25–7/33/6/7/9/43/5/51/9/61/
4/6/71/92, 3602/3/17/32/48/55/88/9/91/6, 3703/7/25/6/
38/9/64 (66). MR 5ft 3in Class 3F: 3191–3, 3200/3/5/7/
8/10/12–4/9/22–6/31–5/7/9–54/6–9/61/3/5–9/71/3–5/7/8/
81–4/6/7/90/2–9, 3300/1/5–10/2–5/7–9/21/3–7/9–42/4/
51/5–7/9/61/4/7–71/3/4/8/9/81/6–9/92/4–6/8/9, 3400–2/
5/6/8/10/1/9/27–9/31/3/5/6/9–41/3/4/6/8/9/53/4/6–9/62–
4/8/9/74/6/82/4/90/1/4/6/7/9, 3502/6/7/9/10/4/5/20–4/9/
31/8/40/4/6/8/50/3/8/62/5/8/70/2 – 5/8 – 87/93 – 6/8/9,
3600/4/5/7/8/12/5/8–24/7/9 – 31/3/4/6 – 9/44/5/50 – 3/6 –
8/60–2/4/5/7–9/73–6/8–84/6/7/90/3/8, 3705/9–12/4/5/7/
21/3/4/7–9/31/4/5/7/42/5/7–9/51/3–7/9/90/2/3/5–7/9/73/
5–9/81–7/9–93/5–9, 3800–15/7–33 (378). MR Class 4F:
3835–4026 (192). Standard Class 4F: 4027–4606 (580)
(Nos 4557–61 ex S&DJR, Nos 4466, 4552/85/98 oil-
burning). L&YR Class 25 Class 2F: 12016/9/21–4/30–
2/4/6/7/41/3–7/9/51/3/6/9/63/4 (25). L&YR Class 27
Class 3F: 12088/9/91–5/8/9, 12100/2–5/7/8/10–2/8–21/
3–7/9/32/3/5–41/3/50/2/4/6/7/9–67/9–72/4–7/9/81–4/6/9/
91/2/4/6/7, 12201/3/7/8/12/5–20/5/9–33/5–40/3–6/8/50/
2/3/5/6/8/60/2/6/8–73/5/8–80/4/5/8–90/3/4/6/9, 12300/4/
5/9/11/2/7/9/21/2/6/8/30/1/3/4/6 – 8/41/3/5/8 – 51/3/5–8/
60/2/3/5/6/8/9/74/6/8/9/81/2/6–90/3/7/9, 12400/1/3–5/7/
8/10–8/22/7–33/5/7–50/2–61/4–7, 12515/7/8/21–7/9
(245). FR Class 3F: 12494/9, 12501/8–10 (6). L&YR
Class 28 Class 3F: 12528/41/2/5/9/51/4/7–9/61/8/9/72/
4–6/8–83/6–8/90/2/8, 12602/7–9/15/6/8/9 (37). CR
Class 2F: 17230–47/9–80/2–92/4–6/8/9, 17300–75/7–
99, 17400–27/9–73 (238). CR 812 Class 3F: 17550–66/
8–97/9, 17600–9/11–28 (76). CR 652 Class 3F: 17629–
45 (17). CR Pickersgill Class 3F: 17650–5/8/9/61/3/5–
74/9/81/2/4/6/8–91 (29). HR Class 3F: 17693–5/7–9,
17702 (7). LNWR 17in Coal Class 2F: 28088/91/3/5/7,
28100/4–7/15/6/28/33/41/52/3/8/66/72/91/9, 28202/5/16/
21/7/30/3/4/9/45–7/51/3/6/62/3/71/95/6, 28308/9/12/3
(46). LNWR 18in Goods Class 2F: 28318/33/5/7–9/45/
50/70/2/85/92, 28403/4/8/15/7/28/30/41–3/50/1/7/8/60/
4/84/7/92/4/9, 28505/7/9/11–3/5/21/5–7/9/31/2/42–4/7–
9/51/3/5/6/9/61/75/80/3/5/6/9/92/4/7/8, 28608/11/6/9/22
(75).

4-6-2T (10) CR Class 4P: 15350–6/9–61 (10).
4-4-2T (68) MR (LT&S) Class 2P: 2092–9, 2100–4/6–9
(17). MR (LT&S) Class 3P: 2110–60 (51) (Nos 2110–
34/51–60 built LMS).
2-6-4T (498) Fowler Class 4P: 2300–2424 (125). Stanier
2-cyl Class 4P: 2425–94, 2537–2672 (206). Stanier 3-
cyl Class 4P: 2500–36 (37). Fairburn Class 4P: 2187–9,
2200–99, 2673–99 (130).
2-6-2T (219) Fowler Class 3P: 1–70 (70). Stanier Class
3P: 71–99, 100–47/9–62/4–8/70–99 (135). Stanier
rebuilt Class 3P: 148/63/9, 203 (4). Standard
Class 2MT: 1200–9 (10).

2-6-0+0-6-2T (33) LMS Garratt: 7967–99 (33).
2-4-2T (167) LNWR Class 1P: 6601/3–5, 26616, 6620/8/
32/5/7/9/43/54/6/8/61/3/6/9/73/6/9–83/6–8/91/2. 6701/
10–2/8/27/38/40/2/7/9/57 (43). LNWR Class 2P: 6762
(1). L&YR Class 2P: 10621–3/5/30/1/3/4/6/9/40/2–4/6–
8/50–6/60/5/7/70/1/5/6/8/81/6/7/9/92/5–7, 10703/5/11/2/
4/5/20/1/5/8/31/2/5/6/8/43/6/8–50/2/5/7/62/4–6/77/8/81/
8/93/5/8/9, 10800–2/4/6/7/12/3/5/8/23/9/31/40/2/4/9/50/
2/5/9/65/9/72/3/5/80/6/7/9/92/6/8/9 (109). L&YR Class
3P: 10835/91/3, 10901/3/9/25/34/43/5/50–3 (14).
2-4-0T (1) LNWR Class 1P: 6428 (1).
0-8-4T (14) LNWR Class 7F: 7930–3/6–9/48/51/4/6/8/9
(14) (All built LMS).
0-8-2T (9) LNWR Class 6F: 7875/7/81/4/5/7/8/92/6 (9).
0-6-2T (94) MR (LT&S) Class 3F: 1980–93 (14). LNWR
5ft Class 2P: 6876/8/81/3/99, 6900/6/9/12/7/20/2/4/6/31

(15). LNWR Coal Tank Class 2F: 27553/61/2/80/5/6/ 91/6, 27602/3/19/21/5/7/35/48/54/69/74/81, 7692/9, 7700/3/10/1/5/20/1/30/3/7/40/1/6/51/2/6/7/9/65/9/73/80/ 2/7/9/91/4/6/9, 7802/3/8/12/6/21/2/9, 27830, 7833/6/40/ 1 (64). G&SWR Class 3F: 16905 (1).
0-6-0T (864) MR Class 1F: 1660/1/4/6/8/71/2/4/6/82/6/90/ 5/9, 1702/6/8/10–4/8/20/4–7/34/9/45/7–9/52–4/6/9/62/3/ 7–70/3/7/9–81/8/93–5/7, 1803–5/11/3/4/8/20/4/6/9/33/5/ 8/9/42/4/6/7/52–7/9/60/5/9/70/3–5/8/9/85/9/90/3/5 (95). Standard Dock Class 2F: 7160–9 (10). MR Class 3F: 7200–59 (60). Standard Class 3F: 7260–7399, 7400–55/ 7–99, 7500–52/4–88/90–9, 7600–6/8–10/2/4–6/8–58/61/ 2/4–81 (412) (Nos 7310–6 ex S&DJR). L&YR Barton Wright Class 2F: 11307/13/6/8–21/3/5/36/8/42/3/5/8/53/ 8/61/71/5/6/9/81/90/6/7, 11400/4/5/8/10/2/3/5/9/23–5/7/ 9/32/6/8/9/41/3–7/53/7/8/60/2/4/7–72/4/5/7/9/81/2/4/6– 92/5–9, 11500/3/4/6/10–4/6/9/21/4/6/30 (96). L&YR Dock Class 1F: 11535–7/44/5 (5). CR Class 2F: 16151– 73 (23). CR Class 3F: 16230–16376 (147). LNWR Class 2F: 27480 (1). LNWR (NLR) Class 2F: 27505/9/ 10/2–5/7/20/2/5/7/8/30/2 (15).
0-4-4T (193) MR 5ft 7in Class 1P: 1239/46/7/9/51/2/5/60/ 1 (9). MR 5ft 4in Class 1P: 1272/3/5/8/87/90/5/8, 1303/ 7/15/22/4/30/7/40–2/4/8/50/3/7/8/60/1/5–8/70/1/3/5/7/9/ 82/5/9/90/6/7, 1402/6/11/3/6/20–6/9/30 (56). LMS Class 2P: 1900–9 (10). HR Class 0P: 15051/3 (2). CR Class 2P: 15116/7/9/21–7/9/30/2–6/8–46/59–62/4–99, 15200– 4/6–40/60–9 (116) (Nos 15260–9 built LMS).
0-4-2T (3) LNWR Bissel Class 1F: 7862/5 (2). LNWR (NLR) Crane Class 0F: 27217 (1).
0-4-0T (62) MR Saddle Class 0F: 1516/8/23 (3). MR Deeley Class 0F: 1528–37 (10). LMS Kitson Class 0F: 7000–4 (5). Sentinel locomotives: 7180–4/90/1 (7) (Nos 7190/1 ex S&DJR). L&YR Pug Class 0F: 11202/4/6/7/ 12/6–8/21/2/7/9–32/4/5/7/40/1/4/6/53 (23). CR Pug Class 0F: 16010/1/20/5–32/5/8/9 (14).

Diesel Locomotives (45)
0-6-0 Diesel Electric 300hp: 7058 (1).
0-6-0 Diesel Electric 350hp: 7074/6/9–99, 7110–29 (43).
Co-Co Diesel Electric 1600hp: 10000 (1).

Rail Motor Vehicles (267)
Steam (2) L&YR: 10617 (1). LNWR: 29988 (1).
Diesel (3) Leyland rail cars: 29950–2 (3).
Electric (262) London (106). Liverpool–Southport (70 + 2 baggage cars). Wirral (19). Manchester–Bury (38). MSJ&AR (24). Lancaster–Morecambe–Heysham (3).

Service Locomotives (12)
0-6-0T (10) LNWR Special Tank 3323; C&W Dept Wolverton, 3/6/7/8 (5). L&YR Barton Wright: 11304/ 5/24/68/94 (5).
0-4-0T (1) MR Saddle: 1509 (1).
Diesel (1) 0-4-0 Diesel Mechanical: ED No 2 (1).
Miscellaneous Standard Gauge Locomotives not included in Stock (2) 0-4-0 MR Battery Electric: 1550. NSR Battery Electric: 1.

Locomotives on Loan (69)
2-10-0 (2) From MOS. WD: 73798/9.
2-8-0 (67) From LNER. Standard Class 8F: 8705–58/60– 72.

Northern Counties Committee

Locomotive Stock at 31 December 1947
5ft 3in Gauge
4-4-0 (27) Class A1: 33/4, 58, 62/4–6/9 (8). Class U1: 4A (1). Class U2: 70–87 (18).
0-6-0 (3) Class V: 13–5.
2-6-0 (15) Class W: 90–104.
2-6-4T (10) Class WT: 1–10.
0-6-0T (2) Class Y: 18/9.
0-4-0T (1) Class N: 16.
Diesel Locomotive (1) Class X: 17.
Rail Motor Vehicles (4) Leyland Rail Cars: 1–3 (3). Diesel Rail Car: 4 (1).

3ft 0in Gauge
2-4-2T (4) Class S: 43, 111 (2). Class S1: 41/2 (2).

Locomotives on Loan (2)
0-6-0 (1) From Harland & Wolff. Diesel Mechanical 225hp: 22.
1A–A1 (1) From Harland & Wolff. Diesel Electric 500hp: 28.

Dundalk, Newry & Greenore Railway
Locomotive Stock at 31 December 1947
5ft 3in Gauge
0-6-0T (5) 1–4, 6.

County Donegal Railways Joint Committee
Locomotive Stock at 31 December 1947
3ft 0in Gauge
2-6-4T (7) Class 5A: 1–3 (3). Class 5: 4/5/6/8 (4).
4-6-4T (4) Class 4: 9–12 (4).
0-4-0 Diesel Mechanical (1) Gardner 75hp: 11 (1).
Rail Motor Vehicles (10) Ford 36hp Petrol: 9 (1). Gardner 75hp Diesel: 7,8,12/4/5 (5). Gardner 103hp Diesel: 16/7/8 (3). Gardner 75hp (ex CVR): 10 (1).
Service Vehicle (1) Ford 26hp Petrol: 1.

Locomotive Allocation at 10 November 1945
1A Willesden: 425/34, 515, 653, 1090, 1105/52/60/5/74, 2354/72/8/99, 2424/43, 2541, 2610, 2787, 2817, 2928/ 31/3/4, 3018/98, 4063/83, 4116, 4345/9/70/84/5, 4438/ 40/94, 5024/7/70/1, 5114/40, 5257/82, 5323/5/6/7/71/8, 5411/3/31/9, 5500/1/3/4/9/10/8/9/45, 5669, 7058/81/2/6/ 96/8/9, 7110/6–9, 7281, 7318/27/42/55/7/61/80/95, 7412/74/5, 7520/31, 7675/6/99, 7700/10/51/7/9/65/87/9/ 91/7, 7821, 8171–4, 8370–2, 8600–5/10–2/24–30/2–4/ 48/9/55–60/79, 8943/53, 9003/12/21/41/62, 9128/39/63/ 4/96, 9272/7/97, 9300/34/93, 9448/53/4, 27553/8/61/71/ 90/7, 27602/9/23/66/74. (173).
1B Camden 5505/7/41/59, 5606, 5735/6/8/9, 6100/1/14–6/ 9/20–3/30/40/1/8/9/50/2/5/9/70, 6202/25–9/37–41/3–8, 7354/6/8/9, 7430/1/67, 7522/7/9, 7667–9/71. (60).
1C Watford 10, 20, 43, 672, 2445/6/82/94, 2589/90, 4372/96, 4443, 6408/9, 6667, 6869/70/1/93, 6909, 8964, 9145, 9262, 9323. (25).
2A Rugby 52, 143, 203, 420/33/50, 508/34/54, 1106/7/13/ 54/73, 2576/7, 3151, 3280, 3479, 4354/87/92, 4456/84, 4511, 4866/7, 4910, 5000/3/4/52/7, 5150, 5250, 5391, 5419/30/96/7, 6601/74, 6701/39, 6912/36, 7360/78/9, 7677, 8892/5, 8901/15/34, 9004/1/3/34/49/61, 9107/33/7/ 52/62, 9229, 9319/36/7/44/68/97–9, 9404/8/10/5/8/33/ 41/6/50/2, 22911, 25722/97, 25802, 27624, 28450, 28529/38/56. (93).
2B Bletchley 2442/4/52/8, 2552/66/82/91, 2600/4, 3347, 5002, 6604/83/99, 7288/98, 7452, 7521, 7742/63/73, 7830, 8894, 8913/25/31/5/52, 9005/7/56/64/76, 9100/27/ 38/73/5/9/93, 9201/8/13, 9332/50, 9403/6/9/16/27, 12086, 12105/7, 12322, 25673/83/94, 25752/91, 25804/ 18/27/45, 28350, 28550/5, 28601. (68).
2C Northampton 412/21, 522, 657/92, 2538, 2602, 3010/ 74, 3168, 3438, 3655, 3841, 4076, 4344/66/95, 4447/61/ 91, 5025, 5191, 6616/41/66/86, 6754, 7299, 7612, 8896, 8914/29/36, 9042, 9103/4/53/7/8/69, 9203/5/49/ 70/1/91, 9321/4/91/5, 9401/3/14/26/40/4, 22913/6. (58).
2D Nuneaton 5, 201/2/4/5/6/8, 430/64, 2777/81/3/6, 2814/88, 2932/41/59/64/73/81, 3084, 3161, 3649, 6636/58/60/80/7, 6704/41/9, 6900/24, 7285/6, 7367, 7594, 8911/54/62, 9068/80/2, 9114/50/67/81/90/1, 9264/ 8/76, 9318/42/5/6/51/2/66, 9400/12/28–30/2/4–7/9, 12141, 12294, 12321, 22902/7, 28333, 28482/7, 28611. (81).
2E Warwick 83, 109/35/44, 3738, 6646/53/73, 6723, 8897, 8910/22/4, 9384, 28315/67, 28532. (17).
2F Coventry 3489, 3518/71, 3691, 3726, 4455, 8926, 9135, 9200/53/78, 9340, 22567. (13).
2G Leighton Buzzard No regular allocation.
3A Bescot 2779, 2851/3, 3061, 4061, 4353, 4873, 5308/ 22/95, 5417/8/99, 7382/96, 7519, 8909/17, 9006/22/5/ 39/45/63/78/81/3/4/9/96/7, 9106/31/42/60/57/7/80/9/95, 9202/11/45/59/65/74/82/6/94, 9301/8/13/28/35/54/61/ 7/71/2/4, 9425/31, 22915/8, 28097, 28139/99, 28261. (69).
3B Bushbury 49, 53/4, 66, 2489, 4027, 4439/92, 5287, 5405/37, 5502/11/3/4/5/22/31/3, 6652, 6933/5, 7397–9, 7413/73, 9011, 9110, 9204/6/33/6/95, 9356, 28209/16/ 30/4, 28403/30. (41).
3C Walsall 9, 11/7/8/9, 45, 69, 462, 501, 2448/66, 2562/ 86, 2627, 3410, 3502, 3786, 4068/9, 4115, 4339, 4441/ 54/88, 4506/7/12, 6661/79/85/9, 8902, 9015/40/8, 9174, 9222/32/48/66/83, 9325/64, 28088/93, 28105, 28246/7/ 51/89, 28313, 28429, 28594/7. (54).
3D Aston 2, 12, 42/7, 2440/1/9/70, 2578, 2616/59, 2782, 2892/4, 2921/63/6, 3008/12/3/4, 3124, 4058/77, 4219, 4302/50, 4490, 4517, 4872, 5015/8, 5132, 5302/40/90, 7363–6, 9017/36/50/99, 9309/27/59/92, 9423, 27591, 28548/59/86. (53).
3E Monument Lane 3, 4; 44/6, 900, 1111/6/53/69, 2450/ 1, 2567/79, 3005–7, 3503, 3915, 4057, 4442, 4514/92, 6876/8, 6922/5/7, 7740, 22904/20/8, 27480/4. (33).
4A Shrewsbury 1725, 2307/62/87, 2404, 3283, 3357/94/

6, 3573/81, 3600/15/8/79, 5180, 5245/81/3/92, 5318/30, 5406/33/4/45/92, 6691, 6740, 7180, 7746/55/99, 7836/ 40, 8307/8/24/69/73–5, 8613/31/88/90, 8945, 9019/28/ 35/7/46/69, 9116/43, 9234/75, 9373/5, 9407/13, 12103/ 31/43, 12233, 12330/49, 12414, 12525, 16027, 27640/ 64, 28153, 28204/56/71, 28308/35/9/70, 28527/33, 28608. (83).
4B Swansea 1676, 2320/60/81/5/8/90/4, 6620, 6757, 7715/41, 7807, 7931/41/8/56, 8175, 8310/25/35/43–5/ 66/7, 8664/5/73/89/91, 8893, 8948, 9033, 9260, 9358, 27621, 28543, 28622. (39).
4C Upper Bank 1769, 1824/52/60/4/93, 7230/2/56/8/9, 7477–81. (16).
4D Abergavenny 7690, 7709/17/72/80, 7816/23/9, 7933/ 5/40/4/5, 8899, 8932/44, 9051, 9243/7/80, 9306/41/88, 20155, 27552/72, 27650. (27).
4E Tredegar 7733/82, 7834, 7932/7/9, 27618, 27663. (8)
5A Crewe North 322, 471/92, 529, 659/60, 1115/56/7/63/ 72, 2323, 2403/47/53/69/87/8, 2544, 2608, 4801/7/8/32– 8/62–5/74–6, 4907–9, 5131, 5255, 5312/4/6/7/54/69/74/ 5/9/81/94, 5403/4/12/22/41/8/95, 5521/3/30/2/9/40/6/8/ 9/51/5, 5601/17/37/66/8/74–6/81/3/4/6–90, 5703/20–2/5/ 33, 6113/25/6/31/2/9/46/7/53/4/6/7/60–3/5–8, 6201/4/6– 12/33–6/52, 6605, 6711/42. (130).
5B Crewe South 402/5/48, 2785, 2885, 2920/46/7/9/50/2/ 5/6/60–2/8/74/80/2/3, 3009, 3412, 3704, 4064, 4126, 4300, 4453, 4595, 5020/8/33/4/7/8/44/8/59/60/4/7/9/72– 4/89/97, 5108/34/43/6/8/81/3/95/7/8, 5235/6/9/40/8/54/ 64/70/1, 5300/5/84, 7074/6/9/87/8/90/1, 7120–4, 7266/80, 7309/30/44/62/84, 7414/6/44/5/51, 7523/4/6, 7602/8/16/33/53/65/80/1, 8326/46, 8687/93, 8906, 9027, 9146/98, 9209/10/30/41/63/96, 9349/57/96, 9445, 22971/8, 28458, 28583, 28614. (128).
5C Stafford 443/61, 2537/65, 2614, 7294, 7588/98, 7606/ 49/70, 8940, 9031/91/8, 9113/44/94, 9320, 25648/74, 25725/49/75/87, 25841, 28592. (27).
5D Stoke 122/3/5–8/56/7, 2305/6/15/6/24/43–5/58/63/4/ 75/6/91, 2430/67/8, 2542/3/64/9/75/84/92/3/8, 2603/5/9/ 28/60–77, 4067/93, 4310/43/63/9/73/7/8/80/1/3/8/91/3, 4448/78/89/96/8/9, 4500/2–4/8, 5278, 5324, 5498, 7320/ 38/70, 7587/96/9, 7609/10/47/8/58, 28442/60/4. (99).
5E Alsager 78, 2309/48, 2471, 2611, 4301/48, 4450–2/97, 7392, 7595, 7661/2. (15).
5F Uttoxeter 85–7, 2303/3/4/46, 2431, 4307. (8).
6A Chester 84, 124/30, 446, 635/99, 933, 1108/12/20/1/ 58/62/4/70, 2425, 2540/68/87, 2617, 5042, 5247/75/97, 5382, 6632/50, 6894, 7051, 7297, 7373–5/83, 7504, 7600, 7795, 12119, 12340/67, 12417, 25297, 25304/21/ 50/76. (46).
6B Mold Jc 2945/53/65/75/9, 4065/73/86, 4367, 4493, 4800, 5190, 5286, 5328/83/5, 7353/71/2, 7530, 7615/50/ 6, 8950, 9047/52/72/7, 9105/12/5/20/82, 9228/35/51/61, 9322/83, 28443, 28531. (41).
6C Birkenhead 101/2/4/10/21/9/31/2, 1714/34/80, 1818/ 53, 2891, 2922/67/9–71, 7160/4/6, 7231, 7324/89, 7439/ 50, 7507, 7655/72/4, 7730, 9244/6/56/8/67/81, 11313, 11441, 12214/32/70, 12364, 12465, 27513/7/22/5/8/32. (51).
7A Llandudno Jc 396, 413, 524, 925/36, 1086/92/8, 1118/9/23/4/50/1/61, 2954/76, 3877, 4072, 4389, 5253/ 94, 5346/70, 6607/59/76, 6725/7/47, 6926, 7796, 7802/ 22/41, 25277, 25373, 25802/3/27/45/62, 28337/85, 28503/ 5/88. (46).
7B Bangor 72/3, 133/4/7, 495, 675, 1093, 2948/51/84, 4305, 4445, 6643/5/69/81, 6710/3/55, 7705/21, 7808/ 12, 12176, 12230, 27604/19/54, 28392, 28404, 28513/ 53, 28618. (34).
7C Holyhead 5110/2/3, 5249, 5313, 6112/27/45, 6899, 7321/68, 7476. (12).
7D Rhyl 479/94, 629/46/58/71, 6628/37/57, 6712/48, 12116/25, 12338/56, 12429, 27562/85, 27606, 28521, 28616. (21).
8A Edge Hill 6/7, 50/80/1, 2426/56/9, 2571/97, 2606/12/ 58, 2848/9/52/4/6/8/9/90, 2925/57/8, 4904/35, 5039/45/ 54/91, 5128/30/45/89/93, 5246/56/98, 5301/3/32/3/43/4/ 7/50/1/76/80/7/92/8/9, 5400/10, 5506/8/14/7/20/5–7/9/ 47/61/86/99, 5613/23/30, 5724/6/37, 6004, 6106/11/8/ 24/9/34–6/8/44/64, 6200/3/5, 6890, 6917/31, 7001/2, 7325/85, 7402/4, 7597, 7603/51, 7711, 7827/70/7/87, 7930/4/8/43/6/9–51/3/5/7–9, 8898, 8908/27/33/66, 9016, 9130/55, 9237/9/42/87, 9333/55/85, 9449, 11221, 11307/18/25/53, 11412/39/45/8, 12111, 27577/96, 27625/31/6/78/82/8/81. (104).
8B Warrington 2583, 3207, 3314/89/98, 3657, 5001/26/ 32/5/95, 5109/49/96, 5252, 5442, 6603/63/88, 6746, 6866/81, 6904/19/20/30, 7268, 7352/76/87, 7591, 7652/ 4/7, 7720/94, 8921, 9008/75/85, 9101/36/68/78, 9411, 12100/18/30/40/75, 12250/69, 12366/74, 12428, 27605, 28117/29, 28262, 28511. (61)

8C Speke Jc 2972/8, 7080/93/4/7, 7284, 7388, 7472, 7875/81/6/91/7/8, 8327/8/47, 8674, 8904/42, 9032/57/ 60/5/6/70/86/94, 9215/8/93, 9302/65, 9447, 11342/97, 11405/27/44/6/69, 12088, 12149/63/7, 12219, 12438, 27580, 27616. (50).

8D Widnes 8, 6906, 7833, 8907/39, 9020/38/58/67/71/3/ 4/9, 9170, 9307, 28095, 28107/45/86, 28221/39/40/53/ 78/88. (25)

9A Longsight 71, 106–8/36, 403, 531/9, 674, 1114/22/59/ 66–8, 1416/20/1, 2351/3/7392/5–9, 2401/2/60/1/3/78, 2580/5/99, 2607, 2775/6/8/88, 2810/3/5/52/4/6/8/9/86/ 7/9, 2923/4/6/9/30/5/7, 3275, 3457, 3717, 4078, 4303/8/ 57/60/97, 4831/70/1, 4937/8, 5094, 5144, 5242/58, 5352/3, 5493, 5552/6/78/91/3, 5603/25/31–4/8/47/72, 5723/34/40–2, 6738, 7267, 7341/3/5/7/69/94, 7400, 7528, 7673, 9002/10, 9108/56/71/83/7, 9226/38/84/5/ 98, 9343/63/80. (125).

9B Stockport 77, 2322/32/50/2, 2772, 2936/8, 3281, 4074, 4340, 4444, 6405–7, 6627, 7289, 7346, 7601, 9043/4/54/92, 9111/84–6, 9227, 9305/69/70, 12407/53, 28338, 28451/7, 28546/98. (38).

9C Macclesfield 51/5, 2319/47/55/6/69/82. (8).

9D Buxton 438, 693, 1278, 2365–8370/1, 2773, 2811, 2939/40/2–4, 3268/9/71/4/8/82/96, 3387, 3842, 4019/ 80, 4309/42/65/82, 4548/9, 6428, 7936/54, 9009/59/93, 9132/40/66, 9212/4/6/20/1/4/5/40, 9315/6/26/31/47/76/ 86. (57).

10A Springs Branch 76, 103, 447, 561, 2455/65, 2539/63/ 72/88, 5019/30, 5129/37/41, 5425/49, 7703, 7803/84/5/ 8/96, 8824/34/58, 8905/30/51, 9014/23/4/6/9/30/53/90, 9118/9/24/5/9/34/41/8/9/59/61/72/6/92/7, 9207/57/99, 9310/1, 9422/4, 12021–5/32/8/9/45/63/4, 12172, 12208/ 25, 12457, 28309/43, 28417, 28524/5/85. (80).

10B Preston 356/77, 483, 5021/46, 5142/85, 5345, 5516/ 24/36/7/44, 6762, 7291/3/6, 7319, 7862, 9219/31/50, 9348, 9417/9–21/42/51, 10639/76, 10793, 11218, 12106/26/34/51/3, 12551, 12605/18/9. (42).

10C Patricroft 138, 207/9, 332, 507/27/8, 628, 2454, 2560/1/73/4/96, 5055, 5111/35/67/88, 5231/59/90, 5304/15/29/77/86/91, 5401/2/8/20/1/4/6/8/44/6, 5528/ 42/3/50, 7876/8/92, 8801, 8903/12/20/41, 9095, 9199, 9254/5/73, 9304/30/53, 9405, 12019/30/1/6/49/59, 28786. (67).

10D Plodder Lane 4119, 4341/52/6/8/79/86, 7401, 7682, 7722/37/56/61/9, 9147, 9378, 10643/4. (18).

10E Sutton Oak 4079, 4125, 4359, 4473, 6656/90/2, 6700/3/22, 7181/3/4, 7393, 7453, 7692, 7752/78, 8918, 9102, 9303/12/7, 11204, 11316/9, 11471/91/5, 12126/ 77, 12280/95, 12393/5/7, 12449, 28152, 28296, 28494, 28509/49. (42).

11A Carnforth 2428/9/32/62, 2581/94, 2601/13/5, 3189, 3237, 3329, 3570, 3757/60, 4060, 4118/20, 4374/5, 4510/3, 5050, 5291, 5306/7/72/3, 5427, 7406/7/9/10, 7605, 9109/17/51/4/88, 9269, 9314/38, 27555/86, 27635/48, 28116/58. (48).

11B Barrow 1, 16/41/67/8, 2308/59/86/93, 2427/93, 2570, 4059/75, 4306/47/51/68/99, 4487, 4594, 6682, 6718, 7287, 7322/3, 20185, 22901/12, 28104/28/33/66/91, 28202/5/26/33/63/95, 28303/12, 28587. (43)

11D Oxenholme 2313/4/7/21, 2457/64, 2595, 7503/25. (9).

11E Tebay 48, 70, 2301/18/49, 4208/92, 4469, 7339, 9088, 9252, 9339. (12).

12A Kingmoor 592/8, 602/3/13/36, 1139–43/5–7, 2742–6/ 8/9/51/2/80, 2802/3/30–7/75–8/80–4, 2905–7, 3868, 3902/22/73/96, 4001/8/9/16, 4181/3/9/99, 4315/24/6, 4877–9/82–4/6/97–9, 4940–3, 5/4, 5005/6/8/10/3/5/7/ 22/3/81/2/96, 5100/18/9/26/7/51/2/69, 5241/66, 5363/ 4, 5429/32/43/82, 5577/9–82, 5713–6/27–32, 7111–5, 16231/5/48/66, 16310/27/32/3/73/4, 16905/11/20/1/2/6. (143).

12B Upperby 397, 652/4/5/73, 4081, 4121, 4346/61/90, 4868/9, 4905/6/36, 5106/33/9/47/84, 5230/43/4/93/5/6/ 9, 5310/1/31/48/68/88/93, 5409/14/6/36/8/50/1/94, 5553/63/4/7/92/5, 5600/24/70/3/7/8/80, 5718, 6110/28/ 33/7/42/51/8/69, 6883, 7295, 7326/40/77/91, 7403/8/15, 7556/93, 7614/8/64/6, 12170, 12201, 12432. (82).

12C Penrith 28318/69, 28420/2/3/92, 28551/75/80/9. (10)

12D Workington 656/94/5, 4192, 4364, 4449/95, 4505/ 93/6, 6654, 6728, 7290/2, 7590, 7604, 12091/8, 12285, 12501/8/9, 28345/7/72, 28401/8/10/5/28/99, 28515/8/26/ 35/42/4/7/61, 28603/10. (41).

12E Moor Row 7317/37/90, 11628, 129090, 12110/84, 12341/94, 12418/94/9, 12510, 28441/84. (15).

12F Beattock 15210/38/40/5/64/81/92, 15217/27/32/7/9/ 62, SRM 29988. (14).

12G Dumfries 170, 566/76/7, 604/5, 902/4/12, 1135/71/9, 2908/9/18/9, 6635/9, 6734, 17230/8/86/8, 17302/29/37/ 43/9/62/78/91/4/8, 17405/9/52/61, 17563, 17600–2/21/3/ 36/86. (45).

12H Stranraer 599, 600/16/42, 1082, 16351/72, 17350/ 75/87, 17421/40/5/58, 17626. (16).

13A Plaistow 1290, 1360, 2097, 2100/5–7/10–8/23/4/6–8/ 30–5/81–90/3, 2330/41, 2523–36/57, 3035, 3358/85, 3478, 3559, 4297, 4530/80, 7235/47/50, 7311/51, 7458, 7561. (70).

13B Devons Rd 7300/2/4/6/7/10/2/4/5/48–50, 7411/82–4/ 6–95/7–9, 7500–2/5/6/11/4–8/58–60/2–4, 9538, 27217, 27509/10/2/4/20. (53).

13C Tilbury 2136–9/41/2/5–53/80, 2522, 4259, 22931. (19).

13D Shoeburyness 2154–60/91/2, 2500–21. (31).

13E Upminster 1261/87. (2).

14A Cricklewood 21–8/31/2/4/5/9, 1294, 1385, 1712/24, 1805/11/29, 2839/55, 2987, 3049, 3150, 3246/61, 3313/ 66, 3400/8/40, 3508/65, 3800/6/58, 3934/47/65/92/5, 4028/9/43, 4228, 4425/57, 4581/2/90, 7200/1/3–27/44/ 51/2, 7433–5, 7621. (85).

14B Kentish Town 29/30/3/6–8/40/64/92, 100/14/48/9/ 66/7, 477, 547, 1051/4/74, 1374/7/9/80, 1660/1/4/8/71/ 2/4, 1713, 1850, 2333/5/83, 2479, 2550/6/8, 2990, 3016/21, 3149, 3764, 3887, 4176, 4229/35, 4470, 4529/ 31/2/63/84, 4601/2, 4806/10/6/7/22/9/30/46/55, 5041/ 65/8, 5267/77/9/85/8, 5342, 5610/4–6/39/50/4/62/3/7/ 82/5, 7229/40–2/5/6/60/2/3/82/3, 7427–9/32, 7640/4/5. (105).

14C St Albans 91, 161, 1854, 2300/2/25/8/9/74/7/80, 3245, 3801, 7261. (14).

15A Wellingborough 116, 1239/46, 1340, 1781, 3796/7, 3808/30/70/6, 3909/77/82, 4033, 4134/60, 4242/87, 4332, 4403, 4574/5, 7238/64/5/79, 7333, 7446, 7543/ 54, 7636/42, 8024/50/82, 8310/28/48/90, 8222/64/78/ 81, 8305/34/8/59/60/3–5, 8492, 8617/44–6/51/71/8/92/4/ 5/9, 9438/43, 9536/44/63/96/9. (72).

15B Kettering 454, 537/50, 1889, 2999, 3011/38/42/95, 3195, 3416, 3525/51/61/6, 3601, 3782, 3888/9/96, 4232/ 78, 4465, 7437, 8285, 8355/6, 8491, 8704, 9501/72/80/ 3, 20216, 22930. (35).

15C Leicester 75, 145/71/82, 536/8/42/3/9/63, 707/38/40/ 63, 1008/10/1/20/3/31/9/41/2/61/71/88/9, 1402/7, 2119– 21, 2331/4, 2791/2/5, 3081, 3166/83/90, 3205/32, 3326/ 33, 3411/23/30/67, 3648/53/76/88, 3710/28/48/90, 3807/ 29, 3937, 4031/4, 4231, 4423, 7248, 7441/2, 7533/4, 8006, 8132, 8211, 8309/68/97–9, 8619/68, 22954. (80).

15D Bedford 141/62/5, 510/48/51, 755/62, 1007/9/13/7/ 34/8/70/91, 1260/72/3, 1302, 1401, 1793, 1810, 3157/ 64, 3222, 3402/28/74, 3707/21/66/8/77/85, 3910/26/67/ 71, 4362, 22933/68. (42).

16A Nottingham 99, 147/60/3/4/72/8/93, 394, 404/11/5– 7/9/27/78/96/8, 502/4/35/40/59/60, 719/39/47/57, 926/9, 1002/12/32/50/94/6, 1230/49, 1344/82, 1409/23/5, 1666, 1727/62, 1826/95, 2096/9, 2101/3/4/9, 2338/9/61, 2555, 2794, 2823/99, 3051/4/73, 3177/85/92, 3249/62, 3324/67/9/77/8/99, 3458, 3511/38/64, 3602/37/96, 3711/ 24/9, 3869, 3933/48/54/6/8/62/9/94, 4030/9/47/55/95, 4107/8/31/2/58/64/80, 4215/23/30/47/64/6/7/75, 4313, 4401/8/12/4/6, 4480, 4533/46/77/8, 4825/7/61, 7277, 7422/38/85, 7539/49/52, 7631/2/7, 8003/70, 8134/ 70, 8206/7/17/8/75/9/82/93, 8380/1, 8614/35/9/66/75, 12121/3/35, 20002, 22941/4, 28507/8. (167).

16B Peterborough 180, 408/10, 520/32/3/46/52/8/69, 756/ 67, 1846/84, 2754/64, 3253, 3317/9/71/95, 3651/2, 3854/9/61/4/98, 3920/1/57/80/1, 4097, 4152/5/72/4, 4218/38/9/73/93/6, 4458/76/80, 4509/18/9/21/2, 7202/ 69/70, 7566, 7622. (57).

16C Kirkby 409/58/82, 568, 630, 3023, 3139, 3424/94, 3572/8, 3759/73, 3894/5, 3907/18, 4005/21/82, 4113/ 40, 4202/5/68/48, 4415/63/72, 4589, 8000/7/9/27/9/92/6– 8, 8100/4/8/9/14/66/91–3, 8214/5/23–5/67–70/2, 8378/9/ 82/3/92/3, 8608/16/41. (67).

16D Mansfield 424, 503, 1297, 1341/50, 1771, 1885, 2093/8, 2122/5/9/40/3/4, 3193, 3239, 3381, 3431, 3587, 3634, 3762/5, 3802/74, 3983/97, 4004, 4394, 8622/43, 22935. (32).

17A Derby 90/8, 111/8, 378, 407/18, 513/6, 632, 734/5/ 43/60/75, 930, 1000/3/33/57/9/60/83, 1252, 1337/61/70/ 3, 1404/8/26/9, 1535, 1695, 1708/26/54/73/9/88/95, 1833/47, 2547, 2758/74, 2847/70, 3083, 3121/3/41/75/ 91/6, 3200/30/64, 3312/5/23/53/64/8/70, 3459/96, 3526/ 36/45/8/50/84/98, 3725/35/45/63/76, 3838–40/81, 4024, 4195, 4214, 4409/19/20/32, 4542/65/6, 4809/15/8/9/39/ 51, 5088, 5261, 5407, 5602/9/36/40/9/56/79/96/9, 8008/ 74, 8265, 8390, 8647/54, 22849, 22934/43/58/9/82. (123).

17B Burton 142/6, 364/95, 426/36/56, 500/25, 631, 1357, 1424, 1516/23/36, 1718/49/70, 1839/59/65, 2094/5, 2757/63/7/8, 2846/98, 3055, 3214/44/7/56/86, 3306/40/ 60/88/95, 3537/82, 3608/19/23/32/46, 3703/9/44, 3815/ 37/47, 3916/30/8/76, 4002/35/46/8/87, 4100/24/66/70/1,

12H Stranraer ... *(see above)*

17C Coalville 79, 541, 1815, 2989, 3001, 3176, 3229, 3429/34/7/45, 3682, 3779/80, 3835/65/72, 3905, 4085, 4103/9/23/48, 4227/52/60/79, 4539, 8106/7, 8273. (31).

17D Rowsley 119/69, 711/41, 1049, 1700, 1875, 2756/60, 2845/72–4, 2902, 3027/45, 3109/13/6/9/27/31/53, 3270/ 90, 3338/42/72, 3485/92, 3543, 3603/16, 3778, 3925/ 55, 4017/8/50, 4101/63/8, 4209/46/9/62/3, 4430, 4540/ 88, 7274, 7457/9–61, 7679, 27505/15/27/30. (60).

18A Toton 325/83, 400/6/22, 526, 2993, 3000/3/50/71/9, 3108/34/54/88, 3211/2/59/87, 3305/27, 3405/20/53/69, 3482/99, 3583/99, 3617/29/31/3/50/68, 3753/87/93–5/8/ 9, 3803–5/10/6–21/3–8/31–4/85/91/2, 3901/14/7/23/9/ 39/61/70/2/4/5/9/88/90, 4011/2/51/2/89/91, 4106/33/6/ 50/6/7/96, 4233/41/50, 4317/76, 4475, 4547/83, 7083–5/ 9/91, 7243, 7447/9/54, 7551/5, 7623/30, 7967/9/70/2/4– 9/81/2/5–9/91/4–6/8/9, 8002/4/33/7/75, 8112/7/9/3/42/4/ 68/78/82/94/6/7/9, 8200–5/21, 8304/30/48–50/61/2/84– 8, 8490, 8606/7/15/8/36–8/62/72/81/3–5/96, 8703, 22921/32/63/74/83, 28512, 28619. (197).

18B Westhouses 414, 2995/6, 3044, 3227/35/54/66, 3331/79, 3580, 3850/60/6/7/80/2, 3966, 4014, 4130/88/ 91, 4243, 4321, 7466, 8011/56/7/60/3/76/83, 8102/15/8/ 25/36, 8212/80, 8333/42/53/8/91, 8494/5, 8620/1/3/50/ 61. (51).

18C Hasland 337/70, 466/90/1, 506/55/6/7, 1518/31/2, 1871/3, 2102/8, 3219, 3318, 3454, 3510, 3622, 3769/71/ 4, 3856/90, 3936/59/68, 4053/4, 4162, 4244/74/88/94, 4410, 7003/4, 7272/8, 7423/6, 7535, 7968/71/3/80/3/4/ 90/2/3/7. (54).

18D Staveley 1528/9/33/4, 1710/1/47/52/3/5/63, 1802–4, 3114, 3224/34/40/2/52/92/4/7–9, 3308–10/86, 3406, 3515/24/46/75, 3751, 3809/57/62/3/86, 3993, 4066/70, 4104/22/9/47/54/82, 4210, 7424/55, 7625–8, 8010/53/4/ 64, 8111/20/2/79/95, 8210/3, 8332/41, 8493, 8609/52/3/ 63/86, 22967. (76).

19A Sheffield 324/62, 401/68, 716/28/9/31/65, 1016/84, 1181, 1768, 1855/7/91, 2761/9/97, 2904/92, 3031/48/66/ 96, 3101/18/26/40, 3241, 3334/43, 3425/68/70, 3512/95/ 6, 3605/7/61/2/83/9, 3715/49/55/72/5, 3844, 4006, 4165, 4211/2/84/5, 4334/55, 4418/26/37, 4550/68/72/3, 4858/9, 5262, 7236, 7328, 7513/45/8, 7624, 8017, 8105, 8219/84, 8314–6, 8642, 22950/1/70. (85).

19B Millhouses 82, 113/39, 487, 545/64, 1019/26/37/47/ 62/3/72/5/8/9, 1286/95, 1342/96, 1403, 3666, 3746, 4860, 5263, 5554/73/85/96, 5607/21/6/64. (33).

19C Canklow 485, 726/7, 1797, 1813/35/69, 2092, 3002/ 47/56–8, 3144/67/71/4, 3208/20/43/65, 3300/25/82/91, 3466/93, 3533/77, 3635/42/60/4/9, 3739/47, 3813/4–43, 3906/27/46/50, 4013/5/26/71, 4127/8/73, 4477, 4537/ 69, 7546/7, 8026/65/7, 8209, 8317, 8682, 9631, 22900/ 26/6/9/75. (68).

19D Heaton Mersey 94/5, 453, 544, 2997, 3078, 3811, 3908/45, 4010/90, 4110/1/7/42/4/77/8, 4237/71/86, 4407/21, 8089/99, 8116/35/90, 8208/16/20, 8329, 8667/ 76/97, 22929. (36).

19E Belle Vue 1690, 1702/48/56, 1814, 2765, 2896, 3361, 3574, 3612/30/8, 3723/56, 3836, 3900/43/52/85, 4022/3/ 5/40, 4114, 4261, 4371, 4459, 4552, 4802/3/45, 5031, 5284, 7336, 7440, 7512. (36).

19G Trafford Park 88/9/93, 168, 1014/21/4/52/66/76, 4236, 4326, 5072/4, 5628/55, 8680/98. (18).

20A Leeds 432/55/89, 519/62/7, 633, 720/5/36/48/58/9, 910/27/8, 1018/40/69/87, 1117/37/44, 1247, 1315, 1422, 1745, 2850, 3401, 3665, 3878, 4020/44, 4151, 4431, 4501, 4820/1/3/4/8/47–50/3/4/6/7, 5040/3/92/3, 5187, 5260/76/80/9, 5534/5/8/58/62/5/6/8/9/87/9/94/7/8, 5604/5/8/11/9/20/48/51/8–60/94, 6103/8/9/17, 7254, 7418, 8001/73/90, 8110/21/4/6–9/37/8/43/76/7, 8306, 10622/30/4/89, 10990. (111).

20B Stourton 1738/9/59/85/94, 1816/38/42/90, 2759/71/ 98, 2816/97, 2998, 3039, 3137, 3267, 3384/92, 3449/56/ 76, 3519/39/79/90, 3636/78/81, 3705/31/7, 3851/2/5, 3931/87/9/98, 4037/94, 4245, 4400/67, 4564, 4605, 7229/71, 7420/63, 7538, 8140, 8276/7/83, 8354, 8640, 9537/40, 22945/76/7. (63).

20C Royston 96, 112/20, 444, 514, 1045/81, 1368/95, 1428, 2326/36, 2551, 2770/84, 2827/57, 2988, 3064, 3233/50, 3332/41, 3446/8/51, 3509/53, 3732/89, 3919/ 42/91, 4003, 4141/3/61, 4446, 7421/48/62, 7581, 7634, 8035/62/95, 8103/13/61/2/9, 8376/7, 8677, 8700/1, 10633, 22927/40. (59).

20D Normanton 140/83, 480, 521, 1067/8, 1686, 1778, 1844, 2747, 2895, 3156, 3301, 3497, 3514, 3639/56, 3714/42/70, 3871, 3903/13/63, 4098/9, 4153/79, 4216/7/ 90, 4335/8, 4404, 4562/70/86, 4603/4, 7334/5, 7405, 8036/84, 8101/23/30/1/9/46/60, 8266/71/4, 8352/7/94–

6, 8670, 8702, 10621/5/86, 10901/3, 12089/95, 12108/
14, 12252/8, 12559. (75).

20E Manningham 184, 391, 1004/43/8, 1255, 1413,
2340, 2545/8/9, 2762, 3351, 3677, 3783, 6400–4, 7255,
7417/9, 10631/6/81, 10714. (27).

20F Skipton 323/51/9, 323/51/9, 452/84, 1253/75/7, 1366,
1681, 1751/67, 1820, 3037/52, 3251/95, 3337, 3477,
3554/8, 3784, 3893, 3960/84, 3999, 4000/7/41, 4197,
4222/76/7/82/99, 4579, 8081, 10623/71, 10795. (40).

20G Hellifield 155, 459/70/2, 932, 1006/56/80, 1430,
2893, 3173/86, 3226/31, 3335/52, 3585/6, 3781, 3904/
44, 4149, 4555/71, 8005, 8145/89, 10842/96/9. (30).

20H Lancaster 353, 488, 565, 931, 1005/22/44/65/95,
1358, 3187, 3293, 3307/30, 4032, 4201/80, 4405/68,
4554/6, 7381, 7468–71, 7532, 8055. (28).

21A Saltley 74/97, 117/75, 326/85, 463/86/93, 505/9/11/2,
715/45, 1015/29/35/55/64, 1338/67, 1411, 1682, 1777,
1856/79, 2327, 2546/54, 2790/3/9, 2828/32/4–6/9, 2900/
3/94, 3085, 3103/10/38, 3201/3/23/5/77/84, 331/21/36/
9/59/74, 3432/3/5/41/3/73/84/90/1, 3516/22/3/7/9/31/5/
40/68/92, 3621/4/44/67/74/80/4/6/90/8/9, 3758/67,
3812/45/79, 3911/2/40/1/9/51/86, 4049/84/8/92, 4137/9/
45/84–6/90, 4200/3/7/13/24/48, 4304/27/33, 4406/13/
27, 4515/6/20/4/5/38/45/67/91, 4811/3/4/40–2/52, 5186,
5265/8/9/73/4, 5447, 5641, 5709, 7239/49/73/6, 7425/
36/43, 7638/9, 8351/89, 8669, 9672–4, 22846, 22946/7/
53/5. (168).

21B Bournville 105/73/9, 439, 517, 917/34, 1073/7, 1699,
2337/42/73, 2559, 3316/55, 3463, 3562, 3675/87, 4138,
4289, 22579, 22630, 22818/34/53/63. (28).

21C Bromsgrove 2290, 3099, 3130, 7234, 7301/3/5/8/13,
7565. (10).

21D Stratford-on-Avon 3210, 3520/1/44/94, 3620/7/73/
93, 3822/73, 4204, 4587, 4606. (14).

22A Bristol 174, 499, 553, 601, 935, 1025/8/30/46/53/8,
1389/97, 1706, 1874/6, 3090/4, 3178/80/1, 3204/28,
3419/36/9/44/64, 3517/93, 3712/27, 3853, 3928/53,
4112/35/69, 4411/22/4/66, 4534–6, 4804/5/12/43, 5272,
5557/90, 5612/8/22/7/9/52/7/65, 7190, 7544/50, 7678,
11212. (65).

22B Gloucester 423/37, 523/30, 1001/27/36/97, 1303/30/
53/65/75/90, 1530/7, 1720/42, 1870/8, 2812, 3062,
3213/57/8/63/73, 3344/73, 3427/62, 3506/7, 3604/45/58/
95, 3754/88/91, 3846, 3924/32/5/64/78, 4045, 4167/75,
4269/72, 4553/76, 7237, 7619/20/35. (57).

22C Bath 115/81, 497, 518, 696/7, 700, 1324/34/48, 3734,
3875, 4096, 4102, 4402, 4523/57–61, 4844, 5056, 5440,
7191, 7275, 7316, 7465/96, 7542/57, 11202, 13800–10.
(43).

22D Templecombe 634/98, 1251, 1406, 3198, 3248/60,
3356, 3792, 4146, 4417. (11).

22E Highbridge 1298, 1307/22/46/71, 3194, 3216/8. (8).

23A Bank Hall 581–3, 937, 1085, 1103, 5202/25–9, 5335/
6, 10669/92, 10766/78/88/99, 10861/79/81, 11206/16/
27/9/31/2/7/46/53, 11371/5, 11512/35–7/46, 12288,
12609. (41).

23B Aintree 4481, 9521/64/6/7/81/5–7/92/5/7, 10648/55,
11336/43, 11413/60/2/75, 11530/44, 12094, 12112/79,
12328/33/7/51/2/62/79/90, 12401/5/56, 13541/82/8,
12607, 12710/23/82/90, 12827/31/8/9/56/7/61/70/7,
12910/35/48/56/62/4/71/81. (61).

23C Southport 678/91, 1186–9/91, 4887, 5200, 5334,
5415/35, 10687/96, 10722/8/43/52, 10844/9/50, 11490,
12102/61/97, 12256/71, 12400/50, 12523. (29).

23D Wigan 2405/9/10, 2631/9–43/79/85, 10664/78,
10707/57/87, 10822/3/47/87, 10923, 11366, 12093,
12152/69/89, 12290, 12312/32/50/60, 12413, 12575/98,
12602, 12725/77/9, 12806/28/167–7. (42).

23E Lostock Hall 2200/1, 2434–7, 2687, 9502/3/23/4/43/
5/52/9/71/98, 9611–7/40/9, 10670/7, 10762, 10801/69,
10938/41/2, 11345, 11423, 11526, 12101/60/71, 12244/
96, 12317/34/6/99, 12431/6/60/7, 12522. (51).

24A Accrington 676/83, 1100–2, 2433, 2634/81, 4225,
4460/79, 5099, 5101, 10674/5, 10703, 10743/5, 10910/
1/35, 11361, 11514, 12216/38/41, 12412/41/52/9,
12821/2/4/5. (34).

24B Rose Grove 2438/9, 2632/5/80, 2726–8/32, 2866/7/9,
7575/6, 9610/68, 10642/53/4, 10885, 10921/53, 11410/
92/7, 12146/83/7, 12220/62/8/78, 12309, 12529, 12841/
73/5/86, 12902/6/13/6/20/8/45/52/8. (47).

24D Lower Darwen 677/84, 2202, 2729–31/3/4, 2821,
3897, 4291, 4483, 10732/5/65/81, 10803/12/75/91/2,
10945/50, 11327, 11467/99, 11506, 12218/53/60/72/89,
12324/63, 12427/44, 12526/62/92, 12608. (40).

24E Blackpool 13–5/63/5, 685/90, 1192–8, 2636–8, 5063/
78/9, 5396, 5571/4/88, 5653/95/7, 5707, 10412/23/9/32/
7/42/6/8/55/60, 10704/19/21/5/49/50, 10800/57/89,
12128/74/94, 12215/75, 12415/30/47, 12542/58/72.
(58).

24F Fleetwood 2712, 2840–2/65, 5217/8, 7161/5, 10640,
10705/20, 10802/25, 11321/76, 11418/77/98, 11516,
12196, 12206/40, 12439/58. (25).

25A Wakefield 586/7, 4462, 4541, 5204–6, 5339, 7577/
80/2, 9505/6/13–9/25/6/9–32/41/3/5/6/50/8/9/62/2/70/
4–8/84/8/9, 9603–5/9/21–3/5–7/9/30/2–5/8/42–8/69–71,
10647/50/6/95, 10742/8/64, 10888, 11358/90, 11415/57/
84, 12046/7/92, 12150/4/86, 12284, 12305/19/69/86,
12433/5, 12561/76. (99).

25B Huddersfield 195–7, 2414, 2861–3, 5061, 5237/8,
5367, 9018/87, 9121–3/6, 9329/60/87, 10694, 10715/7/
77, 10852, 11408/47, 11524, 12182, 12381, 12515/38/
68, 12606. (34).

25C Goole 4062, 4105, 4221, 4474/85/6, 9539/47, 9624,
10798, 10873/97/8, 11207/41/4, 11323, 11432/4/58,
11521, 12037/41/3/4/56, 12133, 12235, 12306, 12454.
(30).

25D Mirfield 4220, 4398, 9500/22/55/79/82, 9600–2/18–
20/58–63, 10712/31/59, 10809/29/43/71/6, 11320,
11443/53, 12166/91/2, 12231/73, 12311/31, 12408/48/
63, 12521/50/83. (43).

25E Sowerby Bridge 1104, 4038/42, 4464, 9507/8/27/8/
68/9, 9606/28, 10665/7, 10711, 10804/6/19, 11381,
11429/68/79/82, 11500/3, 12099, 12243/82, 12375/6,
12574/90, 12614. (33).

25F Low Moor 585/9, 1185/9/90/9, 2796, 2828, 4240,
4471, 5062, 5201/7–12/4/21, 5337/8, 10840/1/55/86,
10909/51/2, 12104, 12217/37/54/5/7, 12354, 12410/20/
2. (39).

25G Farnley Jc 679/80, 4896, 5075–7/80, 5340/1, 5702/4/
5/8, 7567–71, 9055, 9217/23/88–90/2, 9377/9/81/2/9/90/
2/4, 9551–3, 10835/93, 10943/4, 12127/39/55/9, 12388,
12445/64. (47).

26A Newton Heath 580/4/8, 682, 2310–2/84, 2406–8/11–
3, 2553, 2618–26/30/82–4/98/9, 2700–11/3/50/66/89,
2820/71, 2901, 4056, 4311, 4543/4, 4888–95, 5102–5/7,
5203/19/20/2–4/32–4, 5635/42/61/71/98, 5700/1/6/10–2/
7/9, 7386, 7508–10/86, 9504/10–2/20/33/54/6/60/5,
9607/8/36/7/9/50–7, 10737/8/46/76, 10818, 11222/34,
11379, 11400/4/24/5/36/8/70/2/88/96, 11508/10, 12087,
12106/20/4/32/6–8/80, 12205/27/9/39/47/65/6/79,
12300/43/5/55/8, 12424/37/43/66, 12517/8/27/49/57/78/
81. (169).

26B Agecroft 2629/44–50/86, 2714–25/53/5, 2819/38/43/
4/60/4/8, 5215/6, 7572–4/8/9/83–5, 11230/40, 11396,
11464/74, 12162/81, 12203/7/93, 12304/53/68, 12411/6/
61, 12524/87, 12616. (55).

26C Bolton 2633/51–7/78, 9573, 9641/64, 10600/17/46/
60/1/97, 10796, 10807/10/31/59/65, 11348, 11511/3/9,
12157, 12212/36/63, 12348/57/65/83, 12404/46, 12528,
12617. (40).

26D Bury 9557/90/1/4, 9665–7, 10736/55, 10872/4/8,
11338, 11419/81/6/7/9, 11504, 12129/64/5, 12245/6,
12382, 12455, 12554/79/80/4, 12615. (31).

26E Bacup 190–2/4/8/9, 681, 10651/2, 10925/34, 12156,
12224/99, 12440/2. (16).

26F Lees 56–62, 9509/48/93, 12248, 12326/78/87/9,
12403, 12545/69/86. (19).

27A Polmadie 901/8/9/11/6, 1099, 1130/1, 2400/17/76/7/
80/1/3–6/90–2, 2688–97, 5213/51, 5309, 5483–7, 5583/
4, 5691/2, 6102/4/5/7/43, 6220–4/30–2/42/9/50/1, 7331/
2, 7536/7/40, 14441/53/6/9/88, 15116/23/7/41/67/70/9/
83/97, 15201/5/7/21/4/8/65/7/8, 15350–8, 16153–5/9/60/
2/7/72, 16237/9/44/60/1/3/80/92/4/5/8, 16304–8/14/6–8/
22/4/36/7/42/6/53–5/67, 17239/41/68/75/92/6, 17310/6/
7/9–21/47/60/1/5/7/70/81/8/9, 17433/4/6/9/43/4/6–8/59/
64/6/7, 17555/81/7, 17619/41/7/9/61/90. (178).

27B Greenock 2415/6/8–23, 7167–9, 14440/3–5/57/61/8/
79/81/92/7, 14508, 15121, 16030/5/8, 16156/7/63/5/6/
73, 16288, 16349, 17369, 17463, 17551/2/6/64, 17634/
9/82. (44).

27C Hamilton 150–2/4, 2735/40/1, 14648/54, 15118/30/7/
46/74, 15240, 16242/55/6/84/6/7/96, 16303/9/19/20/1/
60/2/71, 17237/42/4/50/60/80/1, 17307/82/4/93/5,
17407/8/10/20/30/1, 17586, 17607/9/63/5, DRC 29950–
2. (56).

28A Motherwell 5120/1, 5488, 8069/78/9/85, 8153–7/83–
8, 14460/2/4/5/98, 14506, 14631/2/4–7/40–3/5–7/9/50–
3, 15134/88/91, 16009/28/9/31/2, 16241/5/7/58/64/5/8–
71/6/7/81/5, 16334/5/6/45/56–8, 17231/47/56/67/70/2/3/
89–91/9, 17301/13/25–8/32/42/4/58/63/77, 17403/4/6/
13–9/32/5/7/62, 17582/4/8/93/5/9, 17606/38/66/8/81.
(119).

28B Dalry Road 919/20, 1175/7/8, 2804/7, 4318, 5029,
7162/3, 8163, 8321, 14442/51/2/78, 14507, 14630/3,
15125/36/9/65/6/9/77/89, 15202/10, 16236/53/83,
16312/3/29, 17550/3/9/65/76/8, 17645/54/9/74. (46).

28C Carstairs 903/7/15, 1136/80, 8301–3/31, 14438/9/46/
9/63/70–2/7/80/4/90, 14505, 15220/61/4, 17298, 17303/

23/40/85/6/99, 17438/51, 17583, 17604/8/13/8/35/55/70/
9. (43).

29A Perth 921–4/38/9, 1125, 3884, 4187/93, 4234/51/98,
4314/22/8, 4885, 5007/11/8/36/85–7, 5125/63–7/70–5,
5357/65/6/89, 5452/6–67/9/70/2–5, 8080/8/93, 8158/9,
8311–3/8–20/2/3/36/7/9/40, 14447/8/58/67/9/76/82/9/93/
9, 14500–3, 15144/63/71/5/6, 15208/9/16/9, 16246/
90, 16328/31/47/8/52, 17374/97, 17449/73. (111).

29B Aberdeen 1134/76/84, 15234, 16240/51/78, 16326/
43/59, 17283, 17339/45, 17400, 17645. (15).

29C Dundee 15173/80/6/96, 15223/6/31, 16323/5, 17450,
17568, 17653. (12).

29D Forfar 14450/4/86, 15160–2/72/84/5/90/4/5/8, 15200/
14/30, 17324/68/76, 17441. (20).

30A Corkerhill 594–6, 611/4/5/9–23/7/37/41/9–51/66,
905/6/13/4, 1109/10/27/48/9/82, 2910–7, 5047/9, 5168/
94, 5489–91, 5560/75/6, 5643–6/93, 7329, 15128/35/43/
82/93, 15206/11/9/25/35/66/9, 16249, 16350/61/9,
17234/49/55/66, 17300/9, 17560–2/6/75/80/5/9/94/6/7,
17624/30/2/42/4/50/73, 17821/9, 17908. (95).

30B Hurlford 570–3/93/7, 612/7/8/43–5/61–3/5/86–9,
3899, 4159/98, 4312/9/23/5/9, 14495, 14504, 15203/36/
60, 16368, 17236/77/8/97, 17308/31/53/83, 17570–4/98,
17620/37/43/51/71/2/88. (55).

30C Ardrossan 578/9, 606–9/24–6/67–9, 2472–5, 16259/
79/82, 16311/64, 17263/74/6/82, 17304/35/48/55–7/9,
17577/9/90, 17622/5/7/9. (39).

30D Ayr 574/5/90, 610/38/40/7/8/84/70, 1132/3/8/55/83,
2739, 2800/1/5/6/8/9/79, 2927, 7182, 14760, 15115/31/
2, 16257/72–4, 16363, 17235/61/2/71/9/84/95, 17312/5/
51/4/64/90/2, 17567/9/91, 17610/1/4–6/28/33/40/69/84.
(61).

31A St Rollox 918, 1126/8/9, 3848/9, 4194, 4253–7,
4880/1, 5115–7/53–9/61/2/76–9, 5355/6/8/9/62, 5423/
53–5/68/71/80/1, 8164/5, 14473–5/83/7/94, 14621,
15129/59/68/78, 16151, 16233/4/52/89, 16370, 17240/8/
51/3/4/69, 17305/11/8/33/52/80, 17453–5, 17554/7/8,
17617/31/87. Works, 16025. (84).

31B Stirling 4283, 4330/1, 14455/66/85/91/6, 15117/22/6,
15212/22/33, 16254, 16340/65/6, 17232/3/43/6/52/7/64,
17402/22–5/60/6/8. (33).

31C Oban 15187, 15204/15/29/63, 17396, 17401/11. (8).

31D Grangemouth 2736–8, 3883, 4320, 8147–52, 15119/
24/42, 15238, 16152/64, 16230/2/43/67/75, 16300/75/6,
17265/85/7/93/4, 17334/8/73, 17412/42, 17603/58/76/
89/91. (40).

31E Dawsholm 153/8/9/76/7/85–9, 200, 4281, 14638/9/
44, 15359–61, 16010/26/39, 16158/61/8–71, 16238/50/
97, 16302/15/30/9/44, 17245/58/9, 17306/14/22/36/41/6/
66/71/2/9, 17426–9/56/7/69–72, 17592, 17605/12/52.
(62).

32A Inverness 4258, 5009/12/4/6/53/66/83/4/90/8, 5122–
4/36/60/92, 5319/20/60/1, 5476–9, 7541, 14332/40/92/
7, 14400/1/3/4/6/8–10/2/5/6, 14681/6, 14762/4/7,
15001/51/3, 15199, 16011, 16262/91/3/9, 16341, 17330,
17693–5/7, 17702/3, 17950–7. (71).

32B Aviemore 5138, 14338/63/79/98/9, 14434, 14690,
15133, 17699, 17700. (11).

32C Forres 14333/7/85, 14678/92, 16301, 17696/8,
17704. (9).

Note: In 1947 Lostock Hall (23E) was transferred to the
Accrington district and renumbered 24C.

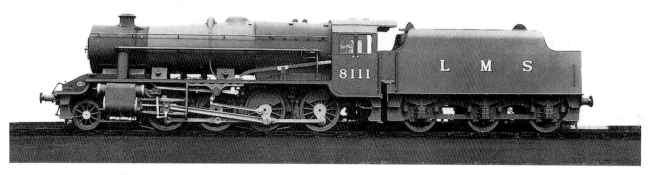

From top to bottom. The ultimate LMS freight locomotive, Stanier Class 8F 2-8-0. Built also as a War Department standard engine for World War II this class saw service in the Middle East – some remained in Turkey until very recent times. A trial version of one of Stanier's most successful classes, the Class 5 4-6-0, fitted with experimental Caprotti valve gear just after World War II. Royal Scot re-built. The double chimney, taper boiler version of the Scot was a magnificent engine turning a competent class into a real success story. Pacesetter for the rebuilding was No 6170 British Legion. Built just into BR days, the brilliant Stanier Duchess Pacific, No 46257 probably Britain's finest express locomotive. Shown here in BR blue livery. One of the two LMS diesel-electric locomotives No 10000. They were the forerunners of the later BR English Electric types.

Farewell Lickey Bankers

Today's 125 HST sweeps across the Worcestershire countryside beyond Bredon Hill and makes for Birmingham, passengers scarcely noticing a drop in speed as it reaches the summit of the Lickey Incline, just over two miles at 1 in 37. But throughout the steam age the incline was famous, more likely notorious, in railway lore, a mistaken view by the early railway engineers that a short sharp shock was better than a longer, steadier climb. Passengers and freights alike had to halt just short of Bromsgrove station to await 'the banker' which would avoid the train engine stalling or ruining its fire.

The Midland had, in 1919, built *Big Emma* or *Big Bertha*, whichever name you preferred best. For many years this 0-10-0 No 2290 was not only the sole decapod working in the UK but the only banker built specially for the purpose – that is until the coming of the Gresley 2-8-0+ 0-8-2 for the Worsborough bank. The nicknames probably came from the fact that in telegraphic parlance Emma stood for M – hence Big Midland or that the engine arrived after World War I when all big things were named after the famous German gun.

Nothing changed much during LMS days trains being banked by combinations of engines according to their loadings – being equal one, equal two, equal three, No 2290 counting as equal two. In 1929/30 the LMS tried out a Bowen-Cooke LNWR design 0-8-4 tank No 7953 and an unhappy trial was made with LMS Garratt No 4998 in 1934. But the time was bound to come when Big Bertha would grow old.

In the mid 1950s eyes alighted on the now redundant through electrification ex LNER Garratt No 69999 then lying at Gorton. The engine was once again (there was a trial in 1949/50) despatched post haste to Bromsgrove but took

Storming to Lickey. An evocative scene showing Jubilee class No 45660 Rooke *heading the 08.45 Kingswear to Bradford (14.20/21 Bromsgrove) routed via Camp Hill and thus avoiding New Street one summer Saturday in 1955. The train is banked by the ex Midland 0-10-0 (LMS No 2290) BR No 58100 'Big Bertha'. Summer Saturdays were an enthusiast's paradise with trains coming up every few minutes – no sooner had one cleared the summit than another set off from Bromsgrove.*

a month to make the journey, suffering a hot box at Burton and a loose pony wheel in the leading unit at Saltley. It began work on 8 August 1955 with complaints from the Bromsgrove enginemen that water levels and steam pressure were difficult to maintain and that even at slow speeds the 178 tons buffering up to passenger trains threw standing passengers.

Next, a BR standard Class 9F 2-10-0 was sent from Wellingborough. The 250lb pressure, self-cleaning smokebox and rocking grate were liked, but while successful on passenger trains the engine was slow on freights, the men saying that the two cylinders would not do the work of four.

But the 9F won and the last banking trip for *Big Bertha* was the Mail on Saturday 6 May 1956 when it lost two minutes on the trip. It left its long time home next morning, running light to

Derby where an official photograph signalled the end. Such was its fame that the media noted its demise in some style. The editor of the *Bromsgrove Messenger* wrote 'No doubt the trains will still run up and down although *Bertha* has gone and some day the noise and smoke, the cinders and the grass fires they cause will all give way to the silent electric engine. But the Embankment will not be the same without her.'

Steam banking continued for another decade, a Churchward 2-8-0 tank No 5226 (which lasted only for the summer of 1958) and the Hawksworth modern 0-6-0 pannier tanks which virtually took over from the Jinties doing stints when the route was switched to the Western. The last big banker to remain on a permanent basis was 9F No 92079 complete with *Big Bertha's* old headlamp. It left Bromsgrove in October 1963.

5
SOME LMS STATIONS

Unlike the Great Western whose stations had grown with the company, the LMS inherited a heterogenous collection. These ranged from the glazed gable train sheds of Euston added piecemeal ever since the completion of the Great Hall (the LMS even spoilt *that* by putting a kiosk in the middle), to the Midland owned S&DJR Bath Green Park (formerly Queen Square), a Bath Georgian building long out of its time. Add to those four odd triangular junctions at Earlestown, Ambergate, Forres and Rutherglen, plus the longest station name in Great Britain, Llanfairpwllgwyngyllgogerychwyrndrobwllllantysiliogogogoch, colloquially known as Llanfair PG, and one can see the variety. Carnforth, stuck in the wilds of North West Lancashire became famous for a short while for it was here (and at Watford Junction) that they made that superb film, *Brief Encounter* while the Midland's fine St Pancras was built on a module to accommodate beer barrels from Burton in the dungeons of its cellars. Preston and Normanton had large refreshment rooms going back to the days when the Scotch expresses stopped for lunch before dining cars came into being, while Inverness had that odd working whereby trains from the South ran over the triangle and backed in alongside the Far North train and vice versa to facilitate transfers.

In the days of the London & Birmingham Railway, Euston was, to be sure, a grand station; so was the other end at Curzon Street, Birmingham, where the elegant three-storey square stone block of offices, though sadly not the train shed, has been preserved and restored by dint of being listed; certainly not by the benevolence of British Rail London Midland Region. Osborne's 1838 *Guide to the Grand Junction and London and Birmingham Railways* saw it that way without doubt but one must bear in mind that Osborne's readers belonged to the age that built the Doric Arch – a time of leisured progress northward with the family coach on the wagon next to the engine, a time when a famous railway manager would exclaim in scorn: 'Carry coals? They will be expecting us to carry dung next!' But then those were the days of 'young ladies accompanied by their Mamas on the one side and lovers on the other, the servant or maid following with band box being saluted and tended until they are safely in their places.'

Today's Euston with its stark concrete and glass entrance hall, where (until public outcry) there were no seats in the actual concourse, is in absolute contrast to Philip Charles Hardwick's Great Hall of 1849 when the largest waiting room in the British Isles opened out of the booking office, its panelled ceiling with bas reliefs representing the principal cities served by the then new London & North Western Railway. In

Long Shriek

It was in the mid-1930s, and the BBC having decided that railways could provide interesting material for outside broadcasts, there was this gathering around a mobile recording unit sited below the embankment of the West Coast Main Line in a very damp field immediately south of Bletchley station. We were awaiting the passage (including the exchange of mailbags at the lineside apparatus) of the 8.30pm Euston–Glasgow West Coast 'Down Special TPO', due to pass at 9.26pm, having already exchanged bags at six previous places.

The driver had been instructed to 'give a good whistle' and everything was ticking over when a distant sound heralded the expectant action. Somewhere about Stoke Hammond, the driver sounded that whistle – and it never stopped. No hooter this, but a good old sustained eldritch shriek, that drowned all other sound as it swept by and on through Bletchley station and into the night, wailing away towards Rugby, with the valve well and truly jammed, having deafened the mike and the postman as they exchanged the Bletchley bags.

For years afterwards, the passage of the West Coast Postal, wailing whistle and all, was dug out by the BBC to simulate the Orient Express, the Trans-Siberian, the Frontier Mail, or whatever the script called for.
D. S. M. Barrie

London Terminus. Euston station departure side showing the down Royal Scot loading ten minutes before departure time. The date must be c1932 as there is one early Stanier coach visible. Even at this time Euston was a very gloomy station and could have done nothing to encourage travellers.

Euston track layout in the 1930s.

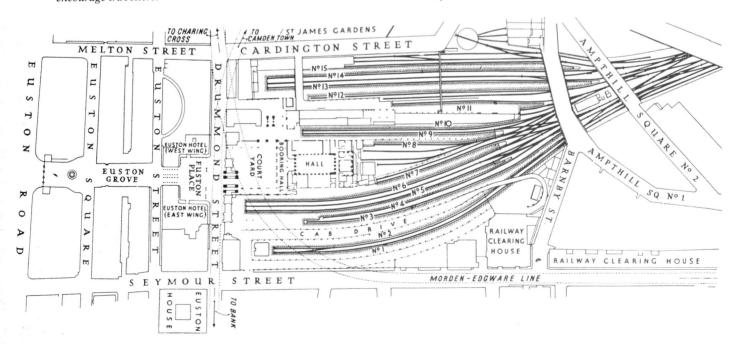

LMS days several of the platforms were still known to the staff by long standing nicknames betraying historic origins – 'The Departure', 'The Kensington Bay', 'The York' – the last named from its having been in 1840 the departure point for the York Mail and other trains to and from what was to become the Midland Railway.

By the late 1930s Euston had attained its maximum extent of 15 platforms totalling over two miles in length and the departure platforms 12 and 13 were lengthened to take trains of 16 coaches. With separate arrival and departure platforms necessitating vast empty stock movements the terminus had its drawbacks and in those pre war days reconstruction was envisaged under a Government assisted scheme to offset unemployment, there being little new in this world. Even then plans of the new station did not include the Doric Arch. A senior railway official was quoted by *Modern Transport* as saying 'We will make a present of the Arch to anyone who cares to take it away'. The *Observer* suggested that 'this splendid creation' should be pieced together on Shap Summit. When Euston was eventually torn apart and rebuilt in the 1960s the Doric Arch disappeared for ever.

Birmingham's New Street was always a bottleneck with its separate LNWR and Midland halves, even if it did have a joint stationmaster. Nothing changes – the old cavernous New Street covered with arches of iron and once clean glass, latterly grime covered or broken, gave place in BR days to a concrete jungle of subterranean platforms just as dingy with poor waiting accommodation and a totally inadequate car park. If Switzerland is the railway turntable of Europe then British Rail has

Gaslight and Gloom. New Street station in the summer of 1927 with a new 'Crab' 2-6-0 standing in the main up platform, No 1, with a semi-fast for Coventry and Rugby. In those days the platform nomenclature would have been platform 1 facing platform 2 as there were only six numbered platforms on the whole station; the ex-LNWR side comprised platforms 1–3 and Midland 4–6. The two stations were separated by a central roadway named Queen's Drive. On the left are the two bay platforms used for Coventry, Walsall (via the Grand Junction Line) and some Sutton trains.

attempted to give New Street a similar claim as the hub of its rail system though the station has been a crossroads since its earliest days.

Major changes in the approach to New Street from the east took place in the 1890s in order to attempt to relieve congestion. Perhaps the one most evident to travellers in later years was the taking of the Midland main line from Derby under the LNWR from Coventry so that Midland trains could reach their section of New Street without confliction with the heavy LNW traffic (opened 17 May 1896). But the bottleneck of the two track tunnels for trains running north and west and platform scarcity remained. Even today it is far from rare for the electric train from Euston to be well on time to Proof House junction and then to wait there for a platform. Trains now take 95 minutes from Euston. In the bad old days of steam it was 115 minutes. The author's father often recalled the time when as a young man he came in to the city on the Harborne branch with the trains held at Icknield Port Road, just before the junction to the north of Monument Lane, awaiting late Wolverhampton trains. To be at work on time they had to jump over the fence and catch the tram into town.

What variety around the system! Holyhead, split down the middle by the waters of the harbour giving arrival and departure sides for the trains as was old Euston, incoming ships after discharge being winched over from the arrival to departure berths. Coventry, until its rebuilding by the London Midland Region, a disgrace to its city. Leeds (Wellington), one of the few stations which the LMS actually rebuilt in the 1930s, is now a parcels depot. Fenchurch Street, London, an untidy anomaly, owned by the LNER but which saw more LMS trains and passengers by way of the Tilbury line.

Then, Crewe. In 1927 LMS figures showed that at peak holiday periods the number of trains dealt with at Crewe in 24 hours was upward of 500; no wonder the lady 'wanted to go to Birmingham' and found herself at Crewe. The main signalboxes at Crewe South Junction and Crewe North Junction had as many as 345 and 265 working miniature levers controlling signals and points electrically, such was the traffic: these were in two tiers to save space and was an LNWR development which became known as the 'Crewe System'. Beginning modestly in 1840 as the junction for Chester on the Grand Junction Railway, Crewe amassed more and more connections until its name became almost a synonym for a railway junction, later taking in Manchester, Stoke-on-Trent, Shrewsbury and, although the junction for Liverpool was at first just north of Warrington (and from 1869 at Weaver Junction some sixteen miles north of Crewe) Liverpool traffic was exchanged in Crewe station and yards.

For most of their length Crewe platforms were covered by all over glazed gable type roofing. Glazed wind screens of characteristic LNWR practice faced platforms 1 and 4, situated between the platform line and No 1 down through line. Where the screen was interrupted for the connections to and from the through line a section was set back to give continuous protection, or, in the minds of some, to block the view of what was going on in the railway's back yard. These screens could also be found at other major stations and junctions such as Rugby and along

Transporter. Manchester Victoria station in 1912, showing the overhead carrier which conveyed baskets of packages from the parcels office beyond platform 17 to all parts of the station. This view from platform 11 looks towards Exchange station and the site of the connecting platform constructed by the LMS. On the right is a mechanical departure indicator, some of which (on platforms 12/13) lasted well into BR days.

Busy Terminus. Glasgow Central in 1939. The station was extended and enlarged by the Caledonian Railway in 1906 to the size shown here and the power signal box on the right was installed in 1908.
The train leaving hauled by a McIntosh class 3F 0-6-0 is the 12.30pm to Kirkhill. The wording on the front of the station building reads 'Caledonian Railway Central Station'.

Liverpool Riverside. Until 27 March 1950 Riverside platforms and the docks beyond resounded to the wheezing chaffs of ex-LNWR 0-6-2 coal tanks and the occasional G2 0-8-0 but the strengthening of the bridge over Prince's Dock changed all that allowing big engines to make the journey through the murky tunnels to Edge Hill and the main line. Jubilee class 4-6-0 No 45567 South Australia heads the first boat train to be hauled by a single engine all the way to Euston and thus marking the end of an era.

Platform ticket issued free at Rugby to patrons of the dining room on the station and to all passengers requiring travel tickets as the booking office was on the platform.

Lime Street Pilot. An unusual class on this job, photographed in June 1939. No 7946 was one of the Beames class of 0-8-4 tanks introduced just after the Grouping period for use over the steep banks in South Wales and also for the Manchester to Buxton passenger trains. Long in the wheelbase they had a nasty habit of dropping in over the sharper points; nevertheless fourteen of the class saw out the LMS.

Stranraer Harbour. The terminus of the short sea route to Northern Ireland before World War II, LMS three-cylinder Compound 4-4-0 No 1177, allocated to Dumfries, is about to leave on the up 'Day Paddy' 12.40pm to Carlisle with through coaches to Euston via the Portpatrick & Wigtownshire Joint Line. It is the mid 1930s and the ex-G&SW engines have been decimated, replaced by newly-built Compounds. Stranraer Harbour is still open but now the London trains have to make the long trek via Ayr and Kilmarnock.

the North Wales Coast at Rhyl and Colwyn Bay; the latter were very annoying to young train spotters stuck on the beach or pier with their parents as it made engine 'copping' just that much more difficult. The approach to North Wales was via Chester, a joint station, as were Carlisle, Perth and Aberdeen in the north.

Situated near the entrance to two valleys through the Southern uplands of Scotland, Carlisle was the natural target for railways seeking their fortunes further north. The lines of seven companies converged there and the variety of liveries and styles to be seen from its station platforms prior to Grouping is part of railway lore. On the LMS side its constituents were the LNW, Midland, Caledonian, Glasgow & South Western and Maryport & Carlisle, while it was also used by Furness Railway locomotives. There were eight platform roads totalling 2,824 yards, the longest of which could cope with two trains together. A glazed roof once covered six and a quarter acres of this site but now as with so many BR occupied stations this passenger convenience has been reduced drastically. A covered way led from the station to the adjacent County and Station Hotel built on land belonging to the Citadel Station Managing Committee: this was let to an independent company.

The LMS had many stations of size and grandeur from its constituents north of the border. Glasgow Central was terminus of the major Scottish expresses from London. It also had characteristics peculiar to itself and the life of the huge city. Serving the piers at Gourock, Wemyss Bay (rebuilt in the heyday of the Caledonian Railway along with Stirling) and Ardrossan, it was the starting point for steamer trips down the Clyde and across to the islands that were the traditional summer excursions, 'doon the watter'. With the entrance from Gordon Street at the north end dignified with columns carrying semicircular arches and an iron and glass portico, Central was – and remains – an impressive station. The concourse sloped upwards towards the platforms, for rail level was above street level and Argyle Street, between Gordon Street and the river, passed underneath it. The hotel was the pride of the Caledonian and was treated with great importance by the LMS, justifying its telegraphic address BESTOTEL.

But Buchanan Street was just a scruffy hole of four platforms and wooden buildings, though its history tells of green carriages and the teak-brown sleeping cars of the Highland Railway. A station of tongues especially around 10 o'clock at night when that notorious caravan of the LMS began its long slow pilgrimage to Inverness. The arched roof of St Enoch was a grand starting point throughout LMS days and well beyond for the alternative route to London – the Midland into St Pancras, the gem of London stations, with its awe inspiring train shed (for a century the world's largest station roof without internal supports) and its now listed though long-closed hotel designed by Sir George Gilbert Scott.

Lancashire & Yorkshire stations were mundane and practical though Manchester Victoria and Liverpool Exchange had attractive tiled maps of the system. Victoria station, Manchester, was certainly their biggest and best though not in the top class. Apart from the fact that it had been

Provincial Terminus. Oxford Rewley Road station on 1 May 1940; the photograph is taken from above showing the ridge and furrow glazing and wooden station buildings so beloved by the LNWR.

An early wartime scene with very few cars in evidence and some of those that are visible show the compulsory white painting of bumpers, mudguards and running boards, also blackout masks on headlamps.

The yard is full of coal traffic while the pooling of private owner wagons is making its presence felt as those visible are from different parts of the country.

Carlisle Citadel. Like York the central footbridge at Carlisle has always been a good spot to stop and take in the character of its station. Unlike York, Carlisle has been more than a major traffic centre, it has also been the meeting place of nations where Englishmen and Scots have celebrated alliances and glowered over rivalries. Right into the early days of BR, Citadel station kept this atmosphere with trains still entering and leaving over the old rival routes hauled by steam engines emanating from rival companies, Duchesses and A3s, Black Fives and B1s, Compounds and Caley 4-4-0s. This photograph, taken in August 1953 shows the station with its overall roof still intact full of the character generated over more than a century.

headquarters of the old L&Y, Victoria had other claims to fame. Under the LMS, platform 11 was linked to the Exchange station's platform 3 giving a continuous platform available for trains throughout its length of 2,916ft which was claimed to be the longest single railway platform in the world, while *The Wonder Book of Railways* and periodicals featured the overhead conveyor serving various points of parcels handling. The operator rode in a position which would frighten a modern-day factory inspector to death as he controlled the hoist of a large basket slung beneath. Victoria equalled Crewe in business. A normal LMS pre-war day saw over 400 trains arriving and departing, not counting many excursions and reliefs. On one Bank Holiday alone in the late 1920s there were 140 specials, 47 of them for Blackpool.

Manchester had one other grand station – Central – almost the twin of the Midland's St Pancras. At least the train shed was spectacular if not the actual station which, so to speak, had no proper front door through which its customers could be invited, nor reception rooms where they could be made comfortable, rather like the average stately home without its columned portico. The wooden booking offices were contained in two short passageways, one of which served the Cheshire Lines (joint with the LNER) and the other the Midland lines. There were a couple of pigeon holes in each passage into which one peered and craned to book a ticket – just adequate for a suburban station but miniscule in scale to prepare one for the tremendous vista that captured the eyes on emerging from this squalid passage on to the concourse. Neither the small book-stall nor the two inadequate refreshment rooms did anything like justice to their surroundings. Only the trains and the huge clock seemed to match this great arch of glass and iron, now an exhibition centre.

And so it went on. There were other great Midland stations at Leicester, Nottingham and Sheffield and the joint station at Bristol

74

County to County

There shall not be more than one train in one county on one line at one time? That might sound far fetched in defining the block system but at the southern end of the West Coast main line in Middlesex it was often literally enforced. Hatch End and North Wembley signalboxes were not always open continuously, particularly in the last years of steam in the 1950s and early 1960s. When they were closed the block sections ran from Bushey (Hertfordshire) to Harrow No 1 (Middlesex), and from Harrow No 1 to Sudbury Junction at Wembley (Middlesex), while the intermediate block signals between Sudbury Junction and Willesden No 7, the next box to the south, were just at the County of London boundary. Northbound express trains climbing the 1 in 330 towards Tring were usually travelling at between 50 and 60mph and if they left Euston at less than 7min intervals they were likely to be checked somewhere in the area. If they were to have a clear run, only one train would be in Middlesex at one time since the train ahead would already be in Hertfordshire while the train behind was still in the County of London.

where the LMS met the Great Western. Trent had one windswept island platform, refreshment room, waiting rooms and a booking office and was virtually isolated. Then there were holiday stations like Llandudno, Colwyn Bay, Rhyl, Blackpool, Morecambe and Largs.

Perhaps the most unusual was Liverpool Riverside, reached from Edge Hill by cavernous tunnels causing untold problems to locomotive crews on the up journeys. The tunnels were cut without lining, the 'six foot' varying from 5ft to 5ft 6in and there were 2,601 yards of 1 in 57. Sulphurous fumes entered the compartments, windows were covered in grime, and the engine crews of ancient LNWR coal tanks emerged at walking pace gasping for breath. On one occasion in BR LMR days a train load of American tourists hauled by an LMS Black Five came to a halt and actually ran backwards momentarily without the driver realising what had happened. Once stopped, another four engines had to be brought from Edge Hill shed to get it moving again. Despite all this the Riverside to Euston boat trains were among the most sought after jobs by train crews who regarded the tunnel as a challenge. Riverside was opened in 1895, a month after the LNWR directors had a lunch in the baggage room and viewed the loading and unloading of the great White Star liner *Majestic*. The LMS was not so lucky, as when peace settled after World War I Cunard and White Star announced that Southampton was to become their principal home, Liverpool's service being secondary. However traffic continued and the station often became very busy; during one week-end in August 1924 nine liners were served by seven special trains. Up to 1938 as many as seventy liners were still making regular sailings from Liverpool. World War II, as the writer can testify, saw troops arriving and departing in huge numbers. In 1941 nine trains each took 500–600 Free French troops, then came the Canadians, then the Americans. It was no unusual thing for a train load of American soldiers to leave the station every hour for thirty hours. Finally the station was called upon to handle the returning troops; altogether 1,747,405 were moved in 4,748 special trains from a station built to deal with only about four trains per week.

Riverside was always kept in spotless condition – usually there were hanging baskets of flowers and potted palms at the buffer end. It actually belonged to the Mersey Docks & Harbour Board which had its own stationmaster (one Captain Pollock in the 1930s), but when there were boat trains Lime Street sent down an inspector, a booking clerk (authorised to accept USA or Canadian dollars) and some casual porterage staff hired by the day. The finale came in the small hours of 25 February 1971 when a Class 40 diesel-electric with a train of troops from Northern Ireland wound its way slowly over the Princes Dock swing bridge, round the dock estate, crossed the deserted Dock Road and vanished into the tunnels. A sombre contrast to the first train for the *Germanic* 85 years previously. Through running of main line locomotives had been possible since March 1950.

New Street Midland Side. The newly restored Midland Compound No 1000 waits at platform 4 with a Stephenson Locomotive Society special for Derby and York. One of the first locomotives to be restored by the then British Transport Commission (under its Curator John Scholes) to full working order, No 1000 was treated by decree with kid gloves; for example coaling had to be done by hand. The picture shows old New Street as it really was – cavernous but with character, even to the top-hatted stationmaster properly dressed for the occasion. The date is 30 August 1959.

THE L.& N.W.R. SCOTCH EXPRESS AT FULL SPEED.

Pre-grouping colours. Reproductions of coloured postcards showing LMS constituent company trains in their pre-grouping liveries. These are typical examples of cards issued, literally, in their millions during the Edwardian and 1920/30 period showing trains of the day. Some were produced by the companies themselves (the LNWR being by far the most prolific) others by such well known firms as the Locomotive Publishing Co, Raphael Tuck, Valentine, and Salmon: others by smaller companies exampled by Knight or Pouteau. Today these are collectors' items, but they provide a very real and fascinating insight into the colourful days of Britain's railways.

The illustrations show, top, an LNWR official card (printed, as were the majority of LNW publications, by McCorquodale & Co Limited – Tuck printed some cards) with a caption 'The L&NWR Scotch Express at Full Speed'. This is one of the relatively few coloured officials showing trains themselves as most were views: there were also ships in colour. The date would appear to be pre-1910 as the locomotive is an Experiment class 4-6-0. After 1910 the George V 4-4-0s would have been more likely . . . in fact a later card illustrated a Claughton. This card also illustrates typically tall LNWR signals, those guarding the slow lines indicated as such by rings on their arms. This one comes from a set of seven cards illustrating 'The Scotch Express'.

Centre. A Locomotive Publishing Co card headed Midland Railway, London, Liverpool and Manchester Express. This is from a painting by 'F. Moore' LPC's legendary artist but actually an oil painting superimposed on a photograph. The date is likely to be just before World War I, and the card illustrates a Midland three-cylinder Compound No 1013 with eight clerestory coaches including a twelve-wheeled diner. It is on the four-tracked section out of London.

VERPOOL-MANCHESTER EXPRESS
LANCASHIRE & YORKSHIRE RLY.

Bottom. A Tuck card from that company's Famous Express Series (No 11) dating around 1910 it shows a Liverpool–Manchester Express headed by an L&Y Aspinal 4-4-2 in gleaming black on a set of troughs. The Tuck trademark 'Oilette' is in the right hand bottom corner.

*Pre-grouping colours.
Reproductions of coloured postcards
showing LMS constituent company
trains in the pre-grouping liveries
representing the more minor
companies – the Furness and two
Scottish lines.*

*Top. A Tuck 'Oilette' card (Famous
Express Series III) showing a red
Furness 4-4-0 headed 'The Furness
Railway Lake District Express, for
Lakeside stations Windermere,
Furness Abbey etc passes through the
country. Along the whole route
charming views present themselves in
quick succession to the tourist'.
Probably circa 1910/12.*

*Centre. An LPC card headed
'12.35pm Oban Express –
Callander and Oban Branch
Caledonian Railway'. It shows a
small wheeled McIntosh 4-6-0 No
54, one of a class specially built for
this road, near Oban with a six
coach train on the single line. Again
by 'F. Moore' it presents a lovely
picture of a dark blue Caley engine
on one of the company's best known
branches. Probably circa 1910/12.*

*Bottom. The Knight series No 987,
'The Highland Mail, 1484ft above
sea-level'. A train halted at the
Druimuachdar summit loop headed
by a green Highland Railway
Castle class 4-6-0 with a train of
mixed six-wheeled and bogie stock.
Colour washed onto a photograph as
usual with this series. Date probably
around 1910/12.*

LAKE DISTRICT EXPRESS. F.R.

THE HIGHLAND MAIL (1,484 Feet Above Sea-Level).

The Knight Series. No. 987

Birmingham New Street, North Western Side. Ex LNWR Prince of Wales class 4-6-0 No 25673 Lusitania (built during World War I and named after the doomed Cunard liner torpedoed by the Germans while carrying civilian passengers) stands in platform 2 facing platform 3, with a semi-fast for Stafford, Stoke and Manchester. The date is 1939 and little has changed at New Street; the footbridge (used as a virtual right of way) linking the two stations is in the background, topped by the clock over the small lever frame controlling the intermediate signals, and the glass in the overall roof is intact and almost clean. LNWR locomotives – Princes, the odd superheated Precursor (but strangely no George V 4-4-0s) and Webb classes still abound while the biggest engines to be seen are Royal Scots and Jubilees.

Scottish Railway Centre. Perth station, which was jointly owned by the LMS and LNER. Jubilee class 4-6-0 No 5579 Punjab is arriving on what is probably an Aberdeen–Glasgow express.

Why are trains which are frequently late not re-timed to be more in keeping with the actual running time?

The LMS run 28,000 passenger and freight trains, but excluding electric trains, daily over their system.

An analysis of the running of trains over a period of 22 days shows that there is nothing constant about them. The 8.15am express from Euston to Holyhead, for instance, during the period from the 1st to the 26th March, 1946, was on time on 12 occasions. On 6 other occasions it was from 4 to 15 minutes late, and on one occasion was 48 minutes late due to a mechanical failure of a locomotive on a preceding freight train.

The facts are that an analysis of the day to day running of trains which is carried out by the operating experts show that different causes for delay occur at different places on different days. Where there are recurring delays from a particular cause which can be overcome, adjustments are made to the timetable and hundreds of such adjustments are carried out.

From The LMS Answers your Questions.

Midland Express. Leicester London Road. A three coach express, possibly for Birmingham, stands in platform 3 in the early 1930s. The locomotive is class 4P 4-4-0 Compound No 1062 from shed 21 – the code for all the former Midland sheds in Manchester. The coaches (two of them ex-MR clerestories) are non-corridor lavatory stock.

The wonders of Euston

There was nothing quite like Euston station, old Euston that is which disappeared in the mid 1960s, for like Topsy it had just grown, bit by bit from the original London & Birmingham station of 1837. Certainly it did not have the splendour of the great arched train sheds of the later St Pancras and King's Cross; for its train shed roof, the design dating from the mid 1830s, was low and pitched, rising and falling like a nursery of greenhouses but with trains and not flowers beneath. But Euston had something that no other station in the country possessed – the Great Hall that could have graced any stately home in the land with a magnificent flat panelled ceiling, the largest in the world some said, and rivalling one in Buckingham Palace. Then there was the unique entrance – the Doric Arch or more properly a propylaeum. Those two features alone characterised old Euston and both were destroyed when today's Euston was beginning to take shape for the modern electric era in one of the greatest acts of official vandalism ever carried out by the nationalised railways and the government of the day. Putting all of today's vandalism by groups intent on wrecking other people's property together is as nothing compared with what went on at Euston with official blessing in the name of progress during the 1960s.

Euston's Great Hall took on a cathedral like quality at Christmas with a carol service conducted by the Vicar of St Pancras church, and a choir including members of LMS staff. Notice the panelled ceiling and the reliefs portraying the principal cities served by the LNWR.

Yet it was just the situation of the Great Hall and the Arch in relation to the tracks and platforms which made Euston what it was, for the Great Hall was alongside what had been the original London & Birmingham departure platform, later platform 6 and almost on the site of today's platform 6 and 7, so that when extensions were called for to cater for newly developing traffic to Derby and York they were on the west side of the Great Hall. Later still more platforms were added on the west side (12–15) for main line departures and others right over on the east side (1, 2 and 3) for arrivals. So the Great Hall was sandwiched in the middle, dividing the station into distinct areas, none visible from the others, with access from the arrival to the departure side through corridors incorporating a booking hall.

Even when passengers reached the departure side they found themselves on platform 13 and if their train went from platforms 14 or 15 there was a further walk round the head end platform behind the buffers to reach them. As for platform 9, used mainly for bank holiday extras, it was tucked down another passageway and probably many intending passengers never actually found it at all!

At Euston you always had to *find* your platform. Nor were there any ticket inspectors at adjacent platforms you could ask, for you had to find those too. As for the scissors barrier gates of Waterloo, they did not exist at old Euston. The barriers were low timber gates on wheels which the platform staff wheeled into position depending on where the departing train was standing, for invariably parcels vans cluttered the buffer stop end of some platforms while some of the outer suburban trains could stand two to a platform at peak times.

But for passengers waiting for their train or waiting for the next one if they had missed their intended train there was the Great Hall. At various times it was waiting room, inquiry and seat reservation hall, model locomotive display area, and used for various other functions. Around it to the outside were other facilities including refreshment rooms – the Royal Scot bar of post war years with fare ranging from tea and coffee, poached egg on toast (1s 6d) to something more substantial. At the top of the great staircase at the north end of the Great Hall was the shareholders' meeting room, sometimes used for exhibitions, while a balcony at first floor level round the Great Hall led to the railway's offices.

But probably the Great Hall was never seen better than at Christmas time when it became a cathedral for the carol service, with a choir drawn from railway staff and St Pancras Church boys. Their voices echoed round the hall mingling with those of the passengers with time to spare. The ceiling was floodlit and lights from the Christmas trees on the floor below created an atmosphere worlds away from a railway station. Charities benefitted from the collection.

The Great Hall and the arch could have been saved – nobody would think of demolishing Buckingham Palace – and the new station designed around them. But nobody wanted to.

6
AN OBSERVER REMEMBERS

Neither the survivors of World War I returning to a changed and changing railway scene, nor the new generation of railway enthusiasts, could find much to enthuse about in train running and locomotive performance in the early, formative years of Grouping. This was especially true of the LMS, where it took four years of doubt, dissension and delay to get on the rails a front-line fleet of locomotives capable of launching, and with their successor types expanding, the largest sustained programme of passenger train accelerations to be carried through before the blackout descended on the Second World War.

Out of Euston on the LMS Western Division as the new regime took off in 1923, the burden was still shouldered by the Claughton and Prince of Wales 4-6-0s, often loaded to well beyond 400 tons and assisted if necessary to a special stop at Willesden Junction to detach the pilot engines used for the 1 in 70 of Camden Bank. And, as Sir Josiah Stamp did not fail to note when he came to Euston in 1925, there was a great deal of piloting of the heaviest trains, either The Irish Mail or the, as yet nameless, Royal Scot with 15 on, having an LNWR 4-6-0 assisted by a 4-4-0 or even one of Webb's famous 'Jumbo' 2-4-0s; this latter breed, incidentally, lasted in regular service until about 1932. They could be seen around Northampton Castle, where one might also spot a Johnson MR 2-4-0 taking the Nottingham through coach off the Sunny South Express on to Leicester via Market Harborough.

At 'the shop next door', St Pancras, an early manifestation of Derby's desire to find fresh fields of operation for various types acquired from neighbour companies was the appearance on suburban trains of an ex-Caledonian 0-4-4T, the driver of which opined that 'the only big thing about it' was the five-digit number on the tank-sides. Equally odd was the brief appearance of an ex-'Knotty' (North Staffs) tank engine at Broad Street, but Derby's greatest effort sadly unrewarded, was to despatch to the Highland section a Kirtley double-framed 2-4-0, MR/LMS No 4. Derby had thought that this might be a good engine for the Kyle line, or perhaps as a banker up to Dava, 1,052ft; the writer last saw it on the back road at Forres Shed, 'awaiting instructions'.

On a more serious scale, by 1928 with the Royal Scot 4-6-0s having been produced in the previous year, and made responsible only two months later for leisurely non-stop running in both directions between Euston and Carlisle, 299 miles – the West Coast main line received additional support in the shape of 20 Claughtons re-built with larger boilers and re-classified 5XP, the first use of that notation. About the same number of unmodified Claughtons were transferred to the Midland

Train Spotting
In LMS days small boys were naturally restricted in their areas of train spotting as fond parents limited their indulgence to a few pennies for trips to the large city stations, the purchase of a second-hand bicycle (it saved school bus fares) and the odd family holiday to the seaside. For a Birmingham boy this meant trips to the local ex-LNWR suburban station at Harborne – 'to see the new red coaches' – or to Somerset Road on the Midland line to the South West. The former had trains which took one to New Street for 1½d *return* (½p) on a cheap day child's ticket.

Generally visits to New Street tended to be to the North Western side as the Midland only produced big engines on the Pines Express and Devonian, the only named trains ever seen. On the North Western there was always a fascinating attraction of smoky haze, 'chaffing' engines and gas-lit homeliness. In the gloom at the south end of platform 3 there was a signalbox with its ringing bells and a milk, fish and parcels bay serviced by a shunter with a horn and a horse. The other side of platform 3 was the road dividing the two stations, Queens Drive: crossing this was like moving into another world. The North Western side had Royal Scots, Claughtons and many other ex LNWR named engines – all worth far more in the notebook than a mere Midland number.

Midland engines could be seen nearer to home, only a 15 minute walk to Somerset Road where very few trains stopped. Trains were watched from the lattice footbridge connecting the two platforms; we had to keep off as the stationmaster did not hold with small boys on *his* patch. Memories remain of the snorting 4-4-0s and 0-6-0s heading for the Cadbury's Bournville estate and beyond with the hidden pounding *continued overleaf*

continued
of horses' hooves on the towpath of the adjacent and parallel canal.

Holidays meant Colwyn Bay where the two tracks beyond Abergele widened out into four to Llandudno Junction. Here, in the early thirties, LNWR engines were very much in the lead and the traffic, particularly on a summer Saturday, simply had to be seen to be believed. Not only did one see the normal Claughtons, Princes, Georges, Precursors, Experiments and lesser LNW breeds, but also Hughes 4-6-0s and Midland 4Fs on excursions plus countless tanks. The only modern engines were the Royal Scots on the Irish Mail – great red engines with white bands on their smokebox doors, some still carrying their earlier names such as *Jenny Lind* though most had the newer regimental names.

A look at a ten year old's notebook for a week in August 1932 shows the following engines 'copped' from the footbridge on the four track section just beyond the station. The figures in brackets () are the shed codes of the locomotives, *viz*: 1 – Camden, 8 – Rugby, 10 – Aston, 10M – Monument Lane, 15 – Crewe, 18 – Birkenhead, 19 – Chester, 21 – Bangor, 22 – Holyhead, 23 – Warrington, 25 – Springs Branch Wigan, 26 – Edge Hill, 34 – Patricroft, 35 – Speke, 37 – Mold Jct, 38 – Llandudno Jct, 40 – Stoke.

Seen Colwyn Bay – August 1932
  Claughton: 5914 *J. Bruce Ismay* (15), 5921 *Sir Arthur Lawley* (15), 5925 *E. C. Trench* (15), 5927 *Sir Francis Dent* (1), 5937 (15), 5943 *Tennyson* (15), 5945 *Ingestre* (15), 5975 *Talisman* (26), 5990 (38), 5991 *C. J. Bowen Cooke* (38), 5994 (38), 5995 (38), 6002 *Thalaba* (15), 6013 (1), 6021 *Bevere* (34), 6024 (34).
  Prince of Wales: 5603 *Coquette* (15), 5611 *Charles Wolfe* (15), 5622 *Charles Kingsley* (15), 5641
continued opposite

Division, mainly for working some of the heavier expresses on the Settle & Carlisle section, and between Leeds and St Pancras, mostly on the night sleeping-car trains; Midland firemen received them with something short of universal enthusiasm. It so happened that several of this batch of Claughtons bore the names of ex-LNWR directors, so the initial appearance of No 5912 *Lord Faber* on a westbound express in Derby station was regarded by the ex-Midland hierarchy who turned out to witness, as something of a gauntlet thrown down . . .

There were other migrations which made life more interesting for observers and recorders. Some of the improved version of George Hughes' 4-6-0s ('Lanky Claughtons' to the LNWR men) came in support of the LNWR 4-6-0s and Royal Scots on the WCML, mostly north of Crewe; off their native heath, they penetrated also to Llandudno and even to Euston on excursions. Time had its revenge in Scotland too. By about 1930 the sturdy and handsome ex-Highland Railway 'River' class 4-6-0s of 1915, which had been sold to the Caledonian after being banned by the HR engineer were back on their native heath, working in company with LMS 2-6-0s of basically L&Y design!

If the 1920s were thus the period of transition, it was the 1930s which became the years of progress towards the attainment of the dominant position in express train running which the LMS was to enjoy before the outbreak of World War II in 1939. The watershed year was 1932, when the company scheduled on its main routes between Euston, Birmingham, plus Liverpool and Manchester a series of intermediate point-to-point runs booked at between 60.3 and 64.5mph start-to-stop, aggregating over 620 miles daily in this speed range, while the total number of runs booked at 55mph or over rose from 62 to 103 daily.

The LMS was also developing charter business. In July 1929 a special train was run from Euston to Scotland for guests of an industrial organisation to visit a coal distillation plant at Glenboig. The return journey by an 11-coach formation, including cinema, lounge, and restaurant cars, made a then record (for an up journey) non-stop run of 395½ miles to Euston behind Royal Scot 4-6-0 No 6127 *Novelty*. (No 6113 had run a down train from from Euston to Glasgow non-stop in May 1928). For three years, 1932–34, a motor group chartered special trains, first class with restaurant cars, for guests to their trade shows at Coventry. The sponsors had asked for 'fast trains' and they got them. Except in the third year, all trains were booked at under even time over the 94 miles to Euston to Coventry and back, with Royal Scot haulage. In the 1933 runs, No 6129 *Comet* travelled 235 miles with an average load of 223 tons at an average speed of 79.1mph. Star turn of all was *Comet*'s final up run, admittedly with only seven coaches, 202 tons tare, 210 full, with driver B. A. Marchant, a member of the great Camden link of that period which included Laurie ('Ninety') Earl, and Frank Brooker. Marchant attained 75mph before Rugby, then ran the 70 miles Welton–Willesden in 47½ minutes at 88mph, maximum 92 twice, including two very slight distant signal sightings at caution to 77 and 70mph, and completing the 93.6 miles to a signal stop outside Euston in 74 minutes 20 seconds, an average of 75.6mph.

A Scot Goes South. An early manifestation of Derby's desire to find possible fresh fields of pasture for various locomotive types which they felt they had acquired from neighbouring companies was the appearance c1926 of red painted ex-Caledonian type (but Nasmyth Wilson built in 1925) 0-4-4 tank on the St Pancras suburban services. It was not popular and soon returned to its tribal zone.

Chester Engine. George Whale's Precursors were built to provide strong reliable motive power for early Edwardian expresses and to cut out double heading endemic in the use of small Webb engines. The driver of No 5300 Cerberus waits for the right away one August evening in 1932. The train is Chester bound. Note the shadows of two small boys with box cameras. The one on the left belongs to one of the authors!

continued
Czar of Russia (15), 5649 *Admiral Jellicoe* (15), 5650 *Castor* (40), 5653 *The Nile* (10), 5656 *Shark* (38), 5659 *Odin* (8), 5673 *Lusitania* (10), 5707 *Hampden* (10M), 5713 (26), 5723 *Stentor* (26), 5730 (34), 5736 *Disraeli* (34), 5748 (34), 5762 (38), 5769 (38), 5772 (15), 5786 (22), 5788 (22), 5789 (22), 5809 (38), 5832 (18).

Experiment: 5551 *Carnarvonshire* (23), 5554 *Prospero* (8), 5474 *Atalanta* (10).

George The Fifth: 5320 *George The Fifth* (8), 5332 *George Whale* (23), 5335 *Miles McInnes* (10), 5341 *Wolfhound* (22), 5342 *Boarhound* (22), 5353 *Staghound* (38), 5354 *New Zealand* (38), 5358 *Malta* (19), 5360 *Beagle* (19), 5362 *Fire Queen* (19), 5365 *Racehorse* (19), 5366 *Roebuck* (19), 5367 *Traveller* (19), 5368 *Perseus* (19), 5369 *Quail* (19), 5386 *Edward Tootal* (26), 5401 *Windermere* (34), 5403 *Leamington Spa* (38), 5405 *Conway* (38), 5406 *Llandidnod* (38), 5407 *Blackpool* (38), 5408 *Holyhead* (38), 5409 *Dovedale* (38).

Precursor: 5200 *Cerberus* (25), 5207 *Eglinton* (34), 5211 *Aurania* (34), 5213 *Emperor* (38), 5215 *Vulture* (38), 5217 *Knowsley* (38), 5222 *Alaska* (19), 5223 *Snake* (34), 5233 *Peel* (15), 5291 *Harbinger* (15), 5295 *Scorpion* (15), 5309 *Fame* (21).

Bowen-Cooke 4-6-2 tank: 6994 (15).

Webb 2-4-2 tank: 6626 (38), 6667 (38), 6734 (38).

Super D 0-8-0: 9104 (35), 9160 (38), 9240 (38), 9272 (8).

Horwich 2-6-0: 13190 (15), 13234 (15).

MR/LMS 4F 0-6-0: 4370 (21), 4373 (37), 4376 (38), 4378 (38), 4437 (38).

Ex ROD (GCR type) 2-8-0: 9476 (37), 9482 (37), new numbering 9661 (37), 9662 (37).

Royal Scot: 6100 *Royal Scot* (1), 6122 *Royal Ulster Riflemen* (15), 6123 *Royal Irish Fusilier* (15), 6159 *The Royal Air Force* (22).
P. B. Whitehouse

Parson's Pleasure. This photograph taken in the late 1930s by the Rev Eric Treacy when Vicar of Edge Hill. It shows Royal Scot No 6142 The York and Lancaster Regiment heading a train of modern coaches at Wavertree on an up London express. At this time D. S. M. Barrie was in the advertising and publicity office and Eric Treacy's superb photographs were a boon to anyone in that job; many appeared in LMS and other publications. It was no light task those days if one was a serious photographer – this print came from a Zeiss Contessa Press Camera (9 × 12) using a Tessar 7in focal length lens, an Agfa glass plate and an exposure of 1/1000 of a second at f5.6.

It was, of course, also in 1932 that (Sir) W. A. Stanier moved from the GWR, quickly producing a succession of six-coupled express passenger and mixed traffic locomotives, plus an eight-coupled design for heavy freight work, all to be extremely successful. A crowning excitement occurred during the two-way demonstration of The Coronation Scot with 4-6-2 No 6220 on 29 June 1937, when a determined attempt was made to establish a new maximum speed record on the descent from Whitmore into Crewe. Speed had touched, perhaps fractionally over 113mph – 114 some said – and as retardation began, and the four recorders were checking their timings, one of them cried out 'God Almighty, that's Mile Post 157!'; with only just over a mile to go they were still doing over 90mph. Seconds later, there was a lurch – from the restaurant car came the cacophony of crashing crockery – and the speaker was rewarded for his profanity by being flung into the corridor and against the coach side as the train rolled through the reverse cross-overs approaching Crewe at way over the speed limit.

The Midland Division was also catching up the rising tide of acceleration. The early dominant partner in the LMS amalgamation had, to a

Track Quadrupling. To assist with the development of main line and suburban traffic over the busy New Street to Barnt Green section the bottleneck of the two-tracked Cofton tunnel (near Halesowen Junction) was demolished over the weekend of 26 to 28 January 1929. The cutting was widened with reinforced concrete-supported sides. This was a fascinating period for the enthusiast with contractors work before and after carried out using vertical boilered steam shovels and an 0-6-0 Manning Wardle open cab tank – maker's number 1793.

Early Treacy

The Rev E. Treacy, of St Mary's Vicarage, 2 Edge Lane, Liverpool 7, is particularly anxious that the enginemen of the trains he photographs should have free prints should they desire them. Mr Treacy proposes to wear a broad white armlet during the coming season when he is taking photographs, and any crews who see that he has photographed them will receive a print each free of charge if they write to him giving the following particulars: place at which photographed; number of engine; their own names and addresses.

LMS Magazine, March 1938.

Camden Shed's Mighty Atom. Driver Lawrence Alfred Earl in the cab of streamlined Duchess Pacific No 6224 Princess Alexandra.

Here Comes the Mail. Colwyn Bay in August 1932 with the down Irish Mail headed by a spotless Royal Scot on the fast line. The excursion behind a Fowler 4F 0-6-0 on the down slow comprises ex-Midland clerestory coaches. The Scot has the smokebox door ring painted white. Both down and up and Mails passed through Colwyn Bay around lunch time, keeping a 10-year old train spotter on tenterhooks with parents demanding punctual meal times. Colwyn Bay station is in the right distance.

certain extent, been hoist by its own petard, for Derby's small engine policy ('M is for Midland, with engines galore, two on each train and still asking for more'), meant that some of the key routes (Derby–Peak Forest, Birmingham–Bath and Bristol) still had weak bridges which had to be rebuilt for heavier locomotives to be used; while there were track bottlenecks, again on the West of England line especially, which had to be obviated at considerable cost, such as blowing up Cofton Tunnel near Barnt Green to make room for four tracks. Locomotive diagramming also had to be overhauled; the frequent use of the relatively small 4-4-0s of Classes 2 and 3 (the latter being Johnson's 'Belpaires') with trains of a certain weight might require four locomotives and sets of men between St Pancras and Manchester, which with the advent of 4-6-0s could be reduced to two, and ultimately to one with lodging turns at Kentish Town and Trafford Park.

As more six-coupled locomotives were drafted in, beginning with the first of the Baby Scot/Patriots in 1930, it became possible to reduce the number of engine-changes, eg a Carlisle 4-4-0 coming off at Skipton and a rebuilt Johnson 'Belpaire' coming on for the short run to Leeds, or a Compound bringing an express from London being relieved by a Class 3 4-4-0 from Leicester to Derby, only for engines to be changed again, with possibly a pilot over the Peak to Chinley or Manchester. On a wind-swept Bank Holiday in 1934 with a down express, well over the single engine-load for compound No 1075, Skipton provided MR 2-4-0 No 214 to pilot the 10-coach train to Garsdale; one could scarcely envy the pilot's crew as they prepared to return to Skipton tender-first in a gale driven rainstorm.

Some of the pilot working that continued after the bigger engines came in was for different reasons; on a mid-day semi-fast from Barrow to

Table A. British Railway Runs Scheduled at 58 m.p.h. and over from Start-to-Stop, August, 1939

Railway	Division	Train	From	To	Distance	Time	Speed
					miles	min.	m.p.h.
L.M.S.R.	Western	6.58 p.m.	Rugby	Watford	65.1	60	65.1
,,	,,	6.12 p.m.	Crewe	Euston	158.1	148	64.1
,,	,,	1.30 p.m.	Euston	Carlisle	299.1	283	63.4
,,	,,	3.17 p.m.	Carlisle	Euston	299.1	283	63.
,,	,,	6.15 p.m.	Nuneaton	Euston	97.1	92	63.3
,,	,,	8.34 a.m.	Watford	Coventry	76.5	73	62.9
,,	,,	6.52 p.m.	Stafford	Euston	133.6	128	62.6
,,	,,	2.58 p.m.	Crewe	Euston	158.1	152	62.4
,,	,,	9.26 a.m.	Willesden	Birmingham	107.5	104	62.0
,,	Midland	11.37 a.m. / 5.14 p.m.	Luton	Bedford	19.6	19	61.9
,,	Western	11.41 a.m.	Blisworth	Euston	62.8	61	61.8
,,	,,	5.13 p.m.	Coventry	Willesden	88.6	86	61.8
,,	Midland	2.22 p.m. / 6.10 p.m.	Kettering	St. Pancras	72.0	70	61.7
,,	Western	10.08 a.m.	Wilmslow	Euston	176.9	172	61.7
,,	Midland	12.10 p.m.	Appleby	Carlisle	30.8	30	61.6
,,	Western	10.16 a.m.	Crewe	Euston	158.1	154	61.6
,,	Midland	9.01 a.m.	Luton	Wellingborough	34.8	34	61.4
,,	Western	11.30 a.m. / 2.25 p.m. / 5.50 p.m.	Euston	Coventry	94.0	92	61.3
,,		12.08 p.m. / 1.23 p.m. / 2.58 p.m.	Coventry	Euston	94.0	92	61.3
,,	,,	10.35 a.m.	Crewe	Euston	158.1	155	61.2
,,	,,	10.34 a.m.	Bletchley	Euston	46.7	46	60.9
,,	Midland	10.00 a.m. / 12.00 noon	St. Pancras	Kettering	72.0	71	60.8
,,	Western	4.35 p.m.	Euston	Blisworth	62.8	62	60.8
,,	,,	2.00 p.m.	Euston	Crewe	158.1	156	60.8
,,	,,	9.16 a.m.	Willesden	Northampton	60.5	60	60.5
,,	Midland	5 trains	Luton	St. Pancras	30.2	30	60.4
,,	Western	4.53 p.m.	Crewe	Euston	158.1	157	60.4
,,	,,	9.28 p.m. / 4.28 p.m.	Rugby	Euston	82.6	82	60.4
,,	,,	1.35 p.m.	Euston	Rugby	82.6	82	60.4
,,	,,	1.15 p.m.	Stoke	Euston	145.9	145	60.4
,,	,,	6.00 p.m.	Euston	Wilmslow	176.9	176	60.3
,,	Midland	8.43 a.m.	Birmingham	Derby	41.2	41	60.3
,,	,,	9.05 a.m. / 2.10 p.m. / 6.20 p.m.	St. Pancras	Nottingham	123.5	123	60.2
,,	,,	11.18 a.m.	Nottingham	St. Pancras	123.5	123	60.2
,,	Western	10.21 a.m.	Mossley Hill	Euston	189.7	189	60.2
,,	Midland	4 trains	Cheltenham	Bromsgrove (a)	31.1	31	60.2
,,	,,	9.05 a.m.	Manton	St. Pancras	90.1	90	60.1
,,	,,	4 trains	St. Pancras	Leicester	99.1	99	60.1
,,	,,	7 trains	Leicester	St. Pancras	99.1	99	60.1
,,	Western	10.00 a.m.	Euston	Carlisle	299.1	299	60.0
,,	,,	12.16 p.m.	Carlisle	Euston	299.1	299	60.0
,,	Midland	5.18 p.m.	Kettering	St. Pancras	72.0	72	60.0
,,	Western	8.43 a.m.	Willesden	Rugby	77.2	78	59.4
,,	,,	6.55 p.m.	Crewe	Euston	158.1	160	59.3
,,	,,	11.58 a.m.	Carlisle No. 12 Box	Euston	298.1	302	59.2
,,	Caledonian	10.42 a.m.	Forfar	Perth	32.5	33	59.1
,,	Midland	2.13 p.m. / 4.13 p.m.	Leicester	Derby	29.4	30	58.8
,,	,,	4 trains	Luton	Bedford	19.6	20	58.8
,,	Western	11.21 a.m.	Northampton (b)	Euston	67.6	69	58.8
,,	Midland	4.30 p.m.	St. Pancras	Bedford	49.8	51	58.6
,,	Caledonian	1.30 p.m.	Glasgow	Carlisle	102.3	105	58.5
,,	,,	6.17 p.m.	Carlisle	Glasgow	102.3	105	58.5
,,	Western	5.33 p.m.	Preston	Carnforth	27.3	28	58.5
,,	Midland	7.22 a.m.	Luton	St. Pancras	30.1	31	58.4
,,	Western	6.17 p.m.	Bletchley	Euston	46.7	48	58.4
,,	,,	4.35 p.m.	Rugby	Euston	82.6	85	58.3
,,	Midland	6.01 p.m.	Cheltenham	Bromsgrove (a)	31.1	32	58.3
,,	Western	6.55 p.m.	Euston	Coventry	94.0	97	58.2
,,	,,	9.03 a.m.	Coventry	Euston	94.0	97	58.2
,,	Caledonian	11.26 a.m. / 2.51 p.m.	Perth	Stonehaven	73.7	76	58.2
,,	,,	3.44 p.m.	Stonehaven	Perth	73.7	76	58.2
,,	,,	11.01 a.m.	Symington	Carlisle	66.9	69	58.2
,,	Midland	9.37 a.m. / 6.29 p.m. / 8.05 p.m.	Leicester	Luton	68.9	71	58.2
,,	Western	8.23 a.m.	Rugby	Bletchley	35.9	37	58.2
,,	Midland	10.50 a.m. / 2.37 p.m.	Mangotsfield	Gloucester	31.9	33	58.0
L.M.S.R.	N.C.C.(n)	8.52 a.m.	Ballymena	Belfast	31.0	31	60.0

Table B. Aggregate Daily Mileage of British Railway Runs booked at 58 m.p.h. and over, August, 1939

Railway	70 m.p.h. and over	67 m.p.h. and over	64 m.p.h. and over	62 m.p.h. and over	60 m.p.h. and over	58 m.p.h. and over
	miles	miles	miles	miles	miles	miles
L.M.S.R.	—	—	223 (2)	1,394 (9)	6,902 (68)	8,928 (99)
G.W.R.	77 (1)	313 (3)	313 (3)	1,083 (12)	2,187 (24)	4,725 (52)
L.N.E.R.	653 (3)	1,293 (6)	1,293 (6)	2,103 (12)	2,896 (23)	4,679 (46)
S.R.	—	—	—	—	—	354 (5)
N.C.C.	—	—	—	—	31 (1)	31 (1)
Total, 1939	730 (4)	1,606 (9)	1,829 (11)	4,580 (33)	12,016 (116)	18,717 (203)
Total, 1938	730 (4)	1,606 (9)	1,829 (11)	4,714 (34)	11,665 (113)	17,924 (187)
Total, 1937	730 (4)	1,606 (9)	1,844 (12)	4,152 (29)	11,228 (107)	16,019 (179)
Total, 1936	542 (3)	778 (5)	996 (7)	2,245 (18)	6,206 (65)	9,116 (105)

Note :—The figures in brackets indicate the number of individual runs making up each total mileage figure

British Legion **Exploit**

Among its express passenger locomotives the LMS possesses two – the 'Turbomotive' No 6202 and the only taper-boiler Royal Scot No 6170 *British Legion* – which have the distinction of being the only ones of their kind . . . That *British Legion* is capable of sound work with heavy loads was demonstrated on a Sunday evening recently when it was working the 6.5pm express from Euston to Liverpool – a 14-coach train of 452 tons tare. With this substantial load, and despite a speed restriction over the new junction then in course of construction at Stafford No 1, No 6170, under the capable management of Driver Williams of Crewe, covered the 158.1 miles from Euston to passing Crewe (at greatly reduced speed) in 166min, representing a gain of three minutes on schedule and an average speed of 57mph. The fastest part of the run was from passing Willesden Junction to passing Hillmorton box, 75 miles at an average of 64.3mph with a particularly good uphill time of 13¾min over the 14.3 miles from Watford to Tring . . . the highest speed attained was 77mph near Leighton Buzzard, while after topping the rise to Whitmore at 56, a maximum of 75 was attained between there and Crewe.

LMS Magazine, 1938 (reported by D. S. M. Barrie and chosen by him for inclusion here 49 years later).

Lancaster a massive ex-FR Baltic 4-6-4 tank might be encountered, in company with a compound or a Class 2 4-4-0 which would otherwise have had to run light engine to Carnforth; between Syston and Melton Mowbray one passed another passenger train to the M&GN behind the unusual combination of a Fowler 0-6-0 and a small ex-GN Ivatt 4-4-0.

Then there were peripatetic pilots, engines which being in the course of transfer from one motive power district to another, were made to work their passage by assisting one or more trains en route, thus avoiding light mileage, and so satisfying some accountancy requirement. Thus, ex-MR Class 2 4-4-0 No 396 was en route from Bath to Kentish Town, and having arrived at Rugby via Birmingham, was directed to assist the 9am Perth–Euston, Royal Scot Class No 6135 on 490/515 tons, the driver of which, Camden's Mighty Atom Lawrence Alfred Earl, emerged from going round his engine to observe No 396 bearing down tender-first on 6135; some humorous oral exchanges ensued before the cortege set off. Earl did not like pilots in front of him!

Ironically, the sweeping Midland Division accelerations of 1937 brought the despised MR-type Class 2P back on to some of the crack St Pancras expresses, especially at weekends when increased patronage required train loads in excess of the 300 tons to which the Jubilees were restricted on the fastest timings. Thus at least two separate maxima of over 90mph were recorded behind 4-4-0 pilots leading 4-6-0s.

Away from the main lines, the enthusiast could still ride behind a considerable variety of engines on some secondary routes. Thus the 32¾ miles of the Crewe–Shrewsbury line could produce LNWR Princes and even an occasional 4-6-2T while that type lasted; compounds, Royal Scots, Stanier 4-6-0s and later Pacifics (the route was often used for final running-in for locomotives after overhauls at Crewe Works) and not least among the performers, Horwich Crab 2-6-0s. Notwithstanding their 5ft 6in coupled wheels, these were fast engines at times, speeds approaching 80mph being sometimes recorded in the dips of the Salop road, while on the former CR Glasgow–Edinburgh line No 13210 (old numbering) was timed with eight on, to average 66.2mph over 20¼m downhill, the maxima before and after the Midcalder Junction slack to 50, being 82 and 76mph respectively.

Another line with a very mixed population in the 1930s was Birmingham–Leicester via Nuneaton, where one might encounter LNWR Webb 2-4-2Ts, two varieties of MR 4-4-0 and two of 2-6-4T, and LMS 2-6-2T; today this route is used on occasion by HSTs diverted by major engineering work between Birmingham and Derby.

A through journey from Stranraer to London in the summer of 1938 exemplified the changes which followed Grouping. Late arrival of the Larne steamer involved a late start for the 'Day Paddy' from Stranraer Harbour; compound No 1177 on six, 194/205 tons, recovered 5min to Dumfries despite a severe relaying slack; the best effort over the heavy grades was to average 33mph up the almost continuous 1 in 80 from Palnure to Gatehouse of Fleet. From Dumfries we were taken on by No 14494, a Caley Pickersgill 4-4-0, which by knocking off the 33 miles to Carlisle in 38min, recovered a further 5min on an easy schedule. At

Carlisle, the Mid-Day Scot had of necessity been held for the Stranraer coaches, and we left 22min late, 13 on, 420/440 tons behind Pacific No 6209 *Princess Beatrice*. To the first stop at Lancaster a generous 85min was allowed for 69 miles, and we ran it in 75min, now 13 late. At Crewe where Driver Jackson took over, they were still some minutes in arrears, but these were knocked off by Rugby, and the train arrived at Euston in just under 150min for the 158 miles from Crewe (63.5mph) 10min under schedule and nicely ahead of time.

Reflections on this journey succinctly focus some changes of Grouping. In just over 400 miles the metals of three constituent companies (Glasgow & South Western, Caledonian, LNWR) were covered; the journey also took in the Midland and the L&Y companies in the Portpatrick & Wigtownshire Joint and the North Union Joint railways (through Preston) respectively. Similarly, the three locomotives used represented the latter-day designs of the Midland and the Caledonian, while No 6209, as a product of the LMS era of big engines and long-distance running at higher speeds all contributed to the half-hour late start being recovered.

Highlander. The up afternoon express leaving Inverness near Millburn Junction (where the Aviemore and Forres lines split) in 1930. The engines are both of Highland Railway origin – a large Ben 4-4-0 No 14422 Ben Na Chaoruinn *double heading Clan class 4-6-0 No 14764* Clan Munro. *The front of the train is LNER teak stock bound for Perth, Edinburgh Waverley and over the East Coast route to King's Cross, the remainder for Euston. The up train was not named.*

91

Signalling and Safety

The LMS might have had the best coaches in the country and eventually some fine locomotives, but in signalling on much of its system it handed over to BR in 1948 a good proportion of the same equipment and operating methods that it inherited in 1923, which relied mostly in strict observance of the rules by signalmen and trainmen. Though the Midland had its rotary interlocking block system, which with track circuits and treadles proved that a train had passed through a block section before another could be accepted, and track circuits were beginning to come into general use in certain locations, these add-on features, together with power operation which had been introduced at a few major stations at the turn of the century, could have provided much needed automation and avoided most of the major calamities on the LMS (and other railways as well). The technology was there but it cost money and with tight economic times that was simply not available for what many in top management saw as luxury safety features. Provided the men out on the line carried out the rules they were not needed.

In hindsight the cost of the major accidents would have gone a long way to paying for the added automation. Even at such a major station as Euston, headquarters of the company, track circuits were sparingly installed, some platform lines as late as 1949 having no more pro-tection than a blackboard chalked up by the signalman when trains arrived and departed as the sole reminder.

The LMS had, though, introduced upper quadrant signals fairly widely, and colour-light signals had made limited appearances. Some colour-light distant signals, installed extensively on the West Coast and Midland main lines, originally showed a double yellow aspect in addition to the normal yellow for caution and green for clear, this extra indication in otherwise semaphore areas meaning 'be prepared to pass the next signal at restricted speed', and was often used where the route was set to cross from fast to slow lines or vice versa. But it led to a major accident at Bourne End in 1945 when an express derailed at 50mph on a 20mph crossover, killing 43 passengers and the enginemen, and the use of double yellow in these circumstances in semaphore areas was abandoned.

Lack of block instrument locking controls resulted in a number of accidents when the wrong block instrument was cleared on multi-tracked sections, or the only instrument was cleared prematurely with a train still in section. The heavily used Liverpool–Southport suburban electric line had no form of block controls and relied totally on signalmen carrying out precisely the block regulations. In contrast the Euston–Watford local electric line was fully track circuited with curious colour-light signals which were not only derived from American practice but

included an automatic call-on feature, and although accompanied by trip apparatus as on the London Underground nevertheless often managed to get more than one train moving between signals, sometimes a queue of trains nose to tail and fortunately on rare but too many occasions one train into the back of another when drivers did not quite appreciate the degree of caution needed.

The Euston–Watford colour-light signals and those on London Transport's District line between Bow and Upminster, which the LMS owned as part of its Tilbury & Southend lines, were simplified versions of a remarkable signalling experiment which the LMS signal engineer A. F. Bound installed at Mirfield between Heaton Lodge Junction and Thornhill LNW Junction. Although block working was retained the signals were American-style colour lights giving speed indications rather than the route the train was to take. The top light applied to the principal high speed route, the second light down to the lower medium speed route although if the signal was capable of showing four aspects the second lens down provided the extra yellow in conjunction with either the lens above or below. At the bottom was a marker light. Drivers could be faced with a signal showing up to four lights, and even at green there were usually two other reds on the same signal above or below. It was a brave attempt to change British signalling. But then Bound was a remarkable engineer. He had been on the Great Central and installed the first three-aspect colour-light signals on a British main line between Neasden and Marylebone in 1923. A decade before that he challenged the then existing signalling thinking by suggesting that traditional block working was out of date and that signalling should be controlled by track circuit block. Sixty years later the whole West Coast main line was controlled by track circuit block, and is the basis of all modern signalling.

The table on page 94 summarises the principal accidents on the LMS between 1923 and 1948 and into BR days on former LMS lines where LMS methods and equipment then survived. The final column suggests what steps could have been taken to prevent a recurrence, taking into account the technology available at the time. This was not necessarily the recommendation of the inspecting officer since attitudes were still largely in favour of keeping the human hand at the controls rather than added automation. References to AWS would until the 1940s have meant the GWR ATC system before the Hudd and later BR magnetic systems were developed, while block instrument locking could have been the Midland rotary interlocking block, or the later variation called 'Welwyn control' following the recommendations after the 1935 collision at Welwyn on the LNER.

A high speed derailment at a crossover when a driver failed to reduce speed at Great Bridgeford in 1932.

Opposite.
The four track main line out of Euston included various places where crossovers linked fast and slow lines. The LNWR provided splitting distant signals for the crossovers as here with Harrow & Wealdstone up distants. The LMS later installed colour-light distants using double-yellow aspects to denote moves over the crossovers ahead, later abolished after the Bourne End accident in 1945. The LNWR Super D 0-8-0s outlasted many later LMS freight locomotives and some survived almost to the end of steam in the West Midlands.

Disaster at Harrow

I was in the middle of breakfast on 8 October 1952 when I heard what seemed to be two distant muffled explosions a few seconds apart, and even when about ten minutes later one or two ambulances passed with bells ringing, nothing seemed exceptional. But then more ambulances, and rumours – and just 40 minutes after the event the BBC 9 o'clock News confirmed that three trains had collided at Harrow & Wealdstone. One was a local train and the first thought was whether my father was on it, quickly denied by a telephone call.

I first saw the wreckage from the road outside the station on the Wealdstone side. It was enormous. Ambulances were lined up in the forecourt leaving under police direction as casualties were brought out. Surprisingly the main road and shopping centre just by were not closed off. Shoppers were subdued but carried on; car drivers were seemingly oblivious of the drama.

From the road bridge at the south end of the station the enormity of the wreckage was only too apparent. The footbridge span across the fast lines linking the platforms and booking halls had disappeared. In its place was a tangled heap of wreckage with sixteen coaches compressed into the length of two spreading over the platforms on to the slow lines on the east side and across the island platform shared with the up dc electric lines on the west. What was left of two locomotives from the Liverpool train lay on their sides across the left hand platform on to the electric lines and into the electric line sidings. One was No 46202 *Princess Anne* only a few weeks out of Crewe works having been rebuilt from the old Turbomotive. In its turbine form it had had a long history of workshop visits to rectify one fault or another. Now it lay wrecked on its

continued opposite

Major train accidents on the LMS and the early years of BR

Date	Place	Type	Cause	Killed	Notes
26/4/1924	Euston	Rear-end collision	Wrong block instrument cleared	5	a
3/11/1924	Lytham	Derailment and fire	Broken locomotive wheeltyre	14	b, e
19/11/1926	Rawmarsh	Derailment and collision	Freight train derailment. Passenger train collided with wreckage	9	
13/10/1928	Charfield	Collison and fire	Disputed distant signal indication, signals passed at danger	17	c, e
8/1/1929	Ashchurch	Collision	Signals passed at danger	4	c
22/3/1931	Leighton Buzzard	Derailment	Excessive speed through crossover	6	c, d
17/6/1932	Great Bridgeford	Derailment	Excessive speed through crossover	4	c, d
6/9/1934	Port Eglinton Junction	Head-on collision on diamond crossing	Signals passed at danger	9	c
28/9/1934	Winwick Junction	Rear-end collision	Wrong block instruments cleared	11	a
13/3/1935	Kings Langley	Rear-end collision leading to other collisions involving four freight trains	Block instrument prematurely cleared	1	a
8/4/1938	Rutherglen	Derailment	Broken axle on coach	2	b
14/10/1940	Wembley	Derailment	Train hit runaway platform barrow	11	
14/9/1941	Holmes Chapel	Rear-end collision	Block instrument prematurely cleared	9	a
30/12/1941	Eccles	Collision on diamond crossing in thick fog	Signalling irregularities and distant signal not observed by driver	23	c
30/9/1945	Bourne End	Derailment	Excessive speed through crossover, double yellow distant signal not acted on	43	c, d
1/1/1946	Lichfield	Rear-end collision	Mechanical failure of point rodding, facing point lock and detector	20	
21/7/1947	Polesworth	Derailment	Poor track because of wartime deferred maintenance	5	
17/4/1948	Winsford	Rear-end collision	Block instrument prematurely cleared with train in section after alarm signal operated	24	a
8/6/1950	Beattock	Train fire	Cigarette end ignited rubbish	5	
27/8/1950	Penmaenmawr	Collision	Rule 55 not correctly applied and interpreted	6	f
21/9/1951	Weedon	Derailment	Locomotive axlebox jammed in horns	15	
8/10/1952	Harrow	Double collision	Signals passed at danger, third train collided with wreckage	112	c
15/8/1953	Irk Valley Junction	Collision	Signalling irregularity and signal passed at danger	10	c
23/3/1955	Sutton Coldfield	Derailment	Excessive speed at permanent restriction through curve	17	g

Possible prevention for the future

a Block instrument locking with track circuits. Although some Midland Railway routes were equipped with rotary interlocking block instruments the later Welwyn or other controls were not introduced until the last years of the LMS and then only on principal main lines.
b Improved materials and testing.
c AWS gradual installation from mid 1950s but even by 1980s less than ²⁄₃rds of lines equipped.
d More positive signal indications. Signalling at junctions particularly distant signal advice has not always

been as precise as it might have been and even now on BR could be improved.
e Elimination of gas lit coaches. Eventually completed by mid 1950s.
f Track circuits. Today continuous on principal main lines.
g Marking of permanent speed restrictions with warning boards, eventually adopted by BR fairly generally with cut out figures from LNER practice in the 1950s and strengthened with distant warning signs and AWS at specified locations from the mid 1970s.

Top.
One of the large LNWR signalboxes inherited by the LMS and handed on to BR, Preston No 1 with its distinctive LNWR levers.

Centre.
Part of the Midland signalbox at Mill Hill with the frame quadrant at knee height. Rotary locking block instruments can be seen on the blockshelf.

Bottom left.
A. F. Bond, the LMS signalling superintendent attempted to change British signalling styles with American pattern speed signals which he tried out in the Mirfield area. The top light applied to the principal high speed route, the lower lights to lower speed routes, while the bottom light was a marker light.

continued

side. Somewhere underneath the mound of debris was *City of Glasgow* heading an overnight sleeping car train from Perth.

112 died and more than 150 were taken to hospital. Walking over the footbridge some were swept away when the span was demolished. Many of those killed were railway office staff who worked at Euston travelling up on the local from Tring. But there were remarkable escapes, such as that of the manager of Wymans bookstall who was safely a few feet away retrieving a newspaper that had blown off when the carnage began and one of the leapfrogging coaches from the second collision ended up against the door of his bookstall; had he been inside when the first collision happened he would have been bound to open that door.

The signalling at Harrow was much the same as it had been from LNWR days except that upper quadrant arms had replaced the lower quadrants and the LMS had installed colour-light distants. There were a few track circuits and block controls but nothing like the Great Western's automatic train control. Drivers depended on spotting and acting on signals. The up Perth had not heeded the colour-light distant signal in fog.

It hastened the adoption of the BR version of GWR and LTS Hudd automatic train control. But ATC (or AWS) apart, there was another result of the Harrow accident, more poignant, for every year for a decade after, a wreath was placed on one of the platforms on its anniversary in memory of some of those killed in what had been the worst accident in peace time in Britain.
Geoffrey Kichenside

Automatic train control LMS style. The visual indicator of the Hudd system installed on the Fenchurch Street–Southend–Shoeburyness line by the LMS in its last years.

7
THE PASSENGER BUSINESS

The 'Sunny South Special'
This train runs through from Liverpool and Manchester to Eastbourne; and a through composite coach from both Liverpool and Manchester to Ramsgate is also attached, making on normal days a load of seven vehicles. The 12.30pm from Birmingham to Ramsgate, with a through coach for Eastbourne, is attached to the former from Northampton to Willesden, the complete train having generally about 12 vehicles in all. Ten minutes are allowed at Northampton for marshalling the Eastbourne portions in front and the Ramsgate portions in rear, so that the two parts may be got away expeditiously from Willesden. In the northbound direction the two trains are run independently between Willesden and Northampton, where they are again marshalled for their northern destinations.
Railway Magazine, 1923.

In 1932, when traffic receipts were at an almost all-time low, the LMS completed its traffic organisation, ending the Midland tradition of the commercial men being subservient to the operators. Now a chief commercial manager and a chief operating manager both reported to the Executive Committee through the vice-president (railway traffic, operating and commercial). The new man in the vice-presidential seat was Ernest John Hutchings Lemon, a career mechanical engineer who after theoretical study at Heriot Watt College, had practical experience with the North British Locomotive Company, Hurst Nelson & Co, and a year's footplate and running shed experience with the Highland Railway at Inverness, of which he could occasionally be persuaded to reminisce both affectionately and entertainingly. From joining the Midland Railway in 1909 as its chief wagon inspector, Lemon had moved in the shadow of Robert Whyte Reid, the brilliant head of C&W with both Midland and LMS. When Reid became a vice-president in 1927, Lemon moved up behind him to head C&W, then succeeded Sir Henry Fowler as chief mechanical engineer in 1931 – clearly an interim move to bridge the gap pending the arrival of William Stanier from Swindon.

Lemon's appointment was initially the subject of some criticism from the traditionalists ('not a traffic man'), but though he might never have designed an express engine, as vice-president he did a magnificent job in charge of the commercial and traffic functions. The two officers who reported to him were disparate in origin and character but both in the right role. As befitted a senior officer of the North Western, Charles Reginald Byrom, the chief operator, had a most dignified presence and bearing. But he could get down to railway work with the best of them; on peak Saturdays he liked to see a bit of the action himself. Once at Euston's platform 15, the uniformed staff noticed him just as they had got the doors shut – and were so overawed by his great presence that nobody blew the whistle or waved a flag. CRB himself looked aft, forrard, checked doors shut, clock, starting signal, and waved the train off.

Ashton Davies, the commercial manager, had homespun Lancashire origins and worked his way up the Lancashire & Yorkshire to become superintendent of the line. To attend a commercial management conference was an object lesson in how to animate people. It was he who postulated traffic movements, asking the operating people what could be delivered. A commercial research section and an expanded sales force with specialist training gave added strength. The traditional vocations of 'canvassers' and 'townsmen' gave way to 'salesmen'.

Trophies were awarded to successful district and individuals, the commercial side's monthly newsheet being appropriately titled *Quota News*; the operators had *On Time*. Customer sales and service requirements were handled at 2,900 goods and over 2,500 passenger stations, supervised by 35 district managers, including dock managers at the company's three principal ports: Barrow-in-Furness, Heysham and Garston. There was a substantial representation in Ireland and even principal European countries and North America.

The resources were enormous. On the operating side at times of exceptional demand, boiler washouts were deferred, passed firemen became drivers and passed cleaners fireman. No question then of turning business away because it was uneconomic to retain carriages only for occasional use. Dozens of fare concessions and excursion facilities enticed traffic, from the universal monthly return (single plus a third) and circular tour tickets (which meant that hardly anyone travelling any distance and back paid the full rate) to cheap day returns, usually single fare for return journey (where bus competition was intense sometimes less), traders' season tickets for nominated employees of firms with large freight accounts, holiday runabout tickets, and special offers to commercial travellers (today's car-borne reps), anglers and conveyers of racing pigeons.

Charter business also became increasingly important. Indeed the LMS was a specialist in mass movement. In one sample year before World War II, the company ran 43 special trains for the Grand National at Aintree and 55 for the Cup Final at Wembley. But these figures pale before the railway effort involved in the Lancashire and Yorkshire Wakes week traffics to the Blackpool area (1,322 trains) or for the

The London Midland and Scottish Railway in brief

Penetrating no less than 32 of the 40 counties of England, the London Midland and Scottish Railway, with its 6,954 miles of track, is the largest railway in Great Britain. Its 2,944 Goods Depots and 2,588 passenger stations are situated where they are of most service to trader and passenger. It provides 291,490 freight vehicles with a total carrying capacity of 3,125,304 tons, and 20,276 passenger vehicles with accommodation to carry 1,123,082 passengers, and 9,914 locomotives to haul them. The annual coal consumption is 6,614,000 tons representing employment for 26,500 coal miners.

It further supplements its services with 29,754 road vehicles and a fleet of 73 fine steamers, together with 97,000 feet of dock quays.

The whole of this vast organisation, with a staff of 263,000 people, is ready to help you and give you Rail Service that is Real Service. *LMS Advertisement.*

LMS weekly season ticket between Wolverhampton and Birmingham issued in July 1937.

Blackpool Autumn illuminations (1,456 trains); in the same year, the company ran 1,800 trains to Glasgow for the Empire Exhibition.

Each year six million people were carried to Blackpool district, and that excluded the substantial season-ticket journeys by the large residential population commuting to Preston, Bolton, Liverpool, Salford, Manchester and other places. During the three months July to September about 2.2 million visitors arrived by rail. On a single Saturday in August, over 460 special and ordinary trains would arrive at and depart from the two Blackpool termini. All passengers by the special trains needed a regulation ticket to secure admission at the barrier to their return service.

It was made possible because there were four tracks (and a set of water troughs) for the first eight miles between Preston and Kirkham, beyond which the routes split into three: two to Blackpool South and Central, and one to Blackpool North as a divergence from the Fleetwood route at Poulton. Specials from north of Preston avoided reversal by running south through the station's East Lancashire platforms, boxing the compass by a maze of junctions and intersecting routes and then passing the station a second time through the northbound platforms. Once over 900 trains used Preston station or passed through it in a single day.

While the Blackpool seasonal traffic was the largest concentration of its kind on the LMS, the expansion of excursion traffic, under the stimulus of a special section established in 1929, was system-wide. Whereas in that year less than 7,500 such trains were run, by 1938 the total had risen to nearly 22,000, and of those equipped with restaurant cars, from 1,700 to 3,000.

With a split of the business between guaranteed, advertised, half-day, and evening excursions – the differences between them being governed by distance, time-scale and fares policy – this range was especially useful to the growing army of railway enthusiasts. At one end of the scale one could enjoy a half-day football excursion from Euston to Birmingham for five old shillings (25p); a similar Sunday trip from St Pancras to Sheffield for eight old shillings. If weekending in Glasgow, the silent Sabbath could be avoided by a half-day visit to Keswick in the Lake District, hauled by one of the batch of Claughtons fitted with large boilers in

A 'Mini' Named Train

Probably the shortest journey made by a standard-gauge named train was the 17½ miles of the Golden Sands Express between Llandudno and Rhyl. It ran in the summer of 1931, its name duly appearing in the public time-tables. A large square Golden Sands Express nameboard on the locomotive smokebox foreshadowed the smokebox nameplates carried by named expresses in the BR years. In the 1930s other train names were displayed only on carriage roofboards. Small name-boards of distinctive shape were fitted into the standard destination board holders on the carriages forming the Golden Sands Express. All lettering was golden yellow. The train made three journeys in each direction from Mondays to Friday, calling at Colwyn Bay, and was allowed 30min for the trip. Motive power was usually a 4-4-0 of the Precursor or George V classes.

1928. This engine, coughing a bit on the steeper parts of the old G&SW main line, would be relieved at Carlisle by the historic combination of an LNWR 'Cauliflower' 0-6-0 (the wooden tender brakeblocks smoking furiously downhill on the Cockermouth, Keswick & Penrith line) and a Precedent 2-4-0. The late Bill Coleby recorded 73mph on one occasion with this train, speeding home downhill from Penrith to Carlisle in the gloaming.

Much further afield, for thirty shillings (£1.50) or two nights in cabins at an extra charge, one could use the LMS/ALA Tilbury–Dunkerque sea route (boat train from St Pancras, complete with restaurant car, hauled by a Fowler 0-6-0) for a day trip into Belgium to visit the Flanders battle-fields of World War I (not realising one would be traversing them again ten or so years later) and to sample the venerable locomotives with which the SNCB powered many of its local trains. For a slightly lesser fare nearer home, but still with two nights in trains, one could travel from Euston to Oban and back, with an optional steamer trip to Iona.

Two-Hour express. For a number of years, until ousted by Class 5XP 4-6-0s, the Euston–Birmingham–Wolverhampton trains were worked by LMS class 4P Compounds. Here No 1169 is seen near Berkswell, probably hauling the 11.30am ex-Euston, a relatively lightweight train of seven coaches including an LNWR 12-wheel dining car.

Successor to the Corridor. The down Mid-day Scot 1.30pm Euston–Glasgow near Kenton on 9 April 1928 hauled by Royal Scot class 4-6-0 No 6110 Grenadier Guardsman *of Rugby shed (8). The train formation is most interesting. Three of the first four coaches are ex-West Coast Joint Stock 65ft 12-wheelers built for this service, the second coach is a WCJS 65ft 12-wheel composite dining car, and these form the Glasgow portion. Then comes the Edinburgh portion, probably the next three, with its own restaurant car and bringing up the rear through coaches to Aberdeen and Whitehaven.*

No wonder that with all these inducements to travel, and despite the inroads made by road transport (including private cars) LMS estimated passenger miles (number of passengers multiplied by the distances they travelled) rose from 6,500 million in 1932, to 8,500 million in 1937, despite a reduction in coaching stock made possible by more efficient repair procedures and tighter diagramming.

But the main plank of LMS commercial policy had to be the radical speeding-up of ordinary services between the main centres of population, coupled with the use of better-class coaching stock, including, from 1928, sleeping cars for third class travellers. Energetically pursued, the programme was not without its problems; introduction of the Coronation Scot in 1937 involved alterations to some 300 other trains, and double-block working (two sections to be clear in advance before acceptance). All through the programme there was a blaze of publicity, with photo-aircraft flying overhead and cameramen in privileged lineside positions; when in July 1937 the LMS briefly captured the British speed record on the demonstration run of the Coronation Scot, one national morning paper devoted the whole of its front page to an illustrated record of the achievement.

Efforts to increase passenger business were well rewarded. Despite intensifying road competition, the total receipts from passenger train traffic (including parcels and mails) increased by £2.9 million between 1932 and 1938. This helped the restoration of dividends on the ordinary shares in 1936, though it lapsed again in 1938, the crisis year with war looming. And progress in traffic efficiency was vital to the war effort.

Before then, however, Lemon's original team had broken up: he himself went on loan to the Air Ministry in 1938 as director general of aircraft production, for which he was knighted. During his absence Ashton Davies was acting vice president; when Lemon returned he was soon disenchanted with the railway companies being under the control of the Railway Executive Committee, and decided to retire; Byrom had already done so under the normal age rule.

Lemon and his predecessor R. W. Reid shared a notable achievement for by 1945, war years included, the LMS since 1923 had built or contracted (thanks to far-seeing financial support from W. V. Wood in particular) nearly 15,000 new passenger train vehicles, just over two thirds of the total stock of some 22,000 plus, while over 68 per cent of the freight rolling stock was also newly built.

Sad Farewell. On 5 October 1930 while on its maiden flight to India the airship R101 crashed at Beauvais in France killing 47 of the 54 people on board.

The bodies were brought back to England for a mass funeral at Cardington, Bedfordshire, on Saturday 11 October 1930. They were conveyed by special train from Euston to Bedford St Johns, thence by road to Cardington. The special train was hauled by Prince of Wales class 4-6-0s No 5684 Persia and 5685 Arabic seen here at Kenton: these were the largest engines allowed over the route beyond Bletchley and those shown were probably shedded there for normal services thence to Oxford or Cambridge.

Glasgow Bound. The 3.40pm Oban–Glasgow passes Oban ticket platform in the late 1930s. The train engine is No 14763 Clan Fraser *and the pilot CR Pickersgill Oban bogie No 14622. This shows one of the results of grouping when the Highland Railway Clan class 4-6-0s were transferred to the Caledonian section for the Oban line.*

Highland Summit. The Stanier Class 5 4-6-0s were universal machines which reached all parts of the system. On 1 August 1939 No 5457, built in 1938, heads a down train (probably 12.10 Perth–Inverness via Forres – the only train around that time not shown to convey a restaurant car) on the Highland Section near the highest point reached by a main line in Britain, Druimuachdar, 1484ft above sea level.

Grand National Special. A Hughes ex-L&Y 4-6-0 at Aintree in 1933. One of the features of these excursions was the 'controlled detrainment' on the track to a special racecourse gate. The locomotive headboard reads 'LMS 767 AINTREE (Racecourse station) at 5.6pm for Manchester (Victoria), Stockport, Wilmslow, Chelford, Alderley Edge, Hazel Grove, Disley, New Mills, Whaley Bridge, Chapel-en-le-Frith, Buxton, Cheadle Hulme, Bramhall, Poynton, Prestbury, MACCLESFIELD'. The engine's shed code is 26A, Manchester Newton Heath.

Tilbury suburban train. A London, Tilbury & Southend section passenger train en route from Southend (via Tilbury) to Fenchurch Street hauled by class 3P 4-4-2T No 2117. The train is a nine-coach set, all ex-LTS vehicles and probably still fitted with the Westinghouse brake. The locomotive was built by the LMS at Derby in 1923. The location may be Grays with the Upminster line branching off to the left.

Named Trains of the LMS

	Between		Between
The Coronation Scot	Euston and Glasgow (Central)	Blackpool & Fylde Coast Express	Euston and Blackpool
The Royal Scot	Euston and Glasgow (Central) and Edinburgh (Princes St)	The Sunny South Express	Manchester & Liverpool and South Coast
The Mid-Day Scot	Euston and Glasgow (Central) and Edinburgh (Princes St)		
The Night Scot	Euston and Glasgow (Central)★	The Granite City	Glasgow and Aberdeen
The Royal Highlander	Euston and North of Scotland★	The Hebridean	Inverness and Kyle of Lochalsh
The Thames–Forth Express	St Pancras and Edinburgh (Wav)	The Lewisman	Inverness and Kyle of Lochalsh
The Thames–Clyde Express	St Pancras and Glasgow (St Enoch)	The Orcadian	Inverness and Wick
The Irish Mail	Euston and Holyhead (for Dublin)	The Irishman	Glasgow and Stranraer Harbour
The Ulster Express	Euston and Heysham (for Belfast)	The Manxman	Euston and Liverpool (for Isle of Man)
The Merseyside Express	Euston and Liverpool		
The Mancunian	Euston and Manchester	The Welshman	Euston and North Wales Coast
The Lancastrian	Euston and Manchester	The Southport Blackpool & Lakes Express	Euston and Southport, Blackpool and Windermere
The Comet	Euston and Manchester		
The Peak Express	St Pancras and Manchester	The Bon Accord	Glasgow and Aberdeen
The Palatine	St Pancras and Manchester	The St Mungo	Glasgow and Aberdeen
The Yorkshireman	St Pancras and Bradford Exchange	The John O'Groat	Inverness and Wick
The Devonian	Bradford Forster Sq and Paignton	The Fast Belfast	Glasgow and Stranraer Harbour
The Pines Express	Liverpool & Manchester and Bournemouth		

★Not named train in reverse direction

Night Mail

'Where's that – Holyhead' shouts the GPO inspector. The cameraman pans slowly down to the gentle 'clonk' of meeting buffers as a 'Baby Scot' drops onto the down Postal, the TPO crew sink their last cups of tea in the refreshment room and bid a cheery farewell to the girls behind the bar, black dressed for respectability behind their glass cases of buns and sandwiches. An unusually clean Horwich 'Crab' 2-6-0 clanks into the adjoining platform – the late running Holyhead Postal has arrived. Amid hustle and bustle the mails are transferred, doors slam shut and the guard in his LMS soft cap holds up the green light. Gently the 'Baby Scot' moves off six beats to the revolution and on into the night. This is Crewe one summer evening in 1936 and they are making the Crown Film Unit's epic documentary *Night Mail*.

Although the film was GPO sponsored it is also a classic record of the LMS in the 1930s just on Stanier's coming. A Royal Scot on the down Postal out of Euston, a Webb 5ft 6in 2-4-2 tank on the auto train shunted at 'the junction' to clear the road, the thrill of picking up and putting down mails, W. H. Auden's poetry and above all the wonderful atmosphere of Crewe near midnight. Only *Brief Encounter* could come within a sight of this and that as second best.

The West Coast Postal or, to give it its official title, the Down Special Travelling Post Office and the up equivalent, has been one of the principal express trains on the main line between Euston and Glasgow with a history going back for 140 years. It is one of the numerous services operated for the Post Office and does not carry passengers although Post Office staff travel on the train sorting mail during the journey. A feature of many of the travelling Post Office trains was the exchange of mail bags between lineside apparatus and the trains passing at speed. As the trains progressed fresh mailbags were picked up to be dealt with by the sorters. At intermediate towns mail sorted earlier on the journey was placed in special pouches and set down on the ends of the traductor arms on the coach side to be caught in the lineside net where the local postmen were waiting to take the mail pouches to the nearby sorting office.

This is the night mail crossing the
  border,
Bringing the cheque and the postal
  order,
Letters for the rich, letters for the
  poor,
The shop at the corner and the girl
  next door,
Pulling up Beattock, a steady climb –
The gradient's against her but she's
  on time.

Past cotton grass and moorland
  boulder,
Shovelling white steam over her
  shoulder,
Snorting noisily as she passes
Silent miles of wind-swept grasses;
Birds turn their heads as she
  approaches,
Stare from the bushes at her blank-
  faced coaches;
Sheep dogs cannot turn her course,
They slumber on with paws across,
In the farms she passes no one wakes,
But a jug in the bedroom gently
  shakes.

Dawn freshens, the climb is done,
Down towards Glasgow she descends
Towards the steam tugs, yelping
  down the glade of cranes
Towards the fields of apparatus, the
  furnaces
Set on the dark plain like gigantic
  chessmen.
All Scotland waits for her;
In the dark glens, beside the pale-
  green sea lochs,
Men long for news.

Letters of thanks, letters from banks,
Letters of joy from the girl and boy,
Receipted bills and invitations
To inspect new stock or visit
  relations,
And applications for situations,
And timid lovers' declarations,
And gossip, gossip from all the
  nations,
News circumstantial, news financial,
Letters with holiday snaps to enlarge
  in
Letters with faces scrawled on the
  margin.

Letters from uncles, cousins and
  aunts,
Letters to Scotland from the South of
  France,
Letters of condolence to Highlands
  and Lowlands,
Notes from overseas to the Hebrides;
Written on paper of every hue,
The pink, the violet, the white and
  the blue;
The chatty, the catty, the boring,
  adoring,
The cold and official and the heart's
  outpouring,
Clever, stupid, short and long,
The typed and the printed and the
  spelt all wrong.

Thousands are still asleep
Dreaming of terrifying monsters
Or a friendly tea beside the band at
  Cranston's or Crawford's
Asleep in working Glasgow, asleep in
  well-set Edinburgh,
Asleep in Granite Aberdeen.
They continue their dreams
But shall wake soon and long for
  letters.
And none will hear the postman's
  knock
Without a quickening of the heart,
For who can bear to feel himself
  forgotten?

W. H. AUDEN.

During LMS years the Down Night Special Travelling Post Office left Euston at 8.30pm and ran non stop to Crewe. On the way it picked up mail from several lineside installations. At Crewe it connected with other mail services from Wales and the Midlands after which it continued to Carlisle and Glasgow, part being detached at Carstairs and running to Aberdeen, with mail being set down at various locations.

Top left: Platform 2 at Euston just after 8pm. Mail is waiting to be loaded in the stowage vans. Like many TPOs mail could be posted directly into a letterbox in one of the coaches provided that they carried an extra 1/2d late fee stamp. Top right: The mailbag transfer arms and the net to catch bags set down from a train at Wembley although it was unlikely for bags to be set down so soon after leaving London. Left: LMS standard Post Office sorting coach with mailbag pick-up net and set down arms, built in the early 1930s.

8
FREIGHT

Mixed Freight. A scene near Miller's Dale on the Midland line through the Peak District of Derbyshire. The main line to Manchester climbs at 1 in 90 from right to left across the viaduct while the freight train heading for Buxton is hauled by Class 3F 0-6-0 No 3271. The Midland route into Manchester Central is now closed.

Midland Division giant. A typical Midland route coal train from Toton to Brent passing Mill Hill in 1939. It is hauled by a Garratt type locomotive No 7994 built by Beyer Peacock & Co in 1930. Originally numbered 4994, the engine was renumbered 7994 in 1939: it later became BR No 47994 and was withdrawn in 1958. It was the last of the class to survive. The Garratts were an attempt to solve the problem of double heading of coal trains on the Midland. They were partially successful but suffered from inadequate bearings. The final solution came with the introduction of the Stanier Class 8F 2-8-0 in 1935.

Freight (the LMS could not make up its mind on terminology and spoke of goods depots and freight vehicles in the same advertisement) accounted for about 60 per cent of the total receipts. And as on the passenger side, they slid downward to a low in 1932, when the company first began reaping the reward of rationalising and modernising the vast business. It averaged about a million tons per route mile annually.

Long distance freight trains were speeded up by the introduction of a new category of train, the 'Maltese Cross' with a minimum of four vacuum braked vehicles connected to the engine. Oil axleboxes were mandatory, thus eliminating special examinations at intervals of 80 miles or so en route. More powerful standard locomotives gave higher speeds and longer non-stop runs. And belt conveyors, electric trolleys and other equipment were increasingly provided in the goods stations.

LMS interest in containers began very early in its life, the first examples entering traffic in 1926. Construction continued apace, especially with insulated and refrigerated designs, until over half the 19,358 containers handed over to British Railways in 1948 had been built by the LMS. Simultaneously the company up-dated and expanded its collection and delivery motor fleet, comprising some 10,000 road motor vehicles, trailers and motor-driven appliances. Operations at many secondary yards were analysed to reduce shunting at intermediate places and Toton Down yard was mechanised. By 1933 the LMS was able to claim that 70 per cent of all freight consignments within its system were delivered on the day after despatch and 94 per cent by the second day.

One solid advantage which the LMS derived from the amalgamation compared with the LNWR was the acquisition of a second trunk route from southern and central England to Carlisle and beyond. Long before the Grouping, the LNWR had been so concerned about the pressures on its line capacity over Shap as to consider seriously an additional deviation line, including a tunnel under the summit.

Before Grouping the Midland enjoyed running powers over the L&Y from Hellifield down through East Lancashire to Liverpool and Manchester, including its own goods depot at Ancoats at the latter place. Now the LMS was able to take up some slack in S&C line capacity, and to increase individual trainloads by the introduction of Horwich 'Crab' 2-6-0s and, later on, Stanier 4-6-0s and 2-8-0s. In 1939, there were some 35 through freight trains daily in each direction on weekdays between Hellifield and Carlisle, not counting some shorter workings, including

Fitted freight. The LMS built up a network of fast freight services throughout the system giving next day delivery at most important centres. The majority ran through the night but here the 11.25am Camden to Carlisle is seen passing Hatch End hauled by Class 5XP 4-6-0 No 5531 Sir Frederick Harrison *built at Crewe in 1933.*

those crewed from Western or Central Division depots to lift stone ballast from the various quarries north of Settle. From passing Settle Junction to reaching the summit at Blea Moor, express goods trains were allowed 24 minutes, to average 30mph up 12 miles, rising almost continuously at 1/100. Most trains were booked to stop for water at least once, usually at Appleby coming south, and Settle or Blea Moor northbound, only 5 minutes being allowed for a water stop. These through trains served a wide variety of starting points and destinations on the former Midland system: St Pancras, Ancoats, Lawley Street (Birmingham), Sheffield, Hunslet and Stourton and on the LNWR/L&Y, Blackburn, Accrington, Rose Grove, Salford, Preston and Aintree. Add to these movements over the S&C another pattern of trains via Wennington to and from Lancaster/Heysham, Carnforth and Barrow-in-Furness over the F&M Joint, and the short stretch between Hellifield and Settle Junction, about 3½ miles, became one of the busiest of its kind on the LMS Midland Division.

Increasingly the trunk movement was by one of the 'fitted freights' or in the case of coal, an 85 wagon load from Toton to Brent about which more in a moment. But in LMS days the end products might well be a raft of two or three wagons delivered by the engine of the pick-up goods

108

to some small country station or suburban coal yard. In the early 1930s the LMS was shifting 85 million tons of coal per annum of which over 9 million tons was export or bunker coal shipped at the company's own coaling appliances; the rest – drawn from some 800 collieries, or in the case of coke, from over 500 coke ovens – ended up at the private sidings of industrial consumers (factories, gasworks, generating stations – many of these the responsibility at that period of local authorities) or at local coal yards for merchants' landsale.

The mass movement of coal and other fuels from the Derbyshire and South Yorkshire coalfields to London and the South was particularly remarkable. Millions of fireplaces burnt their fuel – until the coming of the Clean Air Acts – in open fireplaces by courtesy of the Toton–Brent coal trains. Toton Yard just north of Trent was the gathering ground for coal from scores of collieries, and the point from where, marshalled into trains of very considerable length and weight, mainly composed of private owners' wagons, it started its slow pilgrimage southwards.

The reception point on the outskirts of London was the yard at Brent, between Hendon and Cricklewood. From Brent trip workings ran to the Midland's own London depots, and also to the yards of other railways – Acton for the GWR, Feltham and Hither Green Sidings for the Southern. The LMS had its own coal depots at Walworth Road, Clapham Wharf, Knight's Hill, Brockley Lane and Brixton on the Southern. Roughly midway between Toton and Brent was Wellingborough, where extensive holding sidings were provided, together with a large engine shed for locomotives employed on the freight business. There was also an enginemen's hostel for crews working lodging turns.

Over a good part of the Midland route, separate tracks were provided

Goods Transhipment. The rebuilt goods shed at Birmingham Lawley Street showing sorting deck No 1. Although a relatively modern installation, this picture demonstrates how labour intensive goods handling was, as all traffic was manhandled; it would also appear that many of the delivery vehicles were still horse-drawn in 1948. The old MR goods shed at Lawley Street was destroyed by fire on 23 May 1937, the war delaying the rebuilding. It was officially reopened on 29 October 1945.

*Container Service. The LMS were
pioneers in the use of containers to
avoid unnecessary handling of
freight traffic. A furniture
(household removal) container is
shown here being transferred from a
low-sided railwagon to a lorry. The
date is c1937 and the location the
London area, possibly Willesden.*

*Milk. Much of the country's milk
was carried by rail, modernisation
from the late 1920s brought glass-
lined tank wagons but some still
travelled in churns. This is Aspatria
station, Cumberland, during the
1939–45 war with two LMS lorries
and a mechanical horse and trailer
all loaded with churns and many
more on the ground. There was a
Milk Marketing Board depot in the
vicinity and due to petrol rationing
all the production must have been
sent by rail judging by the number of
churns visible.*

LMS Scheduled Non-Stop Freight Runs Over 90 Miles, Winter Service, 1937–8

Between			Fastest Daily Service				
							No of Runs
	Distance	Train		Class	Time	Speed	Daily
WESTERN DIVISION	miles				min	mph	
Camden–Liverpool	191	7.45pm Camden–Liverpool		FF1	294	39.0	2
Camden–Crewe	155¾	9.28pm Camden–Birkenhead		FF1	243	38.4	1
Crewe–Willesden	151¾	10.30pm Carlisle–Broad St		FF1	211	43.2	2
Crewe–Willesden No 7	151	9.45am Aberdeen to London		FF1	217	41.8	1
Basford Hall–Willesden	150¾	6.5pm Wyre Dock–Broad St		FF1	224	40.4	1
Crewe–Carlisle	*142	2.50pm Camden–Kingmoor		FF1	277	30.4	3
Carlisle–Crewe	140½	10.30pm Carlisle–Broad St		FF1	201	41.9	3
Warrington–Bletchley	135¼	9.5pm Warrington–Camden		FF2	272	29.8	1
Warrington–Carlisle	*117	8.30pm Warrington–Carlisle		FF2	270	26.0	1
Camden–Stafford	132	7.0pm Camden–Manchester		FF1	189	41.9	1
Camden–Tutbury	127½	9.18pm Camden–Manchester		FF1	204	37.4	4
Edge Hill–Carlisle	*125	6.50pm Edge Hill–Kingmoor		FF2	265	28.3	1
Penrith–Willesden	123¼	5.10pm Carlisle–Broad St		FF1	198	37.4	1
Tutbury–Willesden	122½	9.20pm Hillhouse–Broad St		FF1	193	38.1	1
St Helens–Carlisle	*113½	7.50pm Edge Hill–Carlisle		FF2	250	27.2	1
Bletchley–Crewe	110½	7.35pm Willesden–Crewe		FF2	206	32.2	1
Edge Hill–Rugby	110	1.35pm Alexandra Dock–Broad St		FF1	178	37.1	†3
Camden–Stechford	107¾	10.55pm Camden–Curzon St		FF2	178	36.3	3
Bamfurlong Jc–Carlisle	*107½	2.5am Bescot–Carlisle		FF2	228	28.3	1
Crewe–Tebay	105	11.25pm Camden–Carlisle		FF2	203	31.0	2
Heaton Norris–Rugby	100½	8.20pm Moston–Broad St		FF2	170	35.5	1
Rugby–Warrington	98½	11.10pm Camden–Carnforth		FF2	163	36.3	1
Camden–Nuneaton	96	10.40pm Camden–Nuneaton		FF2	175	32.9	1
Coventry–Camden	92¾	8.5pm Curzon St–Camden		FF2	152	36.6	1
Preston–Carlisle	* 90	5.0pm Edge Hill–Kingmoor		FF2	172	31.4	2
MIDLAND DIVISION							
Chesterfield–St Pancras	145	10.15pm Sheffield–St Pancras		–	222	39.2	1
St Pancras–Nottingham	123	10.10pm St Pancras–Sheffield		–	215	34.3	1
Appleby–Masborough	117	9.0pm Carlisle–Leicester		–	181	38.7	1
Leicester–St Pancras	98¼	8.37pm Stourton–St Pancras		–	143	41.2	2
Leicester–West End	95	10.45pm Ancoats–St Pancras		–	162	35.2	1
Wigston–St Pancras	94¾	11.20pm Burton–St Pancras		–	167	34.0	2
Kettering–Masborough	94¾	8.45pm Somers Town–Leeds		–	156	36.4	1
Kilby Bridge–St Pancras	93	6.15pm Burton–St Pancras		–	232	24.0	1
Wigston–W Hampstead	91½	6.45pm Lawley St–St Pancras		–	161	34.1	1
NORTHERN DIVISION							
Glasgow (College)–							
Durran Hill	117	6.25pm College–Carlisle		FF1	227	30.9	1
Petteril Bridge–College	116½	1.20am Petteril Bridge–College		–	230	30.4	2
Buchanan St–Kingmoor	102	7.0pm Buchanan St–Carlisle		FF2	185	33.1	2
Kingmoor–Robroyston	99	8.40pm Manchester–Buchanan St		FF1	160	37.1	1

*Includes a stop at Tebay for banking assistance
†Also two conditional runs

for the freight movement. The goods lines were laid out on a separate alignment from just south of Wellingborough to just north of Bedford, to avoid Sharnbrook summit and its 1 in 120 gradients. Instead, they diverged to the east and enjoyed the benefit of a tunnel under the highest ground, which kept the ruling gradient to 1 in 200. For the rest, such as south from Harpenden, the coal trains shared tracks with the stopping passenger trains, which necessitated frequent refuge loops being provided for overtaking purposes. South of Hendon, at Silkstream Junction, the goods lines diverged and were carried over a flyover to reach Brent on the west side, avoiding conflict with the fast passenger lines.

Land Pirates

Glasgow, Britain's second city until World War II always had a reputation for being a rough place, where the railway was seen as fair game. No question of stabling empty coaching stock between weekend use anywhere in the city limits. It would be either stripped of saleable fittings – mirrors, brass door handles, batteries – or invaded for nefarious purposes; children were conceived and even born on the red and black moquette of LMS seat cushions. So it all had to be worked to country sidings immediately after use, and retrieved for its next job.

Freight traffic was similarly regarded. Leave a van of whisky for an hour to two unsupervised in a yard, and the vultures descended on it. Coal was also prized to keep the home fire burning. In Gushetfaulds coal yard, small boys with buckets were directed by ample mothers leaning from tenement windows in Cathcart Road to stacks of the better quality fuel. Others were more imaginative. On a heavily-graded line through the eastern council estates, the rails would be carefully greased. When a heavy coal train had slipped to a stand, men (and women too!) would climb on to wagons and throw off tons of coal on to the bank for collection at leisure.

Brass commanded a fair price at the scrap yard, making stabled empty wagons a valuable target. A train of 60-odd wagons left at Carmyle over a weekend proved well-nigh impossible to move on Monday, as every bearing brass had been stolen. Nobody, of course, knew anything about it.

Old Electric. Battery powered electric locomotives were not very common on the railways of Britain but the LMS inherited three, one from the L&Y, one from the NSR and this one from the Midland. No 1550 was built at Derby in 1913 and was withdrawn in July 1964 having spent all its life shunting the MR coal depot at West India Dock, Poplar, where it is seen in 1937

Over this route the long caravans crawled at very modest speeds, usually hauled by two 0-6-0 goods engines of varying age and power classification ranging from 2F to 4F. Some were remarkable antiques. The LMS made a few spasmodic efforts to modernise the operation. 'Big Bertha', the 0-10-0 banker from the Lickey incline, was tried on the Toton–Brent run but was a failure. Then some Garratt locomotives were ordered from Beyer, Peacock. The idea was good, but instead of giving Beyers a free hand – which its long experience would have justified – it was told to use standard Midland mechanical design; what emerged was in fact the equivalent of two typical Fowler 0-6-0s, with a predictably unexciting performance. It was Stanier's new standard 2-8-0 that made the first real improvements in motive power.

The engine workings were out-and-home, based on Toton to Wellingborough, or Wellingborough to Brent, returning with empties. At times the congestion became acute. On the goods lines signalling by permissive block was in force and passengers in up expresses nearing Bedford could often see Brent coal trains queuing up almost buffer to buffer, awaiting a path into the station and the passenger lines.

In terms of utilisation the whole operation would not appeal to modern eyes and yet it was probably profitable, simply on account of the heavy tonnages handled – the high 'loadability'. It was moreover almost all in private owners' wagons, so the railway's costs were mainly the provision of engine power, signalling and permanent way.

Many railway workings in Greater London had their interest. By statute or agreement the Midland had established coal depots south of

LMS EXPRESS & CUNARD LINER

The HIGHEST STANDARD OF COMFORT IN RAIL AND OCEAN TRAVEL

A poster of the early 1920s based on the link between the LMS and the Cunard Line then sailing out of Liverpool. The painting shows a Hughes Dreadnought 4-6-0 shadowed by a huge liner such as the Mauretania or Aquitania but is totally mythical. In those days no 4-6-0 could work down from Edge Hill to Liverpool Riverside due to weight restrictions in the Princes Dock area; trains were worked by two elderly 0-6-0 saddle tanks named Euston and Liverpool and later by Webb's 0-6-2 coal tanks hunting in pairs. There is little information on this poster but one of similar design was effected for the Southern Railway and the White Star Line at Southampton: this depicted a liner similar to the Majestic or Olympic with a train alongside hauled by a Lord Nelson which carried a King Arthur number!

YOUR FRIENDS ON THE LMS

'Your Friends on the LMS', top, including a lady porter, a stiff-collared bow-tied waiter (hardly a dining car steward) and a driver in an odd-looking locomotive cab. All very smart. From a painting by Septimus Scot May 1947. Genuine railway personnel were used for this work. The painting of a steel works, bottom, is one of the series involving well known Royal Academicians, pollution et al, scarcely a scene to be welcomed by environmentalists today. It could be Sheffield and the date is 1924.

LMS BRITISH INDUSTRIES STEEL BY RICHARD JACK, R.A.

Fowler's Scot. The first purely LMS 4-6-0 was the 1927 built Royal Scot No 6100. This photograph shows the purported locomotive after its return from the United States and Canada in 1933. The actual locomotive was No 6152 although carrying Royal Scot's number and name.

The last LMS Pacific. Duchess class No 6256 built at Crewe in 1947 was not the final member of its class to be constructed (46257 City of Salford) but the last under LMS auspices.

The Road to Skye. Kyle of Lochalsh, terminus of the ex Highland Railway branch from Dingwall in June 1960. In the platform is the preserved Jones Goods No 103 with the make up for the following morning's mixed train – some empty cattle wagons and BR Mark I stock in LMS maroon – the coach livery for the period. This class and the Cumming Goods 4-6-0s were the mainstay of the line for many years until the former's life expectancy was over and the Stanier Black Five 4-6-0s arrived in the mid to late 1930s. The scene is very much as it had been for well over half a century – the island platform station with the Island of Skye in the background across the water, the small goods yard and the steamship (now a diesel, but performing the same task) alongside the quay. The occasion was historic in that the engine was working normal passenger trains (5.45pm from Inverness and the early morning return to Dingwall) for filming purposes with the BBC Railway Roundabout television team. In the background is a former LNWR coach used as a service vehicle.

Two posters with the emphasis on locomotives. The first shows a streamlined Pacific in Crewe Works alongside what appear to be the frames and cylinders of the unstreamlined version, both with men rather larger than life: this came out in 1937. The second a Duchess in full cry alongside an exploded diagram of the front end: good eye-stopping stuff. This is one of a series of five dated May/June 1947. The others were – the Carriage – sectional views of the new corridor third; Permanent Way – Stafford No 1; The Footplate – cab view of Coronation class with key to the controls; The Track – 4 track main line section through ballast and cess showing drainage.

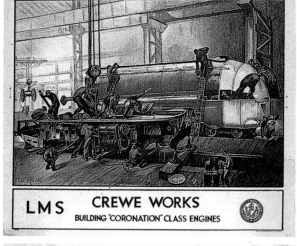

LMS CREWE WORKS
BUILDING 'CORONATION' CLASS ENGINES

LMS 'In perspective' Nº 5
The Locomotive

LMS EXPRESS PASSENGER LOCOMOTIVE
4-6-2 "Coronation" Class

TRAVEL
SPEED **LMS** COMFORT
LONDON MIDLAND & SCOTTISH RAILWAY

Poster boards on stations in the pre-war years were places to linger, for they were covered with eye catching illustrations such as this evocative printing of Royal Scot No 6119 Lancashire Fusilier picking up water at speed – presumably in the Westmorland hills. It was from a painting by Bryan de Grineau, and could well depict Dillicar. Date circa 1933.

the Thames. Passengers on a Victoria–Brighton Pullman might be surprised as their driver eased through Clapham Junction to observe an elderly LNWR 0-8-0 desultorily shunting coal wagons in the LNWR sidings at Falcon Lane; equally, travellers on the London Transport District line between Acton Town and Earl's Court could be disconcerted to see the passage of a 24 wagon coal train behind an LMS or Midland 0-6-0T from Cricklewood shed climbing from the Gunnersbury triangle up to Turnham Green and wending its slightly furtive way to the ex-MR coal depot behind some prestigious shops in High Street, Kensington!

Another category included the express perishable trains for fish, meat and milk over the longer distances. The enthusiastic observer travelling home by the 4.55pm residential express from Manchester Victoria to Blackpool, behind No 5549 in preference to the usual 'Lanky Claughton' might not realise that the 5XP Patriot's next working would be a Fleetwood–Broad Street fish train. And at Appleby on the Settle & Carlisle the amateur had to be alert should the mid-day express from Edinburgh and Glasgow to St Pancras attach two or three glass-lined bulk milk tanks 'inside the engine' for they would thus be on the rear after reversal at Leeds, ready to be smartly detached at St Pancras and tripped to Cricklewood. The Carlisle–London milk, carrying traffic from the Galloway and Maryport lines, the Aberdeen–Broad Street fish timed to arrive for Billingsgate Market, and the meat in time for Smithfield were among the most important and profitable trains always given special treatment. Of such perishable expresses, the 9.45am fitted freight No 1 was scheduled to run the 152 miles from Crewe to Willesden at 46.3mph, while on the Midland Division a fitted freight ran the 145 miles from Chesterfield to St Pancras at just over 29mph.

The railways of course continued to press for their 'square deal', but despite fierce and often unfair competition the LMS had put its freight business substantially in order by the outbreak of war. Then loadings, rolling stock utilisation, receipts, everything increased far beyond what had been foreseen. The vital war time role of the LMS in serving a substantial proportion of the British population would not have been possible but for the valiant efforts of the twenties and thirties.

LMS at the Top

Of fifteen British railway locations 1,000ft or more above sea level, the LMS claimed ten, three of them on the former Highland Railway between Dalnaspidal and Slochd on the HR main line. The highest in England and Wales was at Waenavon, 1,400ft, while on the remote Elvanfoot & Wanlockhead Light Railway (Caledonian) Leadhills Station was at 1,405ft; both the last two are now closed. Of 35 sets of water troughs on the system, the highest were between Hawes Junction and Dent on the Midland's famed Settle & Carlisle line, presenting problems in keeping them ice-free in Winter.

In July 1929 the *LMS Magazine* carried a piece from Mr G. Dobie, stationmaster at Wanlockhead, terminus of the short branch from Elvanfoot, between Beattock and Carstairs, declaring that his station had a special claim to fame as 'the highest railway station on an adhesion railway in Great Britain', 1,413ft above sea level, just beating Waenavon in Wales with a height of 1,400ft. Closed in 1938 this one-time Caledonian Railway branch had a certain homeliness in that, to the end, its coaches had triple footboards which permitted arbitrary halts to be made en route. Another very reasonable rule was that a load of over 105 tons was never despatched unless the consent of the driver working it had been given. During its period of ownership the LMS almost doubled the fare from 1½d to 2½d. This line was one of the first projects in civil engineering undertaken by Sir Robert McAlpine.

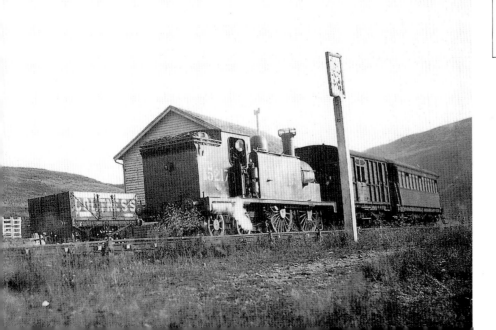

LMS at the Top. Wanlockhead branch, the highest point on the LMS 1498ft above sea level, with former Caledonian railway 0-4-4T No 15217 on the branch train. The stock came from the Knott End Railway in Lancashire and consists of a four-wheel brake van and a bogie coach.

Docks, Harbours and Piers

The LMS owned a total of 28 docks, harbours and piers ranging from major ports like Barrow and Grangemouth through cross-channel harbours such as Holyhead to smaller Clyde piers. Some were used by the company's own vessels and others were commercial ports used by ocean-going vessels.

Holyhead was one of the earliest railway ports and was the LNW's base for Irish services. Their vessels served Dublin North Wall and Greenore, and the City of Dublin Steam Packet Company – which until 1920 held the mail contract – sailed to Kingstown (Dun Laoghaire). During the 1920s the services were rationalised; the mail passenger sailings were now to Dun Laoghaire with North Wall and Greenore being cargo and livestock only. There were day and night sailings to Dun Laoghaire with connecting boat trains.

Heysham was a product of the Midland's expansionist policy and was opened in 1904 with services to Belfast, Londonderry (Burns & Laird Ltd) and Douglas. The Londonderry sailings were withdrawn and the Belfast service finally succumbed to 'the Troubles' in 1975. Heysham is now the principal port for the Isle of Man.

Fleetwood was both a packet harbour and one of the most important fishing ports in Great Britain but after the transfer of the Belfast service to Heysham in 1928 the only cross channel vessels to use the harbour were the Isle of Man Steam Packet Co's ships to Douglas.

Garston on the Mersey, four miles up stream from Liverpool, was mainly a coal exporting harbour but bananas and other fruit were imported and there was a banana ripening shed on the quayside of Stalbridge Dock, the nearest of the three docks, opened in 1909.

Sketch map of Tilbury Docks

LIST OF LMS DOCKS, HARBOURS AND PIERS

FURNESS
Barrow

LONDON & NORTH WESTERN RAILWAY
Deganwy Quay
Foryd Pier
Garston
Holyhead

LNW & L&Y JOINT
Fleetwood

L&Y
Wyre Dock

MIDLAND
Bristol (Avonside + Kings Wharf)
Heysham
Tilbury (Riverside) landing stage
Gravesend (Town and West St piers)
Poplar

NORTH LONDON
Poplar

SEVERN & WYE JOINT
Lydney

SOMERSET & DORSET JOINT
Highbridge

CALEDONIAN
Bowling
Grangemouth
Oban (Railway Pier)
Alloa

Clyde Piers
Gourock
Wemyss Bay

GLASGOW & SOUTH WESTERN
Ayr
Troon

Clyde Piers
Fairlie
Largs
Renfrew

HIGHLAND
Kyle of Lochalsh

PORTPATRICK & WIGTOWNSHIRE JT
Stranraer

(Note the NL and Midland owned separate docks at Poplar)

Control

The LMS was always proud of its Control system. Looking back from today's standpoint, with power signalboxes controlling scores of miles of busy main line, it is perhaps not easy to visualise the difficulties for signalmen in a plethora of small signalboxes in obtaining a comprehensive picture within even a small area as a basis for making decisions on train running. In the early years of the century the Midland had been first in setting up an organisation to improve chaotic freight train working in the South Yorkshire/Nottinghamshire/Derbyshire area. There were occasions of freight train crews being relieved in sidings, only for the relief crew in turn to be relieved after eight hours without the train having moved an inch, due to congestion.

So grew up the Control system, founded on telephone communication between District offices and all signalboxes, stations, yards and engine sheds; it recorded details of train movement, loads, power, trainmen's hours and delays, and took suitable action to keep things on the move. Initially confined to freight train working, it was some years before the system also embraced express passenger train running.

At the British Empire Exhibition at Wembley in 1925 the LMS showed full replicas of the passenger control tables at Derby and Crewe. Clips (commonly referred to at Derby as 'donkeys') holding colour-coded cards with train information were moved along rails mounted on the desk top to give a picture of the state of the line. Presumably it was felt that to show this, rather than a freight office, would put over more effectively the message of a caring organisation. As the explanatory booklet boasted: 'Even a moment's delay at a signal is known at the Control office almost before the train has restarted, and an explanation has to be forthcoming promptly.' It went on to explain the Control function in arranging the 'strengthening of trains at stations where advices show that this will be necessary'; how many people, one wonders, realised that this piece of jargon referred to adding extra coaches and not to pieces being riveted on to make them less prone to damage!

Old photographs of the freight control office at Masborough (Rotherham) at this time are eye-opening to those familiar with modern office practice. With a head controller, relief assistant and four assistants on duty, the first two sat at a central desk. The rest walked round, speaking to signalboxes and so on from a series of telephone cubicles arranged along the walls. The information they gleaned was transferred by card to two pegged train boards, which bore no geographical resemblance to the routes concerned. Masborough was just one of 24 district control offices on the Midland Division alone, and their locations – Cudworth, Gowhole, Chaddesden, Toton, Coalville et al – emphasised their primary function with freight. With such spartan facilities they oversaw all freight traffic and the provision of engines and men to shift it. There were special trains to arrange, often at short notice, and empty wagons (these were the days of privately-owned coal wagons bound for specific collieries) to get to loading points at the right time and in the right quantities. Marshalling yards had to be kept fluid despite traffic fluctuations, and specially important loads 'chased' along their route.

By contrast, the divisional control at Manchester, which gave centralised supervision of the entire L&YR section, was high technology personified. The booklet explained that it was located in a room 'circular in shape, on the walls of which were indicated the tracks . . . Below

INTER-DISTRICT CONTROL TELEPHONIC COMMUNICATION

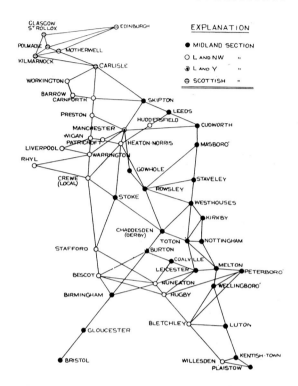

Traffic Control (LNWR). In the early 1900s freight traffic had increased to such a level that some form of supervision and regulation was essential. The Midland Railway was the pioneer of traffic control and other railways soon followed suit. Control offices were connected by telephone to all signalboxes, marshalling yards, locomotive sheds and other locations. The controllers received reports from signalboxes on the running of trains and from marshalling yards giving details of traffic on hand thus enabling them to make the best use of locomotives and train men, avoiding congestion at depots and excessive overtime.

Train boards such as the one at Bescot were used to give a visual indication of the position of all freight trains in the district by means of different shaped (for different classes of train) and numbered pegs. Tickets were hung on these pegs giving the locomotive number and details of the train men.

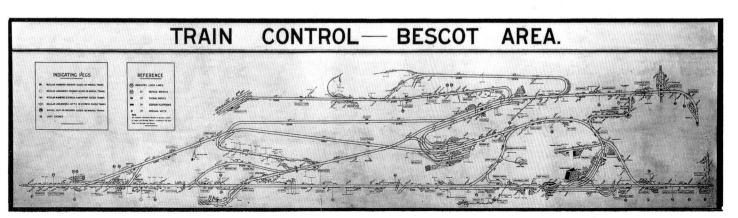

TRAIN CONTROL — BESCOT AREA.

CHADDESDEN CONTROL AREA (Local Trips).

No. 4.							No. 11. (8)							No. 18.							No. 24.					
From	Bkd.	Act	To	Bkd.	Act		From	Bkd.	Act	To	Bkd.	Act		From	Bkd.	Act	To	Bkd.	Act		From	Bkd.	Act	To	Bkd.	Act
St. M.	6.25		WIRKS	7.15			CN.	9.45		LNW. Jc.	10.17			CN. M	5.40		RIP.	7.30			St. M.	8.35		A'GATE	9.4	
WIRKS'H	10.0		ENG SDS	12.8			LNW. Jc.	3.10		CN.	3.33			RIP	7.54		Pass. to Derby.				AE.	9.38		BUTT'Y	10.0	
ENG SDS	12.27		St. M	12.35										CN.	10.8		L.ETN.	10.28			BUTT'Y.	10.7		B'HOL	10.13	
St. M.	1.10		WIRKS.	2.30				No. 11 S.O.						L.ETN.	11.40		CN.	12.0			B'HOL.	10.23		H.S'HAY	10.38	
WIRKS	5.58		L.ET N.	6.32			CN.	7.42		LON RD.	7.57			CN.	12.44		L.ETN.	1.2			H.S'HAY.	11.50		A'GATE	12.6	
L.ET'N.	6.45		St. M	6.52			LN RD.	8.12		TELE S	8.14			L.ETN	1.40		CN.	1.55			AE. S	12.27		BUTT'Y	12.45	
			To Shed.				TELE S	8.19		OS RD	8.21			CN L.E. S	2.10		L.ETN	2.23			BUTT'Y S	12.46		B'HOL	12.53	
							OS. RD	9.15		LNW J	9.18			CN SO	2.36		L.ETN	2.54			B.HOL S	12.52		H'TS'HY	1.2	
No. 6.							LNW	1.55		CN.	2.20			L.ETN	3.55		CN.	4.18			H.SHY S	1.25		AE	1.40	
St. M.	6.40		RIP'Y	7.43										CN.	5.52		L.ETN	6.14			AE. SO	1.29		B'HOL	1.35	
RIP'Y	8.15		L.ETN	11.0				No. 12.						L.ETN.	6.40		CN.	7.0			B.HOL SO	1.39		AE. COLL	1.42	
L.ETN	11.40		RIPY	1.35			CN.	10.48		WORTH'N	12.40										AE C SO	2.0		AE.	2.5	
RIP'Y.	2.20		L.ETN	3.50			WORTH'N	4.40		CN	6.38				No. 19. M.O.						AE.	2.10		PENT'H.	2.18	
L.ETN SO	5.0		CN.	5.13										CN.	6.5		SM.	6.18			PH	3.0		AE.	3.10	
CN. SO	6.30		L.ETN	6.49				No. 13. (8)						St. M.	6.45		CN.	6.55			AE E.& B.	4.0		SWAN.	4.12	
L.ETN	6.20		CN	6.35			CN	8.20		OSM. RD.	8.52			CN	7.35		BM. YD.	7.50			SWAN	4.55		AE.	5.10	
L.ETN SO	7.40		CN	8.3			OSM. RD.	10.15		CN.	10.30			BM. YD.	8.55		CN	9.10			AE.	5.53		CN	6.28	
No. 7.							GN	11.42		SPON J.	11.47			Then as required.							No. 25.					
CN	7.8		DEN	8.4			SPON J	12.32		CN.	12.40										CN.	8.45		SHIR	10.15	
DEN.	8.18		L.ETN	9.59			Relieves Con No. 5	12.55 to 2	10					No. 20.						SHIR	11.40		AE.	11.56	
L.ETN	9.21		RIP	10.35										CN.	3.32		D'NBY	4.28			AE. SO	2.42		SHIR.	3.50	
RIP.	11.10		L.ETN	12.40				No 13. Night.						DEN.	4.50		DY. Sth	4.52			S'HIR SO	4.50		AE.	5.27	
L.ETN.	1.4		DEN	1.20			OS RD (M)	2.15		CN	2.30			DY. HLL	5.30		L.ETN	5.50			AE. SO	6.53		MAT'K	7.18	
DEN.	1.35		L.ETN.	2.54			CN (M)	3.0		OS RD	3.14			L.ETN	6.22		RIPLEY	7.33			MAT'K.SO	8.30		CN.	9.30	
L.ETN	3.15		RIP.	5.3			OS RD (M)	4.25		SHED	4.30			RIP	8.31		CN	10.0			AE. S	4.0		W'WELL	4.40	
RIP.	6.10		L.ETN	7.7				No 14.													W'W'L S	4.35		AE.	4.52	
																				AE. S	6.3		BULL.B	6.x	

Local freight trip record for Chaddesden control area.

these are miniature track plans, and in front of them desks for the controllers . . . Still closer to the centre are the sectional controllers' desks, and in the centre . . . the chief controller. As trains are reported to the proper control officer, he plugs in on the miniature board, and simultaneously a coloured light appears on the line diagram, this moving forward (as the control officer) receives advice of the train's progress . . . it is a picture reminiscent of fairyland.' Many railwaymen might cynically agree that was an apt description!

Gradually these important offices settled down into a more or less standardised form, with telephone consoles for seated controllers and a retreat from moving cards about on maps or boards. A high proportion of control staff came up through the clerical grades and their operating knowledge was (at least at first) limited. Often they had never seen the lines over which they exercised jurisdiction, which did not endear them to the men on the ground. There was a story, perhaps apocryphal, of a driver advising Control that his engine was a complete failure, having dropped a lead plug. He was asked if he could not go back and look for it, put it in again and be on his way!

With the spread of power signalboxes after 1945, each covering large areas, oversight of train movement by Control gradually diminished. The signalman in a modern power box, with his panel diagram before him, was better placed to anticipate conflictions and delay than someone in an office twenty miles away, depending on telephone reports and perhaps an updated train graph. Inevitably, therefore, Control offices manage by exception; more and more they have reverted to dealing with freight in all its facets, and with large-scale arrangements to deal with hold-ups, accidents, diversions and the like.

9
IRELAND

The LMS was as much part of the Irish as of the English, Welsh and Scottish scene. It of course provided the busiest ferry services on the shortest crossings, and one of its two real Irish railways boasted high-quality expresses and well-organised commuter services as well as rural backwaters and narrow-gauge appendages. The first of the LMS's predecessors on the scene was the London & North Western, intent on strengthening its already powerful hold on the Irish traffic through the two quickest sea routes, Holyhead–Dublin and Fleetwood–Belfast. The Dundalk, Newry & Greenore Railway was built with great enthusiasm, as was an extended port complete with hotel for the steamer service from Holyhead. From sheltered Greenore the railway ran to meet the Great Northern's Dublin–Belfast main line at Dundalk to the south and Newry to the north. Though of course built to the Irish standard gauge of 5ft 3in, the twin routes were equipped by Crewe including Ramsbottom/Webb 0-6-0 saddle tanks complete with names, six-wheeled carriages painted in the LNWR's purple brown and spilt milk livery and full signalling. The atmosphere was pure LNWR.

Though technically this was the shortest route to Belfast, the hotel and station never saw great passenger activity. The railway, however, lived on well after the passenger service ceased to become one of Ireland's charming anachronisms.

While live cattle continued to be exported to England and carried to market by rail, Greenore remained an active port, the Webb saddle tanks shunted around the yard and almost equally ancient Great Northern 2-4-2 tanks trundled the ageing 'sax walers' still painted in LNWR livery in the 1950s from junctions to port. It was a fascinating experience to lie in a bath in the Greenore Hotel, the window overlooking the station platforms, sniffing the smoke from below and listening to the familiar chaff, CHAFF, chaff, chaff, of an elderly Webb engine.

The LMS also inherited from the LNWR the Dublin North Wall steamer berths, warehouses and hotel, and a short section of railway.

The Midland did much better. Unlike its rival, it did not build but bought its way in, purchasing the Belfast & Northern Counties Railway in 1903. On amalgamation, this became the LMS (Northern Counties Committee) later part of the Ulster Transport Authority and now Northern Ireland Railways. The only remnants of a railway system in the north today are the old Great Northern main line from Belfast to Dublin and its Antrim branch, parts of what was the Midland Railway (Northern Counties Committee) and the Bangor line of the former Belfast & County Down Railway.

Opposite: Traffic Control (LMS). Birmingham New Street control office in April 1942. The Bescot office closed in 1928 or 1929 and the staff were transferred to New Street. During the blitz of October to December 1940 the old control office was burned out and staff worked permanently in the air-raid shelter until October 1941 when the new one was opened with improved desks and telephone facilities.

The various posts on the photograph were, reading from left to right: (curved desks) guards relief controller, assistant controller (loco), locomotive controller, passenger train controller, (desks along wall) freight train controllers. Section C Coventry exclusive to New Street, Aston to Lichfield, Stechford to Bescot and Soho Road line. Section B New Street to Stafford exclusive, Bescot to Bushbury and branches. Section A Wichnor exclusive to Dudley, Walsall to Rugeley & branches.

Cross Country local. One time Belfast & Northern Counties Railway 2-4-0 compound as LMS/NCC No 57 Galgorm Castle *leaves the main line from Belfast to Londonderry at Cookstown Junction on 20 June 1935. Note the jacks carried on the front of the locomotive, the LNWR type cast iron numberplate and the somersault junction signal to the rear of the train.*

The NCC Looks Ahead. The Northern Counties Committee experimented with internal combustion as can be seen by this photograph of the first railcar, No 1, built in 1933 and originally driven by a petrol engine. The station appears to be Carrickfergus on the Larne line. No 1 was subsequently fitted with a diesel engine and ran until the 1960s.

The Midland having dived in with both feet found itself not only with a good mileage of Irish standard gauge track carrying profitable traffic but also with some extremely doubtful narrow gauge lines. The Belfast & Northern Counties had several of them under its wing (all 3ft gauge) including the Ballymena & Larne Railway and a section of line from Londonderry to Strabane. The latter ran parallel with the Great Northern line from Belfast to Derry, on the opposite bank of the River Foyle. Strabane was also an end-on junction for what became, in 1906, the largest narrow gauge system in the whole of Ireland, the County Donegal Railways Joint Committee in which the LMS inherited a half interest via the Midland. This was incorporated to control all lines to the west and indeed all narrow gauge tracks in County Donegal except those of the Londonderry & Lough Swilly Railway. The Midland (of England) and the Great Northern of Ireland became joint owners.

So the LMS inherited an interesting (to say the least) parcel of lines, and to add to the variety in 1924 the ailing narrow-gauge Ballycastle Railway was taken over. Looking back one can see what a delight it must have been to the historically minded enthusiast, made even more fascinating by partition, which drew borders across the Dundalk, Newry & Greenore south of Newry and the County Donegal just west of Strabane. There were also narrow gauge boat trains from Larne to Ballymena; these, in the early days, had to be seen to be believed. With the Ballymena & Larne section the Midland had inherited not only the first 3ft gauge railway to carry passengers in Ireland but also the only narrow gauge line in the British Isles to run an express, though it was not until the twilight years under the LMS that an attempt was made to provide comfort anything like equal to the standard gauge. In 1928 new corridor coaches were specially constructed at the Belfast works of the NCC

Ulster express engine. No 97 Earl of Ulster was one of the 2-6-0s built specially at Derby for the 5ft 3in gauge NCC: the class was used for the fast Belfast to Londonderry expresses. Note the LMS crest on the cabside, the cast number plate with the Celtic figure 7 and the catcher for exchanging tablets at speed.

123

Coincidence

The grim grandeur of the Barnesmore Gap was impressive enough, but what most excited me was the last section, along the rough, tortuous and quite undeveloped Atlantic seaboard. The diesel horn echoed: the crossing keepers opened the gates; mothers and children rushed to the doorways of the whitewashed crossing cottages; and labourers digging tiny patches of peaty soil at the cliff's edge set their watches as we rollicked by. The driver apologised for the rough riding: I should have come when the track was as good as anything I would have seen in England, he said. Talking about England, 'My daddy once went there. I've never been myself, of course'. And so into the dilapidated little port of Killybegs, where the most modern object was an oil tank wagon, a neat miniature of Esso's British wagons, standing in the siding.

David St John Thomas on the County Donegal.

providing a short-lived service for, in 1933, passenger traffic was transferred to the standard gauge.

The County Donegal was in a different field for, cherishing its relative independence from 'across the water', this superb piece of railway retained a charm of its own right up to closure in 1959. The Donegal system made history in 1926 when its manager, one Henry Forbes (Irish pronunciation Forbess), a man of great character, respected rather than liked, introduced a passenger service using petrol railcars purchased from the Derwent Valley Light Railway in England. Once the problem with the Free State customs had been overcome (the vehicles were said to be buses on which duty was payable), these proved to be a continuing boon, their successors in diesel railcars literally saving both the passenger service and the line beyond normal expectation. In the event, the border, the road improvements and need for extensive re-laying of the permanent way as well as joint state ownership saw an impossible future.

Thus the LMS, having only one narrow gauge railway in England, the Leek & Manifold Valley in Staffordshire, had plenty on its hands over the Irish Sea.

But if the minor lines were sometimes a joke, the same could certainly not be said of the NCC as a whole, either in Midland or LMS days. The Belfast to Londonderry, Portrush and Larne trains, ran as real expresses to smart timings. Motive power in earlier years included some interesting two cylinder compounds built for the BNCR but Midlandisation was rapid with typical Derby-built 4-4-0s (named after Castles) soon taking over. The LMS added some large 2-6-0s and later, into nationalisation, some 2-6-4 tanks.

The total track mileage of the LMS–NCC was a few chains over 245 though this included nearly 43 miles of 3ft gauge. Its services gave connections between the two principal cities of the Six Counties – Belfast

The Dundalk, Newry & Greenore Railway was a microcosm of the LNWR. The coaches were pure Wolverton and lasted until the closure in 1951 while the indigenous locomotives were a 5ft 3in gauge version of the Ramsbottom/Webb special tanks. The GNR (I) took over the working of the line in 1933 using its own 2-4-2Ts on passenger trains but the remaining 0-6-0STs continued to work the freight service. No 6 is shown here at Newry on 30 May 1932 – the last year of totally independent working.

and Londonderry, with branches serving a number of relatively important seaside and market towns. Boat trains ran from Larne Harbour to Londonderry loading at times to as many as seventeen bogies. The company also owned hotels at Larne (Laharna) and Portrush (Northern Counties).

The main line left Belfast York Road station with its locomotive shops and shed, and made its way north-easterly along the northern shore of Belfast Lough to Bleach Green Junction where the Larne line diverged with the main tracks carried over Valentine's Glen by the well-known Greenisland viaduct, completed in 1934 at a cost of £200,000 – a vast sum in those days. These works incorporated a flying junction whereby the main line passes over the down Larne line. This concrete structure, the only civil engineering monument to the NCC, obviated the necessity for all main line trains to reverse at Greenisland, effecting a considerable saving of time and such was the traffic that substantial resignalling was undertaken, allowing three minute headways. From this point of view the exit from Belfast was indeed more modern than from either of the main London termini.

Perhaps nowhere in the British Isles is there greater nostalgia for pre-war train services than in former NCC territory, for especially after the Greenisland scheme (and doubling of part of the Larne line) there was considerable pride in what seemed to achieve the best of both worlds:

Donegal Baltic. County Donegal Railways Joint Committee 4-6-4T No 10 Owenea takes a Stranorlar bound train out of Strabane on 14 April 1937. This was the largest 3ft 0in gauge system in Ireland and was jointly owned by the LMS (once Midland) and the Great Northern (Ireland). The section from Londonderry to Strabane was pure LMS. Strabane was the junction with the GNR (I) and the customs post for narrow gauge trains leaving for Eire. There were two separate stations joined by a covered overbridge. On the opposite side of the CDRJC island platform was the line to Letterkenny. Locomotives were painted geranium red, coaching stock red and cream – a livery virtually copied by BR in its primeval years.

Narrow Gauge double header. A pair of compound 2-4-2 tanks Nos 101 and 102 built for the Ballymena & Larne Railway but transferred to the 3ft 0in gauge Ballycastle section by the LMS, head the 3.58pm train for Ballymoney, the junction with the Londonderry to Belfast main line, on 12 July 1935. The coaches are also ex-Ballymena & Larne, built by the LMS in 1928 for the boat train specials: they were the only 3ft 0in gauge corridor vehicles in Ireland and were extremely comfortable. They ended up on the County Donegal Railways Joint Committee where they ran until 1959.

part and parcel of the overall LMS with all the familiarity and comfort that provided and excellent local management. The Second World War brought even greater traffic pressure to the main NCC routes than it did to most main lines in England, Wales and Scotland. Northern Ireland was important to all three of the armed forces, one RAF runway indeed extending across the main Derry line and requiring special signalling. With shipbuilding and industry on peak production, commuters poured into Belfast from both the main and Larne lines.

Great efforts were made to restore things after the war, when record crowds were taken from Belfast to Portrush both for holidays and day trips, but when most of the LMS went into BR's London Midland Region, Ulster took charge of its own railways with a generally sad tale since including bombing of the once-smart York Road terminus (no longer used by Londonderry trains). Because the County Donegal Joint Railways, mainly in the Republic, could not be handed to the Ulster Transport Authority, a share of that alone of the Irish possessions passed to British Railways.

10
LOCOMOTIVE TRIALS

In the early days of the LMS, locomotive testing was somewhat rough and ready, relying on two inherited dynamometer cars. At the end it had become a highly sophisticated process, using a new dynamometer car with three mobile testing units – while the locomotive testing station at Rugby was well on its way, though not into service until nationalisation. The vagaries of dynamometer car testing on service trains, subject to uncontrollable outside influences, was replaced by testing under carefully regulated conditions of speed, output and firing technique. And the risky interpretation of coal and water consumptions related to drawbar horsepower, which could vary by up to ten per cent, gave way to more scientific data on output, consumption and efficiency over the whole range of an engine's workings.

It started with an evaluation of the express passenger engines of the constituent companies between December 1923 and May 1926, using the difficult routes between Leeds and Carlisle, and Preston and Carlisle and pitting Midland 4-4-0 compounds and a 990 against LNW Prince of Wales and Claughton 4-6-0s, L&Y 4-6-0 Dreadnoughts and Pickersgill 4-4-0 and 60 class 4-6-0 representatives of Caledonian practice. Ostensibly it was to be a guide to future building policy, though existing management prejudice had already decided this. The dice were loaded from the start; the Claughton used over the Settle line was a 'dud' transferred in for the tests and handled by men strange to the class, while the Caledonian and L&Y engines showed hearty appetites for coal. The remainder, *including four of the five compounds* used, gave results in the range of 4.15–5.1 lb coal/dbhp hr (drawbar horsepower hour) quite representative of contemporary performance. The fifth compound gave untypical results mainly in the 3.65–3.97 lb/dbhp hr range; by this was the design vindicated for further building.

The next notable test, during the run up to the decision to build the Royal Scots involved a borrowed GWR Castle running between Euston, Crewe and Carlisle, on timings of 175 minutes Euston–Crewe and back with up to 450 tons, and taking 400 tons between Crewe and Carlisle. The performances were competent without being spectacular, and coal consumption was lower than had been demonstrated earlier that year with the pre-grouping types. It reinforced the decision to build the new 4-6-0s and to kill Fowler's project for a big Pacific.

In the freight field the problems of working coal trains from Toton Yard to Brent by the Midland route would not go away, and trials went on intermittently for years. As has been mentioned elsewhere, almost everything that was available ran the course – Class 4F 0-6-0s in pairs, a

THE ROYAL SCOT CROSSING THE CANADIAN ROCKIES (5,600 ft.) WITHOUT ASSISTANCE.
INSET BELL PRESENTED TO LOCOMOTIVE "ROYAL SCOT" BY THE CANADIAN PACIFIC RAILWAY.

Showing the Flag. 1933 saw an 11,000 mile trip round the United States of America and Canada by the locomotive No 6100 Royal Scot and an eight coach train of the latest LMS stock (the locomotive was in fact No 6152 disguised). The train is seen here at North Bend, British Columbia, on the Canadian Pacific Railway.

borrowed S&DJ 2-8-0, an LNWR 0-8-0, Garratts, Fowler Class 7F 0-8-0s and latterly Stanier 2-8-0s – even in desperation the Lickey banker. From the coal consumption aspect the outstanding machine was the Fowler 7F, with the Stanier 2-8-0 little inferior.

At about this time the dynamometer car people were hoist with their own petard, and there were very red faces all round. Some tests on the new Royal Scots had produced an incredibly low consumption figure of about 2.7 lb/dbhp hr, which could have been valid in freight service but would have demanded a superlative machine in passenger service. Pride goeth before a fall! Nigel Gresley was suspicious and baited a trap by asking for a loan of the No 1 dynamometer car to calibrate his old NER car. Fowler fell in head first. Trials between Doncaster and Peterborough with the two cars coupled back-to-back showed that friction in the specially calibrated drawbar spring of the LMS car was causing gross over-recording of drawbar pull. Applied to the Royal Scot tests the true consumption was about 3.5 lb/dbhp hr, which was reasonable but no ground for crowing. Curiously, the initial tests with the low superheat Princess, Class 5s and Jubilees in 1933 all gave unnaturally low consumption figures which were increased substantially as testing continued. It was never explained but just quietly dropped!

Testing was a well nigh continuous process, in between the more spectacular trials. Many were the devices tested which were claimed to produce economy – exhaust steam injectors, feed water heaters, and the

128

like. More radical departures from the conventional locomotive were scrutinised; they included the Beyer–Ljungström condensing turbine locomotive, the ultra-high pressure *Fury* and Stanier's 'Turbomotive'. Few of them lived up to their claims.

The mid-1930s saw an intensive programme as Stanier set about bringing the locomotive fleet up to date. There was a three-pronged attack, directed to getting new engines (mainly the Jubilees) to steam satisfactorily, getting the coal consumption figures down by raising the superheat, and lastly (following the other two) proving the feasibility of accelerated timings. Taking the Jubilees as an example, the steaming was brought up to standard by redesign of blastpipe and chimney, including elimination of the jumper blastpipe, and the superheater was stepped up from 14 to 24 elements; the effect of all these was tested step-by-step on the road, bringing consumption on the fast Euston–Birmingham service down from around 4.2 lb/dbhp hr to 3.16 lb. The way was now open for the two series of tests to confirm the proposed timings for the Midland Division accelerations of 1937 and 1938. The most spectacular was the second series, using Jubilee No 5660 *Rooke* with a 300 ton train. It was pushed very hard indeed, especially on the southbound climb from Carlisle to Ais Gill summit, when 900–1,250 horsepower was produced almost continuously.

But it was the prelude to the Coronation Scot which captured the public imagination. First, in November 1936, No 6201 *Princess*

Scot on the Southern. The newly formed British Railways instigated a series of locomotive exchanges in April, May and June 1948 to ascertain the best types of locomotive for future development.

One of the classes selected was the LMS-rebuilt Royal Scot. No 46154 The Hussar (a star of Camden shed) is seen here leaving Waterloo on the down Atlantic Coast Express, 11.00am Waterloo to numerous destinations in Devon and Cornwall.

This is a preliminary run in June 1948 as there is no Dynamometer Car on the train. The locomotive is attached to an eight-wheel tender from a War Department 2-8-0 as extra water capacity was required because there were no water troughs on the Southern. The tender is spuriously lettered LMS!

When the train-sets for the Coronation Scot service reached completion at Wolverton Works, a special train notice came into the office ordering two high-speed test runs (additional to normal running-in trips, Wolverton–Crewe and return, some 200 miles in all. The gentleman in the Crewe timing office who got out the notice was either slightly naïve or an enthusiast of the first order, because he had written-in the magic (to us) words Bletchley P meaning that Bletchley mpd would provide engines and men for these trains required to average over 60mph and to touch about 80.

Now the most powerful passenger locomotives in Bletchley's allocation were ex-LNWR Prince of Wales class 4-6-0s, used then only on secondary, excursion and relief trains, and including one or more of the small batch of this class which were fitted with the Beames-Walschaerts outside valve gear to inside cylinders. Owing to the rapid syncopated action of this valve gear at high speed, these locomotives were known to the staff as the 'Tishy engines', after a somewhat notorious racehorse of that name, immortalised by *The Daily Mail's* famous cartoonist Tom Webster, as being prone to cross its legs during a race.

Oh, yes, we've got the notice,' confirmed Bletchley on the phone, 'Yes, we're preparing two Class 4's (Princes). Our men are very keen.'

But it was not to be. Somebody at a higher level, and with a closer knowledge of locomotive allocations than the compiler, had read the special train notice, hence a further, somewhat rueful call from Bletchley: 'Camden have been instructed to send a Pacific' – though the caller did not so describe it! – for this job. Sorry!'
D. S. M. Barrie

Elizabeth ran a proving trial for a tentative six-hour timing between Euston and Glasgow, 401 miles. It did not materialise because of increase in weight of the train formation, but 6201 improved on the timings, particularly southbound. There was, of course, a price to be paid for high speed; whereas Princesses on the heavy Royal Scot train had recorded figures as low as 2.86 lb/dbhp hr, No 6201 needed 3.68 lb northbound and 3.48 southbound. Then, before the new streamlined Coronation Scot service opened, a press demonstration run of the new train from Euston to Crewe was made in June 1937, at which a determined attempt to beat the world speed record of 112½mph was made. On the gentle descent from Whitmore to Crewe the Hasler recorder on the engine showed a maximum speed of 114mph to have been reached. In practice, the work of independent recorders suggests a figure of only 113mph – enough for a record, but only just!

It is now well known that Riddles, in charge of the trial on the footplate, delayed braking for the Crewe stop in order to reach a record speed, and only by great good fortune did not pile the whole train up on the south junction at Crewe. Sixteen months later a spectacular trial was made between Crewe and Glasgow to assess the new Pacific's capability for fast haulage of 600 ton trains, on a seven-hour Euston–Glasgow timing. In practice it was as much a test of the firemen's muscle as of the engine, for the coal consumption of No 6234 *Duchess of Abercorn* was high by current standards; speed with heavy loads is not bought cheaply. But the outstanding feature was the sustained high power outputs on the severe northern climbs, successively producing maxima of 2,300–2,500 horsepower at the drawbar. Nothing like it had ever been seen before. Yet at one point it was touch-and-go whether the test would have to be abandoned; the train reached Symington for a special water stop with the tender tank *empty* and water out of sight in the bottom of the boiler water gauges.

Not all testing involved power and consumption monitoring. Work had started on assessing the forces generated between locomotive and track, an area of scanty theory. Engines had developed rough riding since time immemorial, and the reasons were less than clear. So the old LNW dynamometer car was converted for continuous recording of the forces between wheels, axleboxes and frames, and hooked up by a festoon of electric cables to a rebuilt Royal Scot – a class once notorious for rough riding – for testing on the curvy route from Derby through the Peak District to Manchester. Data emerged which guided bogie and other modifications to minimise the problem.

All this testing work was done at considerable cost, and the benefits mainly accrued to the CME's design effort. But the motive power department looked for information which could be applied to the more basic problem of training men how to drive the engines and handle the shovel to produce the most economical results, and reports of dynamometer car tests did not fit this bill. So in the late 1940s four special tenders were built whereby a locomotive inspector could weigh the complete coal bunker before and after a journey. Routine testing no longer needed prior planning, and produced immediate answers. They could

also be used to evaluate different coal supplies. Alas, they were only put to limited use.

By the demise of the LMS, the new Rugby Testing Station (with its older GWR Swindon counterpart) were poised to take over the testing of the important classes of locomotive. Thereafter the dynamometer car was used mainly for confirmatory testing on the road of engines which had already been put through their paces on the rollers. The Skipton–Carlisle route was a favourite for Rugby-tested engines. LMS types which were put through this ordeal included a Duchess, rebuilt Royal Scot, Jubilee, several class 5 4-6-0s, and 2-6-0s of Hughes, Class 4, and Class 2 types. In many cases a desire to improve steaming, particularly with lower-grade coals, was the prime aim. It was during such testing that the Duchess was pushed to a *sustained* steaming rate of 41,500 lb/hr at Rugby, the highest output ever recorded in this country; even then the boiler limit had not been reached.

The old No 1 dynamometer car had its last independent fling in 1948, during the BR-initiated interchange trials, when a Duchess, a rebuilt Royal Scot, Class 5 4-6-0 and Class 8F 2-8-0 were pitted against comparable engines from other regions. The results were hardly conclusive, for a variety of reasons; suffice it to say that the LMS designs acquitted themselves honourably, while at times the Royal Scot stole the show on performance from the bigger passenger engines. The LMS could be justly proud of their representatives at these trials.

Trial for the Western. During the summer of 1949 a couple of mini trials were made on the suburban services from Leamington to Birmingham Snow Hill using ex-LMS engines: the classes used were the Fowler 2-6-2 tank and the Stanier 2-6-4 tank which were pitted against the standard Churchward GWR 2-6-2 tanks which regularly worked this service. On 14 August 1949 2-6-4T No 42577 of 2A shed (Rugby) takes the 3.53pm out of Leamington Spa (General). There is a great deal of interesting detail in the photograph: on the left is the LNWR Leamington Spa (Avenue) station serving Kenilworth and Coventry at one end and Rugby or Weedon at the other – this station is now closed but the connection from Kenilworth is now used by express trains from Birmingham New Street to Paddington and other stations via Oxford.

Crewe

How oft since childhood have I wished I knew
What lay behind the mystery of Crewe!
It was a name on every cryptic mouth
Of those who talked of journeys North or South
And long before I knew what travelling meant
Crewe was a word of magical content
'We change at Crewe' said grown-ups yet they came
Back from adventure looking just the same
And when at length to travelling years I grew
Time but intensified the thrill of Crewe.
It stood for haste for making in the night
For lamps and noise for terror and delight
For urgent porters breaking up a dream
For shrieking whistle and for shuddering steam
For monstrous engines thundering and ablaze
For criss-cross metals in a shining maze
For trains illumined sliding out and in
And high-piled barrows charging through the din,
For guards magnificent as man may be
For bolted buns and gulps of scalding tea.
Crewe stood for trains, in splendour, pomp, and glow –
Trains – and aught else?

Ah, how I longed to know!
Above this vast and clamour – echoing roof
Did old familiar stars look down aloof?
If from this hurly one adventured out
And, startled by strange stillness, stared about
What would one see? Was there a town of Crewe
Nowise concerned about my passing through?
Did folk alight and live at Crewe? How strange
To settle down where others came to change!
As I grew up I swore that I would try
To solve Crewe's brooding mystery by-and-bye
Its secret – some day – I resolved to know
And, boldly letting some connection go,
Forth from the station vowed to seek a way
(If such there were) and find what further lay.
I've never done it. As the years go past
Conviction calms my questioning at last
My childhood's maddest guesses must be true
Only the engines know the way to Crewe.
Crewe is a fantasy of traveller's brains
Born of the night, of Bradshaw, and of trains.

W.K.H. *Punch*, 6 September 1922.

THROUGH COACHES 1939

CREWE to

Aberdeen 2.2 a.m., 1.9, 4.26 (Sats. excepted), 4.52 (Sats. only), 10N29, 11.11 p.m. (Sats. excepted). (Suns. 2.2 a.m. and 11.11 p.m.)

Aberystwyth 2.5 (Mons. excepted), 9.25 a.m. and 1.15 p.m.

Barrow 10F58, 11G5 a.m., 2.9, 4.26, 8.0 (Sats. excepted) and 8.32 p.m. (Sats. only). (Suns. 3.27 p.m.)

Bath 10.45 a.m.

Blackpool (Central) 3.42, 10C58, 11G5 a.m., 4P17 p.m., 8.0 (Sats excepted) and 8.32 p.m. (Sats. only). (Suns. 4.7 a.m. and 3.27 p.m.)

Blackpool (North) 9H46, 9J50, 11H15 a.m., 2K9, 3E44 and 3H58 p.m.

Bournemouth (West) 10.45 a.m.

Brighton 11B41 a.m.

Cardiff (G.W.) 1.25, 10.32 a.m., 1.10, 4.7 and 8.17 p.m.

Cheltenham (Mid.) 10.45 a.m.

Dundee 2.2 a.m. (Suns. 2.2 a.m.)

Eastbourne 11B41 a.m.

Edinburgh (Princes St.) 1.45 (Mons. excepted), 2.2 (Mons. only), 9.27 a.m., 12L40, 1L9, 1M15, 4.40 (Sats. excepted) and 4.52 p.m. (Sats. only). (Suns. 2.2 a.m. and 3.5 p.m.)

Exeter 1.25, 10.32 a.m. and 4.7 p.m.

Glasgow (Cen.) 12A50 (Mons. and Sats. excepted), 1A4 (Mons. and Sats. excepted), 1D17 (Sats. only), 1.22 (Mons. only), 3.0, 9.27 a.m., 12L40, 1L9, 1M15, 4.40 (Sats. excepted), 4.52 p.m. (Sats. only). (Suns. 1.10 a.m., 3.0 a.m. and 3.5 p.m.)

Glasgow (St. Enoch) 3.27 a.m.

Hastings 11B41 a.m.

Heysham 9.5 p.m. (Sats. excepted), 9.40 p.m. (Sats. only). (Suns. 9.33 p.m.)

Inverness 10N29, 11.11 p.m. (Sats. excepted). (Suns. 11.11 p.m.)

Kendal 1.25, 10F58, 11G5 a.m., 2K9, 4.27 (Sats. only) and 5.50 p.m.

Llandrindod Wells 1.10 p.m.

Llangammarch Wells 1.10 p.m.

Llanwrtyd Wells 1.10 p.m.

Morecambe 5.50 and 9.5 p.m. (Sats. excepted), 9.40 p.m. (Sats. only).

Newcastle-on-Tyne 12.5 a.m. (Mons. excepted). (Suns. 12.5 a.m.)

Newport (Mon.) 1.25, 10.32 a.m., 1.10, 4.7 and 8.17 p.m.

Oswestry 9.25 a.m. and 1.15 p.m.

Paignton 10.32 a.m. and 4.7 p.m.

Penzance 1.25 a.m.

Perth 2.2, 9.27 a.m., 1.9, 4.26 (Sats. excepted), 4.52 (Sats. only), 10N29, 11.11 p.m. (Sats. excepted). (Suns. 2.2 a.m. and 11.11 p.m.)

Plymouth 1.25, 10.32 a.m. and 4.7 p.m.

Southampton 10.45 a.m.

Southport (Chapel St.) (via Edge Hill) 5.37 p.m.

Stirling 2.2, 9.27 a.m., 1.9, 4.26 (Sats. excepted), 4.52 (Sats. only), 11.11 p.m. (Sats. excepted). (Suns. 2.2 a.m. and 11.11 p.m.)

Stranraer 11.20 p.m. (Sats. excepted), (Suns. 11.11 p.m.)

Swansea (Victoria) 1.10 p.m.

Taunton 1.25, 10.32 a.m. and 4.7 p.m.

Torquay 10.32 a.m. and 4.7 p.m.

Truro 1.25 a.m.

Turnberry 11.20 p.m. (Sats. excepted).

Weston-super-Mare 1.25 a.m., 1.10 p.m.

Whitehaven 10F58, 11G5 a.m., 2.9 and 4.27 p.m. (Suns. 3.27 p.m.)

Windermere 1.25, 10F58, 11G5 a.m., 2K9, 4.27 (Sats. only) and 5.50 p.m.

York 12.5 a.m.

A Except Dec. 22nd and March 22nd.

B Sats. only, runs until Oct. 28th, 1939, and commencing April 6th, 1940; also runs Dec. 23rd, 1939, and March 21st, 1940.

C Sats. only and commences Oct. 28th.

D Also on Dec. 22nd and March 22nd.

E Dec. 22nd, 23rd and March 21st only.

F Sats. only.

G Sats. excepted.

H Sats. only until Oct. 21st.

J Runs Sats. excepted, until Oct. 9th; also on Mon., Oct. 16th.

K Except Dec. 22nd, 23rd and March 21st.

L Except Dec. 21st, 22nd, 23rd and March 21st.

M Dec. 21st, 22nd, 23rd and March 21st only.

N Dec. 21st, 22nd, March 20th and 21st only.

P Dec. 22nd, 23rd, and March 21st. only.

LNWR in 1930. Crewe on 15 June 1930 with ex-LNWR George V 4-4-0 No 5341 Wolfhound (note the big bosses to the driving wheels) and an unidentified Prince of Wales class 4-6-0 on the 4.25pm Crewe to Chester standing in No 8 bay.

The 4-4-0 has acquired a tender of Great Central design from a former ROD 2-8-0 which had been purchased at a knock-down price from the Government Disposals Board. On the platform there is a hand-operated rotary pump for filling carriage water tanks.

Old Crewe. A view of Crewe in LNWR days but one virtually unchanged until recent times. The picture clearly shows one of the huge island platforms protected (as were so many LNWR stations) by large glass screens. The various notices indicate refreshment rooms for the appropriate classes.

133

Freight at Crewe

Although Crewe became a famous name as a passenger junction few gave much thought to its role in respect of freight. The LMS felt the need to draw this to the attention even of its own staff through the April 1935 issue of its house magazine *On Time* when it pointed out the work carried on at Basford Hall sorting sidings, Crewe North, Stafford up and down, and Gresty Lane up and down sidings. Over 200 inward freight trains and local trips detached on average 7,000 wagons every 24 hours and despatched on a similar number of outward freight trains. In addition approximately 400 wagons of 'smalls' were handled through Crewe tranship shed.

During the heavy Easter, Whitsun and August holiday periods, and at weekends from spring to late autumn, station avoiding lines were further occupied by a number of passenger trains travelling via Basford Hall Junction, Sorting Sidings Middle and Salop Goods Junction from the Stafford direction to Manchester, Liverpool, the North, Chester and North Wales and vice versa. This obvious relief to Crewe station saw over seventy passenger trains working over these lines during the August bank holiday period 1937.

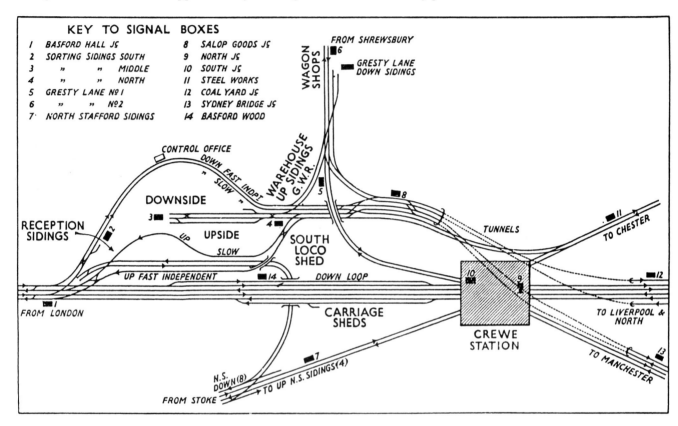

Route plan of lines in the Crewe area, 1938, showing freight routes.

11
PUBLICITY

Publicity played a vital – but ever changing – role in the life of the LMS. And note that it was LMS as distinct from L.N.E.R., indeed the only one of the Big Four not to put full stops between its initials, a distinction carefully followed even when the four took joint ads. (But there was not always consistency in the use of the initials or the company's full name, London Midland and Scottish Railway, still with no punctuation.) In its quarter century, the company's publicity function had to deal with the complicated creation of the new organisation, the General Strike and acute depression, the Square Deal and other campaigns, the resurgence of passenger and freight business culminating in the Coronation Scot, of course the railway's centenary of which much was made including a large exhibition of ancient and modern, many technical innovations with practical implications for the railway's users such as the container, the war with its 'Is your journey really necessary?' campaign, and those few post war years of expectation ever punctured by bleak reality when the task was to explain why things were not yet better.

Much of the publicity was highly successful, not least in persuading the vast staff that the LMS was a natural entity getting places, an employer of which they could become proud. The posters that literally brightened many square miles of passenger platforms cheered passengers and staff alike as they told of the railway's achievements and the golden countrysides it could whisk them to, often at very advantageous fares.

The Big Four went about their publicity tasks in very different ways. The LNER had both an advertising manager and an information agent in charge of the Press office; the GWR a publicity agent in charge of both functions and ready to exploit the company's continuity through Grouping and to make it perhaps the best-publicised commercial undertaking of all time; the Southern brought in J. B. Elliott from Fleet Street to tackle a bad Press and public discontent; and the LMS appointed a Midland man, T. C. Jeffrey, as advertising and publicity officer, placing him in the chief general superintendent's office at Derby. It was not a good start, though not until 1927 did the department come back to the old LNWR address at No 2 Euston Square (to be moved across the road at Euston House in 1934). That coincided with Jeffrey's retirement; his deputy G. H. Loftus Allen, took charge until his untimely death in 1945.

Well connected, immaculate, always apparently relaxed, at home in society but also within his team of varied talents, where he was always clearly and effortlessly the boss, he was the ideal man for the challenge. He had joined the LNWR as a probationer in 1913, had done well as an army officer in the war, and had a taste for the arts which was reflected in

Finding an Image
In the early years of the LMS the publicity department must have debated the choice of a locomotive to typify the size and strength of the new organisation. Evidently the Hughes Lancashire & Yorkshire 4-6-0 appealed, for although not familiar outside its home ground it gave an impression of rugged power and dependability. A 1935 brochure titled *Travel LMS – The Best Way* showed a passenger train headed by one of the 4-6-0s on the cover and again on an inside page, where the caption read 'The last word in comfortable railway travel'. On another page an engine of the same class was captioned 'LMS express passenger locomotive'. Something went wrong at this point, for the second picture on the page, captioned 'LMS express freight locomotive', was unmistakeably the Lickey banker.

DAILY SKETCH

No. 8,787   WEDNESDAY, JUNE 30, 1937   ONE PENNY

FIRE THREATENS A ROYAL HOME

Left Euston at 9.50 a.m.

114 M.P.H. BY RAIL!

BRITISH RECORD

On her record-breaking run between Euston and Crewe yesterday the new L.M.S. "Coronation Scot" is seen in this DAILY SKETCH picture thundering past Watford at 70 m.p.h. Driver Tom Clarke estimated his speed at one point on the trip to Crewe at 113 miles an hour. On the return journey from Crewe (158.1 miles) he averaged 80 m.p.h., his actual time being 119 minutes as against 133 minutes in November. The train was also 11 minutes ahead of schedule. **Outward Journey:** 2 hours 9½ minutes. **Home Journey:** 1 hour 57 minutes. World's Record (Germany): 119.8 m.p.h.

Arrived at Crewe (158.1 Miles) at 11.59¾ a.m.

Left Crewe At 1.55 p.m.

And here—are the two heroes of the day, Driver T. J. Clark and Fireman J. Lewis. They certainly deserved the congratulations of the stationmaster at Crewe.

Arrived at Euston at 3.54 p.m.

Mr. F. A. Lemon, vice-president of the L.M.S. toasts the train's crew on arrival at Euston. Left to right: John Lewis (fireman), F. F. Brockbank (guard). Tom Clark (driver) and footplate inspector S. E. Miller.

WIRELESS ON PAGE 16

the high quality of LMS posters. To concentrate on that aspect for a moment, to help make the best of its substantial investment in pictorial posters, the company employed a distinguished art adviser in Norman Wilkinson. It sponsored posters by Charles Pears and many members of the Royal Academy – seventeen were working on commissions simultaneously – depicting industries, towns, castles and other historic sites, and holiday regions served by the LMS in all four countries of the United Kingdom. As *The Railway Magazine* put it: 'Beyond indicating the place or industry that they wish to advertise, the LMS are giving the artists an entirely free hand. There is another important question, that of reproduction in poster form. The company are quite alive to that, and neither money or trouble will be spared to ensure the best reproductions possible of these notable contributions to every man's open-air picture gallery.' Many of the posters were launched at an exhibition. Altogether they portrayed the LMS as a go-ahead, caring railway and added an extra dimension to many a schoolchild's lessons. Copies of some posters were indeed cherished in many a class room well beyond the LMS's own life.

Perhaps by the very nature of the work, and the varied sources from which the participants came, an advertising department included an interesting collection of characters. From Derby there came Murray Secretan, a gifted artist in painting or colouring locomotive photographs, who in his spare time did some beautiful work for the Locomotive Publishing Company; in 1937 he did an excellent coloured cover of the

Irish Mail Packet. A painting by Norman Wilkinson used for a poster to advertise the Holyhead–Dun Laoghaire service. One of the four 1920–1 vessels, Hibernia, *built when the LNWR regained the mail contract is shown backing out of Holyhead inner harbour. The station hotel is the building in the background and on the right is the coaling barge* Pick-me-Up. *Opposite.*

Scoop. It must be rare for a railway speed record to occupy the whole of the front page of a national daily but this tremendous achievement was set up by the LMS press office in 1937. The paper was one of the two national tabloids then on sale, the Daily Sketch, *and the occasion the epic trial for the Coronation Scot on 29 June 1937 when No 6220* Coronation *managed 114mph and just kept to the rails south of Crewe. Driver Tom Clarke, fireman J. Lewis and footplate inspector S. E. Miller.*

137

Brighter Stations
Following a series of experiments, the LMS have adopted a range of six standard colours for painting their 2,500 passenger stations in a more cheerful and more attractive style than has hitherto been employed. These colours include two light shades, either of which can be used in conjunction with any one of three dark shades. The sixth colour, golden brown, is being used sometimes by itself and sometimes in conjunction with another paint; it is particularly useful at stations where there are electric trains, for there the air contains a certain amount of iron dust, which causes a rust-like stain on paint work. The effects of this are reduced when golden brown paint is used. Ultimately all LMS passenger stations will be painted in accordance with the new colour scheme.
Meccano Magazine, November 1938.

streamlined No 6220 *Coronation* for the booklet *Modern Locomotives of the LMS*, sponsored by the company but produced by LPC with text, thirty illustrations, and a list of named locomotives; it cost just one shilling. Secretan later moved on to the LMS trade advertising section, which was hived off from the advertising and publicity department to become a separate branch of the commercial function. (Under the Midland and early LMS regimes, the letting of advertising spaces on stations and bookstall contracts had all come under the advertising department.)

A well-remembered personality who took a notable part in the expansion of the department was W. C. (Bill) Brudenell, whose father had been employed by the Duke of Buckingham on the Oxford & Aylesbury Tramroad, and later became stationmaster at Rickmansworth on the Metropolitan & Great Central Joint Line. Bill used to recall how his father had regularly to watch the passage of GC expresses as they swept through the Rickmansworth curve, and to report by telegram any instance of bits being nicked out of the wooden platforms!

In the field of book publicity the LMS tended to rely largely on outside authors. In connection with the British Empire Exhibition at Wembley, a 35 page (art) booklet about the train control system, *The Magic Wand of Transport* was produced for the company by *The Railway Gazette*; it sold at sixpence. The celebrations of the Liverpool & Manchester Railway Centenary in 1930, organised by the City of Liverpool in conjunction with the LMS, included a big exhibition in St George's Hall, a railway fair and a nightly pageant at Wavertree Park, while the well-known historian C. F. Dendy Marshall was commissioned to write a 62-page booklet *One Hundred Years of Railways* published by the company at a shilling. Edmund Vale was another author commissioned to write *Ships of the Narrow Seas* and edit a series of route-descriptive guide books beginning with *The Track of the Royal Scot*. The last pre-war title in this series, *The Track of the Coronation Scot* (1937) reflected the growing interest in railways *qua* railways by including details of the train equipment and tables of the up and down passing times. The centenary of the London & Birmingham was celebrated with *A Century of Progress*, 44 quarto pages plus colour cover for sixpence, children half price. A collectors' item, its price has more than kept pace with inflation.

As a sequel to the North American tour of The Royal Scot, the LMS published a commemorative booklet titled *The Triumph of the Royal Scot* and the publicity people got one of their oddest assignments: to design within the specified dimensions of the engine nameplate commemorating the tour, a caption under the engine name recording concisely as much data as possible in letters of specified height: the department duly obliged!

The LMS had a particularly heavy commitment to joint publicity activity with its many holiday resorts. Providing the railway's name was mentioned it contributed to the resorts'-run advertising, took pages in their guide books and laid on many a preview trip. Close relationships were maintained with the principal resorts' tourist organisations: if the

LMS needed the Blackpool traffic to survive, Blackpool was even more dependent on the railway whose stationmasters were indeed honoured citizens.

By 1929 the LMS was issuing a million and a quarter guide books, covering all kinds of holiday resorts served by the system. Biggest item within this output was the annual *Holidays by LMS* (6d), containing over 700 pages, 200 of them illustrated, with a list of over 10,000 hotels and boarding houses: the revision and up-dating was rather like painting the Forth Bridge – the work took most of the year between publishing one issue and completing the next one for press. Stationmasters were expected to play their part in securing advertisements and of course selling copies to likely passengers.

1932 saw the beginning of a great upsurge of activity in the departments. With the appointment of Ernest Lemon as vice-president in charge of both the commercial and operating aspects of the railway traffic, with Ashton Davies leading the commercial push under him, the philosophy was to go out and get business. That meant advertising directly and indirectly for passengers and freight as never before. But the greatest pressure fell upon the hitherto small press section. This was first enlarged by the appointment in 1932 of a seasoned Fleet Street journalist who was also a contributor to the railway technical and enthusiast press, D. S. M. Barrie (later to become general manager of BR's Eastern Region). This was nicely in time for the first major acceleration of

Showpiece. An ex L&Y horse trailer carrying a set of LMS posters specially commissioned from eminent artists at Blackpool around 1924. The posters included one showing Aberdeenshire countryside, a mounted Lifeguard, the Peak District, a driver's cab at night (almost certainly an LNWR Claughton) and a station scene.

139

LMS THE PERMANENT WAY
RELAYING
BY STANHOPE FORBES, R.A.

The Permanent Way, by Stanhope Forbes RA. An example of LMS posters of the mid 1920s. The company commissioned a number of famous Royal Academicians to paint posters under the aegis of their Advertising & Publicity Officer, G. H. Loftus Allen. The location appears to be the north end of Tring Cutting with Pitstone Cement Works on the right.

passenger services and for the trial runs and subsequent record breaking performances of Stanier's new locomotives. By this time Lemon, who had a great appreciation of the value of publicity, swiftly and firmly removed some rather traditional barriers of reticence and reluctance. A photo-news capability was undertaken by Leonard Croft; this not only won front page pictures in more than one national daily, but also built up an effective photographic library.

Expansion was far from confined to the function of Press and BBC relations; two new activities were to be launched through staff newspapers and films. The LMS already had a house magazine (also available to the public) which traditionally covered a pattern of staff changes, ambulance and temperance movements, horticulture, 'fur and feather', short articles and other recreational and entertainment activities. The management felt that this valuable medium should not be used as a propaganda vehicle, but instead, two free circulation staff newspapers should be introduced for the operating and commercial departments respectively, *On Time* and *Quota News*, the latter symbolising Ashton Davies' quota system. Targets were set for every station and district, the competitors being grouped in leagues, each with its trophy for best performance. (The best quota story was that of a relatively small goods station which unexpectedly became the destination of a large and long-lasting traffic in pipes consigned 'carriage forward' the receipts thus credited to it, submerging its otherwise modest quota. A bewildered stationmaster/goods agent was eventually summoned to Euston to collect a handsome shield before a distinguished but equally bewildered audience.) *On Time* in addition to reporting on the performance of divisional and district leagues for punctuality, improvement in the rate of engine failures and so on also contained all-line and localised feature articles.

Then the department became responsible for the production and distribution of cine films, (both training and instructional for the staff, and general interest for the public) largely supplanting sets of lantern slides. These films were produced to the company's requirements by a professional film unit, a satellite of the photo agency Topical Press; the department was responsible for distribution and showing. It established a cutting-viewing theatre in the basement of Euston House and two mobile cinemas (ex-LNWR vehicles converted) which travelled the system showing films – numbering about 150 by 1939 – to staff, their families and the public. Films like the lantern slides could also be rented by interested organisations. Much concerned with these distributions and showing arrangements was A. J. (Charlie) Potter, whose career eventually ended as distribution manager for British Transport Films. He still recalls his department's achievement in persuading the operating management to close the Western Division North Wales main line between Colwyn Bay and Llandudno Junction on a Sunday morning to enable the film crew, suitably but somewhat perilously mounted on a flat truck, to film two period and one modern locomotives following on adjacent tracks. At that time the Sabbath was still well kept on the North Wales Coast and one senior official refused to break it for mere publicity people. The job was given to the Llandudno Junction shed foreman.

The outbreak of war greatly affected the department; between one third and half the staff went on active service, some immediately while, with the exception of a very small section which remained at the emergency office in London to deal with the newspapers, BBC and the Ministry of Information, the rest functioned from huts in Hertfordshire. The work content was greatly changed: both the departmental journals and the *LMS Magazine* were suspended, but in order to keep the staff informed of what could safely be published, a news-sheet was soon started for all-line free circulation; its apt title was *Carry On*. Advertisements were now on behalf of the Railway Executive Committee.

Sadly, both Loftus Allen and his deputy died during the war, and both Publicity and the ERO (paper and printing) departments came temporarily under the direction of J. O'Neill, a (needlessly) feared character. It was the LMS practice for formal correspondence between departments to be signed in the name of the head, so occasionally there were

Higher Speed at Reduced Cost

The term 'permanent way' is a serious misnomer; it needs constant maintenance and periodical renewal. But in the inter-war years it did tend towards permanence in two important respects, track technique and layout.

The use of bullhead rail secured in cast-iron chairs on softwood sleepers was standard on the LMS as in Britain generally. Rail had increased in weight to an almost universal 96lb/yd section for main lines, and – pioneered by the LNWR – in length to a common 60ft. The main weakness was at rail joints, which became dipped due to bending of the rail ends, ballast settlement and fishplate wear. The use of short two-bolt fishplates, allowing the joint sleepers to be brought close together, was tried to get better end support, but was unsuccessful due to difficulty in effective ballast packing under these sleepers. The LMS was prominent in another solution, installing in 1936 experimental main line lengths of heavy flat-bottomed rail; a new (to Britain) 113lb/yd section was used, with cast iron base plates and bolted fastenings. This was the forerunner of the flat-bottomed track now standard.

Layouts changed little, and there were many relics of early railway construction which had become an embarrassment. In the mid-1930s the LMS developed a new type of junction turnout which, while retaining long crossing timbers, allowed cant (tilt) to be provided for the diverging road and thus an increase in speed. The secret was the use of two-level chairs. The crossing timbers were themselves canted in the ballast, with the crossing and its closure rails supported in a tapering series of thick-base chairs to keep the straight road level. A further development was the use of switch diamonds on flat-angle crossings to give support to the wheel at all times.

The Day Begins. A 1947 LMS poster by Terence Cuneo painted in the round-house at Willesden, a depot which did not normally see the Class 7P 4-6-2s. The Duchess Pacific is shown in LMS post-war lined out black livery.

hilarious situations where the publicity assistant signing 'for Jos O'Neill' a memo requesting something to be printed, was to receive an answer turning the proposal down, or demanding some change to be made before printing, also addressed to, and signed by or 'for Jos O'Neill'.

There were many administrative wrinkles but nobody could doubt the publicity's success in putting the railway on its feet and there remain many fond memories of famous LMS headlines, posters and films. Especially an enormous amount was done to arouse the interest and competitive spirit of the staff.

 THE DAY BEGINS

12
THE FINEST COACHES
IN THE COUNTRY

Whatever problems the LMS might have had with personality and policy clashes in the field of locomotive design from 1923, the carriage department had a much more painless succession. R. W. Reid the Midland carriage superintendent took charge – and everyone knew that in carriages the Midland was supreme. Midland carriages indeed had an impeccable pedigree right from the 1870s when in a social revolution the Midland had abolished second class, upgraded third class and admitted third class passengers to all trains.

From then on general purpose Midland carriages were without doubt the best in the country. Perhaps the only features on which the Midland could be criticised were its reluctance to introduce through gangways between coaches and its passion for gas lighting. Although corridor trains with restaurant cars did appear on the Midland many of its expresses of the new century until World War I were formed with non-corridor stock, even with restaurant cars in which passengers sat for the whole of the journey or joined at an intermediate station – a feature influencing LMS thinking in later years. As to the technicalities of carriage design, having reintroduced the clerestory roof in the mid 1890s the Midland was reluctant to let it go and not until the World War I period did the semi-elliptical roof appear on main line corridor stock, long after other 'clerestory' companies had abandoned it. Midland stock built after World War I designed by Reid – only the third Midland carriage superintendent in the 50 years from 1874 to 1923 – set the pattern for the first LMS coaches of the new era.

What of the coaches of the other companies? The largest number – over 5,000 – of course came from the LNWR. Certainly the LNWR and the West Coast Joint Stock fleet had some of the most magnificent coaches ever built in Britain with the sleeping and dining cars, the massive 12-wheel corridor coaches built for the 'Corridor' (the early afternoon Euston–Glasgow/Edinburgh/Aberdeen train) and the Euston–Liverpool American boat sets. In contrast, while the LNWR had some very adequate general purpose corridor and non-corridor stock it also bequeathed the LMS an extensive fleet of antiques dating from the 1880s and 1890s.

In Scotland the Caledonian, too, was a railway of contrasts. There were many non-bogie coaches on suburban and branch routes but the prestige Glasgow–Aberdeen services had been equipped with splendid 12-wheel corridor coaches – the Grampian stock – from 1905. The Caledonian did not own any restaurant cars other than its share of the West Coast Joint Stock cars and just before World War I used Pullman

Midland Diner
The Midland had not been able to beat the LNWR in speed between London and Manchester; but it wooed the public with excellent meals, a scenic route and a useful facility for seats in the dining cars, first and third, could be reserved the day before by telephoning the stationmaster's office at St Pancras or Manchester Central. No charge was made.

You could stay in your seat throughout the journey, consuming morning coffee, a solid five-course lunch, afternoon tea or dinner, or a combination of these delights. All credit to the LMS for retaining for a long time this splendid alternative to the Euston route, and even publicising it in a booklet *The Track of the Twenty-Fives*. The Manchester trains left St Pancras at two-hourly intervals virtually throughout the day, starting at 8.25am.

The LMS carriage line of descent: With the last of the Midland's carriage superintendents, R. W. Reid, taking on LMS coach design inevitably Midland practice predominated in the early years of the new company. Top: Midland corridor first with clerestory roof built in 1912. Right upper: LMS corridor brake third of the mid 1920s with side doors to each compartment. Right middle: One of the luxury coaches of the late 1920s with end doors, and large picture windows to each compartment, with a deeper window level and no waist panel. Right lower: Corridor composite of the Stanier era built in the mid 1930s, the basic design of which with detail modifications lasted the LMS for the rest of its existence.

cars for dining services on its principal trains. Surprisingly the Highland Railway, despite the length of its main lines with trains taking several hours between Perth, Inverness and Wick had few corridor coaches and no restaurant cars, while the Glasgow & South Western, like its Caledonian neighbour, had a variety of stock including a handful of restaurant cars.

Back in England the Lancashire & Yorkshire with its cross country and complex suburban services handed over some passable but not outstanding corridor coaches and many non-corridors old and new. The Furness, North Stafford and London, Tilbury & Southend lines were primarily local in character with mainly non-corridor stock although the Furness had a few corridor vehicles for longer distance through services over other railways, while the Tilbury line had its unique sets of corridor stock for through working over the District Railway to Ealing, some of the coaches from which ended their days in military use on the Shropshire & Montgomeryshire Railway. Some delightful oddments were inherited by the LMS such as the open end balcony coach from the Garstang & Knott End Railway and the four Indian looking saloon coaches with balconies from the narrow-gauge Leek & Manifold Valley.

That then was the picture of coaches taken over by the LMS in 1923, with a wide variety of sizes – 8ft to 9ft in width and lengths from 26ft to 65ft – in broadly three groups, non-corridor, non-corridor lavatory stock and corridor stock. Reid was faced with producing fairly standard stock to suit everybody, and with LMS refinements of basic Midland designs he succeeded by using side door side corridor compartment coaches for main line services and non-corridor compartment coaches for suburban

144

or local services, some of which had between compartment lavatories. However another type of general-purpose coach also appeared for long distance services, the open saloon coach with end doors – vestibule coaches as they were called by the LMS – and on many services passengers had the choice of side corridor compartments or open coaches although many of the open coaches were intended for dining purposes, being marshalled next to kitchen or restaurant cars.

A distinctive design feature was the twin window arrangement at each seating bay with one window being a droplight, above which were ventilating windows with rotating glass vanes which could be set by passengers to face or trail the airstream. On a few of the first class vestibule coaches there was an element of double glazing, for inner and outer droplights were provided. In the third class, seats were in bays of four, mostly with tables, while in the first class the seats were in facing pairs on one side of the central passageway and in fours on the other. Some third class coaches had the two plus four arrangement for dining purposes.

The coaches had timber bodies with wood framing, and outer panels covered by wooden mouldings, the latter finely picked out in black and gold lining edged with vermilion, which set off the crimson lake body

Mass production of timber-bodied coaches in the mid 1920s after Reid streamlined building methods. The different parts of the body were jig built and assembled more or less as a kit.

colour in much the same way as the Midland Railway livery had done for more than half a century. The coaches were carried on steel underframes but the principles of the timber body construction had not changed since the dawn of railways and the road mail and stage coaches before that. But early on in LMS days Reid reorganised carriage construction methods at Derby and Wolverton on mass production lines with pre-fabrication of major components, final erection being effectively a bolt together operation. Yet while streamlining production of timber-bodied coaches the LMS also entered the field of all-steel coaches, partly because of the need to build coaches more quickly than the capacity of its own works allowed and partly to provide work in the steel industry. Orders for more than 200 open saloon thirds and brake thirds and 300 full brake/parcels vans went to outside industry. They had steel body framing and flush steel panelled sides yet they appeared in the ornate fully lined livery with non-existing panels picked out almost exactly as though they had the mouldings of the timber bodied coaches.

Although following Midland design and practice, the LMS had adopted a length of 57ft and a body width of 9ft for much of its general purpose stock, a length which had been used by the LNWR and Caledonian for some years before the Grouping, and adopted also by the Midland right at the end having used 54ft for many years before that. Restaurant and sleeping cars though had been much longer, up to 65ft in length and carried on six wheel bogies. Suburban stock had been much more variable and there were still large numbers of non-bogie four- and six-wheel coaches on such services at the grouping. Indeed some new four-wheel stock of Caledonian design was put in service on the Balerno branch services just around the time of the grouping. Even though the LMS used the 57ft length for much of its new non-corridor stock it still produced 54ft coaches for a few specified services – even a handful of 51ft coaches for new set trains on the Carthcart Circle service in Glasgow.

On the Tilbury and Southend services the LMS provided more than a dozen lengthy 11 coach sets of non-corridor coaches seating more than a thousand passengers in each, with just over 900 third class and 120 first class. In deference to the outer suburban nature of the journey of up to an hour or so toilets were provided in two coaches – but serving just two compartments in each coach, meaning that at most only 20 third class and 14 first class passengers could avail themselves of the facility. Even then they would have had to be fairly skilled in quickly identifying the coaches concerned particularly if joining at an intermediate station! Much has been written about the Great Eastern Jazz service out of Liverpool Street in shifting thousands of city workers each day, but less than justice has been done to the LTSR and its successors in transporting much of the population of Southend-on-Sea to and from London every day.

Until the mid 1920s the LMS had largely continued what had gone before in carriage design. But from 1927/8 it took the next step forward which moved passenger comfort on the LMS into a new area and set the pattern for the next three decades. The principal change was in side

How the LMS 8F Went to War
In addition to all its exertions within the British Isles, the LMS played an unusual part overseas, for the Stanier Class 8F 2-8-0 was chosen by the War Office as its standard locomotive. This decision was made as early as 1939, too late for the completion of the 240 locomotives concerned to be sent to France – perhaps a blessing in disguise. In the interim ancient stalwarts such as the GWR Dean Goods 0-6-0s had to fill the gap. But that is another story.

So prior to the introduction of the Riddles Austerity 2-8-0 and 2-10-0, also built for wartime use, and later the huge input of USA 2-8-0s built for the second front invasion of Europe, the Stanier 8F, constructed in many railway workshops round Britain, was to be the motive power for the War Office support services. But in which theatre of war? By dint of necessity this was to be the Middle East as everywhere else (by 1941 when shipments began) was occupied by the Germans. Thus 22 LMS type 2-8-0s, fully erected along with their tenders, were shipped out; eighteen reached Egypt and Palestine taking the long journey via the Cape, though four were lost with their ships. The railway authorities received them with open arms and the class was used not only on the Egyptian State Railway's extension into the Western Desert but also on the Suez line and the newly-constructed link which crossed the Canal at El Kantara to the tracks of the Palestinian Railway, trains running to Lydda and Haifa. A further 24 engines went into service between August 1941 and February 1942: some were fitted with armour plating covering the boiler and part of the cab.

Another batch of 8Fs built in 1940–41 entered the war on a quite different basis. In 1939 the Turks had ordered 37 large
continued overleaf

continued

2-10-0s of German design (almost identical to the Reichsbahn Class 50) from British manufacturers but war meant that the British need came first. While not fighting companions, the Turks generally supported the Allies and were naturally a little upset. Embarrassment increased when the Germans offered to do the job promptly. So Britain despatched 22 LMS 8Fs, the long way round (for ease of shipping partly dismantled) by way of the Cape, the Red Sea and the Suez Canal. Sadly the war moved too fast.

The locomotives were discharged on to islands near Port Said and at similar dumps at Alexandria and Haifa. Twelve locomotives, all in bits, were stranded for six months or more with parts needing to be identified, let alone cleaned of corrosion. Eventually they reached the Turkish Railways workshops at Sivas and two LMS representatives went to oversee the work (one of them R. G. Jarvis).

By October 1941 the various parts began to arrive at Sivas; it needs little imagination to envisage the bumps and distortion which took place on the way let alone the corrosion necessitating chipping off layers of thick rust, regrinding valve gear and other moving parts. But the task was completed by early November when TCCD No 45151 all smartly painted was put at the head of the 18.45 'Posta' piloting a massive looking Swedish 2-8-0.

The 8F was not the engine that the TCCD really wanted – the originally ordered German machine was 50 per cent larger! But it was a good try, appreciated by the Turks who nicknamed the Stanier engines the 'Churchills'. Over forty years later the 8Fs were still at work as yard shunters. Thirty-seven German type 2-10-0s were eventually supplied from Britain in 1948.

corridor stock by the elimination of side doors to each compartment, for henceforth the LMS built only coaches with end doors. Second was the introduction of single wide picture windows to each bay or compartment and third was the improvement in internal decor with selected Empire timbers for partition and wall facings, in later years labelled to show the type of wood. Seating moquettes were thoughtfully chosen and seat cushions, especially in the first class were well sprung and padded, a total contrast to the stuffed horse-hair seats used by some of the LMS constituents.

The first coaches to the new pattern were built only in small quantities and were effectively luxury coaches – a lounge first class coach with guards' and luggage accommodation, a semi-open first class coach, and a more conventional seven-bay open saloon coach seating 42. The lounge brake coaches seated 10 passengers in low leather upholstered armchairs and settees but the semi-open firsts had conventional seats in three compartments and three bays in the open saloon. The compartments seated only four passengers so that all had a corner seat but the open bays were arranged with seats in twos and fours on each side of the passageway. The 42 seat open coach was unclassed but was used for third class dining. The new coaches were introduced to the Euston–Glasgow Royal Scot service and then to other principal expresses. Unlike the LNER and GWR, the LMS (with one exception) never built complete sets of coaches for its principal express trains so that newer coaches were often (indeed usually) mixed with older stock.

The new pattern stock was further refined in 1929/30 by having the wide picture windows made deeper at 3ft instead of a little more than 2ft 6in. Windows in compartments and some windows in open coaches were made as frameless balanced droplights so that the whole window could be lowered into the lower part of the body. Small batches of both open and side corridor third class coaches were built to this pattern on 60ft underframes which meant that there was much more leg room between seats, the third class compartments being 6ft 6in between partitions instead of the usual 6ft. First-class compartments were by now 7ft 6in between partitions, a length which remained standard until World War II. However the third class coaches at 60ft length were probably too luxurious and full thirds and third brakes soon reverted to 57ft with a reduction of compartment size to about 6ft 3in.

But fine though these coaches were LMS carriage design was to undergo further changes with the arrival in 1932 of William Stanier to head the LMS mechanical engineering department. Although coming from the GWR Stanier did not pursue GWR carriage design practices – indeed it would have been a retrograde step had he done so – other than to adopt steel panels on timber framing for the external finish not only for the sides but also the ends and roof. Steel bodyside panels had been used for a year or two before Stanier's arrival but window frames, roofs and ends had continued to be of wood. Stanier's designs were completely flush-sided, with rounded window corners and for the first time with sliding window ventilators in the upper part of the main window in corridor and open saloon stock. Thus there were no mouldings and

Survivor. During World War II the Stanier 8F class 2-8-0 was used by the War Department as one of its standard types, locomotives going as far afield as Persia (Iran). Most ended up in the Middle East (Palestine and Egypt) but some were sold to the Turks as compensation for German classes lost to them by hostilities. Known as the 'Churchills' some of these locomotives lasted in service until the mid 1980s. TCCD No 45151 (co-incidentally an LMR number of a Stanier 4-6-0) is seen here shunting at Irmak in April 1977.

Stanier Coronation class Pacific No 6230 Duchess of Buccleuch *in full cry up the steep climb towards Shap summit having spurned banking assistance at Tebay. This was the first of the five locomotives originally built in non-streamlined form in LMS days. Reproduced from* The Railway Paintings of Alan Fearnley *by permission of Alan Fearnley.*

*Stanier's Greatest. In BR red livery
the originally blue and silver
streamlined Pacific No 46229*
Duchess of Hamilton *passes
Wennington (between Carnforth and
Settle Junction) heading a SLOA
special from Carnforth to Leeds on
12 April 1982. Now preserved and
cared for by the Friends of the
National Railway Museum, the
engine has a fascinating history.
Sent to the USA as No 6220*
Coronation *in 1939 on a goodwill
tour, it returned to Britain during
hostilities due to shortage of motive*

*power, was de-streamlined in
January 1948 and eventually
withdrawn from regular service on
15 February 1964. Purchased for
static exhibition by Butlins it was on
display at Minehead until 13 March
1975. It was placed on loan to the
Friends of the National Railway
Museum in May 1976 and restored
to working order. Butlins are seeking
to dispose of its locomotives during
1987 and it is hoped that York will
retain No 46229 for future
generations.*

panels yet the livery still had the lining applied to provide a modified panelling style, although within a year or two a much simpler lining style was introduced which did away with panels and gave just two single gold lines above the windows and below the roof respectively and gold/black/gold lining at the waist. Economy dictated the use of deep yellow paint in place of gold on some coaches. Soon after the formation of the LMS the daughter of one of its officers designed a circular motif – certainly it could not be called a coat of arms in the heraldic sense. It incorporated the rose of England, a dragon wing (crest of City of London) and the Scottish Thistle and adorned the sides of most gangwayed coaches.

From the early 1930s once the Stanier designs had been evolved – and most continued the internal layouts and dimensions of earlier coaches – the experiments with small batches were virtually over. Lengths became more or less standardised at 57ft for most general purpose corridor and

Luxury on suburban services – one of the saloons built for the Manchester–Blackpool club trains.

153

THE FINEST COACHES IN THE COUNTRY

Opposite. Train formation of the 1937 Coronation Scot. Note the two kitchen cars and the high proportion of open saloon seating.

non-corridor stock, although even in the Stanier regime two 11 coach trains of 54ft coaches were built for the Tilbury and Southend lines, 60ft for corridor composite first and third class coaches, 62ft for a particular type of brake composite, 65ft for a few open firsts and some third class sleepers, 68ft for restaurant/kitchen cars and sleeping cars, and 69ft for sleeping cars, the latter two lengths on six-wheel bogies.

At the other end of the scale were the 50ft full kitchen cars which were fitted not only for gas cooking but had gas lighting as well, the only LMS built coaches to be so fitted. Gas lighting though was still used on a large number of coaches handed on by the LMS constituents. Although electric lighting had begun to be used fairly widely from the turn of the century not all railways wanted to get involved with the added weight of dynamos and batteries which meant greater train weight overall taxing the small locomotives of the time. The Midland had two bad train fires following collisions before World War I but did not heed the lessons while Midland gas lit coaches were again involved in a fire after a collision in LMS days at Charfield on the Birmingham–Bristol main line. There was an unsolved mystery following this accident when two children's bodies were discovered amidst the wreckage but could not be identified as belonging to other passengers nor were they claimed by anyone else afterwards.

The Stanier era heralded more comfort for third-class passengers in side corridor stock for all new vehicles were fitted out to carry only six passengers in each compartment instead of eight hitherto, and moreover armrests were provided to divide the three seats on each side. The armrests did however fold up into the seat back so that four passengers could be seated if the train was full but passengers already seated three-a-side were usually reluctant to lift the armrests to squeeze another passenger in. The Stanier coaches continued a feature introduced a year or two earlier in which the corridor doors to the compartments were formed as twin doors both of which slid open, instead of the single door flanked by side windows, the conventional arrangement on other railways – except on some Southern corridor electric stock which also had the twin sliding doors.

The typical LMS express usually included both open and side corridor first and third class accommodation, some of the open coaches being used for dining purposes. Some of the business expresses between Euston and Birmingham, Liverpool or Manchester did substantial dining trade with as many as four dining vehicles. One or two even had two kitchens to cope with the numbers, particularly on the Mancunian and the Merseyside Express, the latter sometimes loading particularly on Fridays to 16 coaches. Some of the seats in the dining car could be reserved for the entire journey, as in the days of non-corridor dining cars, but others were left fluid for casual trade from the rest of the train.

The LMS carriage seat on the whole was very sympathetic to passenger shape and accommodated the ins and outs of most passenger bodies very well, unlike Great Western seats which went in when they should have gone out and vice-versa, or the LNER bucket seat of much of Gresley's corridor stock which really felt as though it was a bucket.

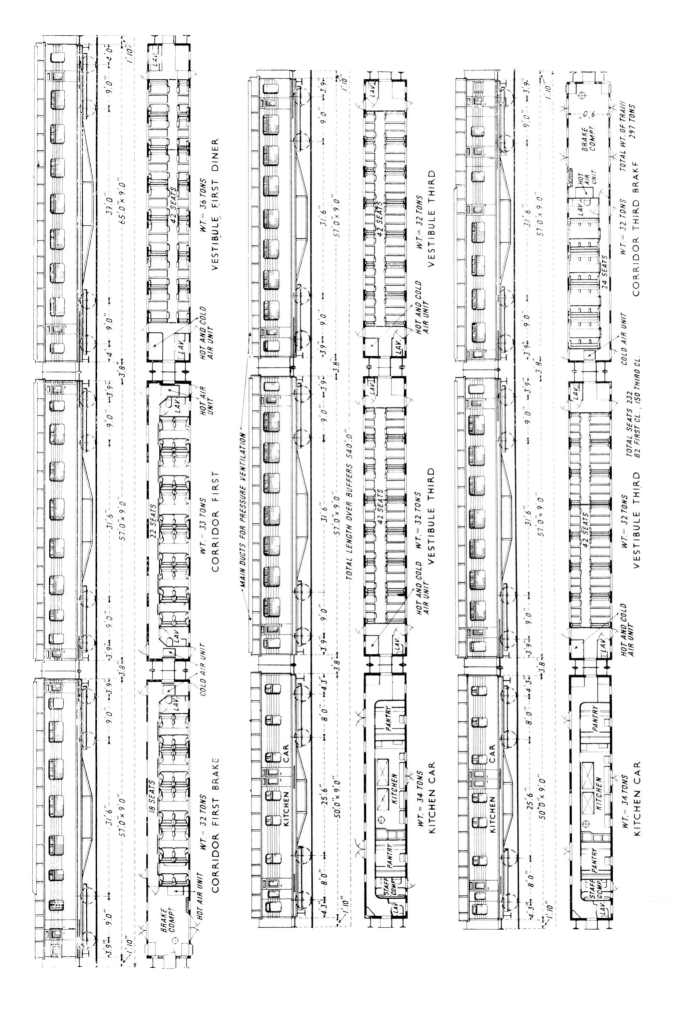

VESTIBULE FIRST DINER
WT = 36 TONS
42 SEATS
HOT AND COLD AIR UNIT

CORRIDOR FIRST
WT = 33 TONS
22 SEATS
HOT AIR UNIT
COLD AIR UNIT

CORRIDOR FIRST BRAKE
WT = 32 TONS
18 SEATS
BRAKE COMPT
HOT AIR UNIT

MAIN DUCTS FOR PRESSURE VENTILATION

TOTAL LENGTH OVER BUFFERS 540.0"

VESTIBULE THIRD
WT = 32 TONS
42 SEATS
HOT AND COLD AIR UNIT

KITCHEN CAR
WT = 34 TONS
KITCHEN
PANTRY
STAFF COMPT
LAV.

VESTIBULE THIRD
WT = 32 TONS
42 SEATS
HOT AND COLD AIR UNIT

VESTIBULE THIRD
WT = 32 TONS
42 SEATS
HOT AND COLD AIR UNIT

KITCHEN CAR
WT = 34 TONS
KITCHEN
PANTRY

CORRIDOR THIRD BRAKF
WT = 32 TONS
24 SEATS
BRAKE COMPT
HOT AIR UNIT
COLD AIR UNIT

TOTAL WT. OF TRAIII 297 TONS
TOTAL SEATS 232
82 FIRST CL., 150 THIRD CL.

Luxury for the ordinary traveller – Stanier corridor coaches included armrests and reading lights in third class compartments. The large windows of late 1920s stock were modified in the Stanier coaches to include sliding ventilator windows in the top part. Decor was in wood veneers from 'Empire timbers'.

Even in suburbia the LMS commuter was in much more luxurious accommodation with soft seats and nearly 6ft 3in between partitions more than 1ft wider than the cramped sit up and beg seats of the Gresley Quad-Arts out of King's Cross or the Quint-Arts at Liverpool Street where passengers in a full train were faced with interlacing knees with the passenger opposite them, and standing passengers had to decide on whose shoes they would stand, for there was hardly any room for standing feet to fit in between the seated ones. On the LMS it was much more gentle. Around Manchester it was even more so for there were the club trains, the luxury long distance residential services to Blackpool, Southport and Llandudno which included first class club saloons, armchairs, reserved seats and stewards to serve liquid refreshment.

As for the LMS in its later years the general run of the mill coaches changed little, all-steel bodies came again just at nationalisation, round porthole toilet windows on post World War II corridor stock but no real differences. There was though one more flight of fancy with the Coronation Scot trains of 1937. They were not new but were mostly refurbished existing coaches although two types were built specially. First class compartments seated just four passengers like the luxury stock of the previous decade but while the Coronation Scot trains did not show quite the advances of the rival LNER Coronation sets, they did not need to, for LMS general purpose coaches were far and away superior to similar LNER and GWR stock. True the Coronation Scot sets were strikingly liveried in blue with broad silver lines at window level and they were pressure ventilated internally. But that was as far as they went and the service itself lasted only for two years. Even though further Coronation Scot coaches were built specially, one set going to America for the New York World Fair in 1939, and others completed at the end of World War II, they never ran as a train and as articulated pairs with non standard seating they could not be used on seat registered services and were a general nuisance to the operating department. Most finished up on long-distance residential or holiday relief trains.

The LMS also dabbled in articulation for pairs of vestibule coaches for excursion use and for a few three-coach suburban sets. Lightweight all-metal construction techniques were also tried, particularly in the new suburban electric stock for the Wirral and Liverpool–Southport lines in 1938/9. The latter could provide BR with some design lessons for high density seating in open saloons combined with air-operated sliding doors.

Most LMS-built coaches survived well into BR days, some into the 1960s. Even some of the pre-grouping coaches had long lives, Midland clerestories lasted into the 1950s, Caledonian Grampian 12 wheelers were seen at odd times on Birmingham and London suburban services, and even a North Stafford coach on the Tilbury line, all late in the 1950s. Certainly the early BR coaches were no better than their LMS predecessors and mostly rode much worse. Indeed except for air conditioning and sound insulation on today's trains LMS coaches would stand comparison with anything built by BR in recent years in standards of comfort, especially seat comfort, but not in strength, for the BR Mk III coach is probably the safest in the world.

Electrification

The LMS inherited a small portfolio of isolated electrified networks: the suburban lines from Euston to Watford, and Broad Street to Richmond, used third and fourth rail at 630V dc. On Merseyside the ex L&Y line from Exchange to Southport and Crossens, and to Ormskirk was electrified on 600V dc third rail. By contrast, in Manchester the L&Y had put in a unique third rail system using 1,200V dc with side contact to Bury, and Holcombe Brook. The latter branch was originally electrified on the 3,600V dc overhead system. Further north the trains on the Midland's line from Lancaster to Morecambe and Heysham collected current at 6,600V single phase ac from an overhead catenary.

Getting further electrification projects to the starting gate was as difficult as with the most recalcitrant horse – as H. E. O'Brien, the new company's electrical engineer, discovered to his cost. Almost from day one he worked on proposals to electrify the West Coast main line between Crewe and Carlisle, no less, at 1,500V dc with overhead catenary. Tests were run to assess power demand and diagrams produced of a Swiss-style 2-D-2 locomotive to handle heavy trains over Shap. He referred to the scheme in some detail in a paper to the Institution of Electrical Engineers in 1924. This brought down the wrath of the Euston hierarchy on his head, and he resigned.

If there was one section of the *continued overleaf*

The LMS inherited several isolated suburban electric systems. In London the LNWR's electrification of the Broad Street–Richmond/ Euston–Watford lines was completed just before the Grouping of 1922. Although the LMS built new compartment stock to increase service frequency much of the stock was built by the LNWR, magnificent open saloon coaches in three coach sets, perhaps slow in unloading and loading through the end sliding doors but with the most comfortable seating of any suburban electric stock in the country, including arm chairs in the first class. This train at Richmond in 1925 includes a set still in LNWR livery at the far end.

Highlight of LMS-built electric stock was that for the Liverpool–Southport line built in 1939/40 to replace the original L&Y trains. Lightweight and with air doors they had high density seating yet were a neat design inside and out.

continued

LMS which cried out for electric traction it was the London, Tilbury & Southend, a real operator's headache. It carried a heavy, intensive passenger service, running at tight headways in the peaks, and hauled by moderate size engines supplied with bad water. Tentative electrification schemes were discussed but were relegated to dusty shelves.

Just two new schemes did come to fruition. The first was the 8¾ miles of the Manchester, South Junction and Altrincham line, jointly with the LNER, which was electrified in 1931 on the 1,500V dc overhead system. This was the first fruit of the Government-appointed Weir Committee, whose recommendation of this system remained valid for nearly thirty years. The other was the

Wirral lines from Birkenhead Park (where they made an end-on connection with the independent Mersey Railway) to West Kirby and New Brighton, just over 10 route miles. This was done under a Government Loan Guarantee scheme. The Mersey Railway used the third and fourth rail system at 650V dc and the LMS trains had to be equipped to suit, but they also had earth return through the wheels since the LMS Wirral lines proper had only the outside positive third rail and track return. To balance the working of LMS trains over Mersey tracks the Mersey stock normally worked the New Brighton branch belonging to the LMS, so that Mersey stock also had to be equipped for running on third rail only as well as its own third and fourth rail system.

13
RUNNING SHEDS AND WORKSHOPS

The steam locomotive running shed – later it acquired the more up-market title of 'motive power depot' – may have been Mecca for young railway enthusiasts but it sorely tried the enthusiasm of those who worked there. The preparation, disposal, cleaning and repair of its charges were carried out under conditions which, fortunately for the management were not governed by the Factory Acts and would have been the despair of the modern Health and Safety Inspectorate.

Sheds varied widely. The generality were either dead-end or straight-through (the latter including the east wind) usually gloomy beneath a low roof of limited light penetration. The G&SW was a notable exception in providing some with a high roof, improving light and smoke clearance. By contrast with these straight sheds, the bigger Midland sheds were usually formed of one or more square 'roundhouses' with central turntable and perhaps 24 radial stabling tracks of varying lengths. Some of these could take on a positively cathedral-like atmosphere to the superficial observer. However, those who worked in them saw other, less desirable features – vicious draughts, bitter cold in winter, gloom, uneven floors, leaky roofs and, when the washout engines were being fired up from cold in the early evening, an atmosphere that would blunt a sharp knife. In the Manchester area, where before clean air legislation there was much chronic bronchitis, sufferers in the footplate grades were taken off locomotive work and put 'on the brush' sweeping up in such hell-holes!

Most work on servicing locomotives was not done in the shed anyway, but in the great outdoors of the shed yard. Methods here had barely changed in a hundred years, and the disposal of engines, including coaling, cleaning fires, ashpans and smokeboxes, could only be described as degrading hard labour performed in an atmosphere of heat, heavy lifting and flying ash and grit. Little wonder that after World War II, with full employment, staff for such work could be difficult to recruit and even harder to retain.

The LMS inherited around 260 assorted establishments; their unsatisfactory features were instantly known, even if their rectification came low in the order of priority. In April 1923, Derby's district locomotive superintendent told the local engineering club: 'There is an urgent and immediate call to take action to improve locomotive shed working. Methods are in use which would not be tolerated in any modern engineering plant.' Only five depots, all of LNWR origin, possessed mechanical coaling plants; that at Edge Hill exploited a unique site which allowed hopper wagons on a high level siding to discharge direct into storage bunkers above the locomotives.

Shed Life

Shed life was seldom straightforward and often adventurous. One thinks of the engines which ended up in the turntable well due to carelessness and bottled up the shed for hours. Then there were the ex LNW G2 0-8-0s in Midland hands forgetful of the regulator which worked the opposite way from standard; the number which backed off the roundhouse turntable and accelerated noisily through the shed wall was not negligible! One recalls the Newton Heath bank engine at Victoria one Saturday night, whose fireman used the lulls between trains to imbibe freely in the refreshment room bar and, when challenged by his long suffering driver, laid about him with the shovel and put him in hospital. There was a depot, which shall be nameless, where the shedmaster was also a scoutmaster and on occasion was wont to come on duty in Scout uniform, shorts, woggle et al, to the prejudice of good order and staff discipline. Then more than one mechanical foreman, in charge of the breakdown crane on a lifting job (which not infrequently pushed the crane beyond its designed limits) finished up with his crane on its side; his future career prospects were permanently stunted. And there was Trafford Park, nominally a single shed providing power for Cheshire lines and Midland Division trains. Because the CLC staff worked under GC workshop conditions while LMS staff came under normal conciliation grade conditions, the shed was divided by an invisible but impenetrable wall.

REORGANISATION OF THE MOTIVE POWER DEPARTMENT
LONDON MIDLAND & SCOTTISH RAILWAY

Map showing locations of main and garage depots throughout the system

Numbers of Motive Power Depots

No.	Depot
1A	WILLESDEN
1B	Camden
1C	Watford
2A	RUGBY
	Market Harboro'
	Seaton
2B	Bletchley
	Leighton Buzzard
	Oxford
	Newport Pagnell
	Aylesbury
2C	Northampton
2D	Nuneaton
2E	Warwick
2F	Coventry
3A	BESCOT
3B	Bushbury
3C	Walsall
	Dudley
3D	Aston
	Monument Lane
3E	Albion
	Tipton
4A'	SHREWSBURY
	Trench
	Coalport
	Ludlow
	Clee Hill
	Craven Arms
	Knighton
	Builth Road
4B	Swansea
	Carmarthen
	Llandovery
	Upper Bank
	Gurnos
	Brecon
4C	Abergavenny
	Hereford
4D	Blaenavon
4E	Tredegar
5A	CREWE NORTH
	Whitchurch
5B	Crewe South
5C	Stafford
5D	Stoke
5E	Alsager
5F	Uttoxeter
6A	CHESTER
6B	Mold Junction
6C	Birkenhead
6D	Birkenhead N.
7A	LLANDUDNO JUNCTION
7B	Bangor
7C	Holyhead
7D	Rhyl
	Denbigh
8A	EDGE HILL
8B	Warrington
	Arpley
	Over and Wharton
8C	Speke Junction
8D	Widnes

No.	Depot
	CARNFORTH (Contd.)
11D	Oxenholme
11E	Tebay
12A	CARLISLE, KINGMOOR
12B	Upperby
	Penrith
	Workington
12D	Moor Row
12E	Beattock
	Leadhills
12G	Dumfries
	Kirkcudbright
12H	Stranraer
	Millisle
	Newton Stewart
13A	PLAISTOW
13B	Devons Road
13C	Tilbury
13D	Shoeburyness
13E	Upminster
14A'	CRICKLEWOOD
	Kentish Town
14B	St. Albans
14C	
15A	WELLINGBORO'
15B	Kettering
15C	Leicester
15D	Bedford
16A	NOTTINGHAM
	Southwell
	Lincoln
16B	Peterboro'
16C	Kirkby
16D	Mansfield
17A	DERBY
	Burton
17B	Overseal
17C	Coalville
17D	Rowsley
18A	TOTON
18B	Westhouses
	Hasland
18C	Staveley
18D	
19A	SHEFFIELD
	Millhouses
19B	Canklow
19C	*Heaton Mersey
	*Brunswick
19D	†Widnes (M)
19E	*Belle Vue
19F	York
19G	*Trafford Park
20A	LEEDS
	Stourton
20B	Royston
20C	Normanton
	Manningham
20D	Ilkley
20E	Skipton
	Keighley
20F	Hellifield
20G	

No.	Depot
	BRISTOL (Contd.)
22D	Templecombe
22E	Highbridge
	Wells
23A	BANK HALL
23B	Aintree
23C	Southport
23D	Wigan (C)
23E	Lostock Hall
24A	ACCRINGTON
24B	Rose Grove
24D	Lower Darwen
24E	Blackpool
24F	Fleetwood
25A	WAKEFIELD
25B	Huddersfield
25C	Goole
25D	Mirfield
25E	Sowerby Bridge
25F	Low Moor
25G	Farnley Junction
26A	NEWTON HEATH
26B	Agecroft
26C	Bolton
26D	Bury
26E	Bacup
26F	Lees
27A	POLMADIE
27B	Hurlford
	Muirkirk
27C	Beith
	Edinburgh
27D	Carstairs
	Girvan
27E	Ayr
27F	Dalmellington
27G	Greenock
	Ardrossan
27H	Corkerhill
27J	Dawsholm
	Dumbarton
	Airdrie
27K	Yoker
28A	MOTHERWELL
28B	Hamilton
28C	Grangemouth
29A	PERTH
	Crieff
	Balquhidder
	Aberfeldy
	Blair Atholl
	Methven
29B	Stirling
	Loch Tay
29C	Dundee
29D	Blairgowrie
	Forfar
	Arbroath
	Montrose
	Brechin
	Alyth
29E	Oban
	Ballachulish
29F	Aberdeen

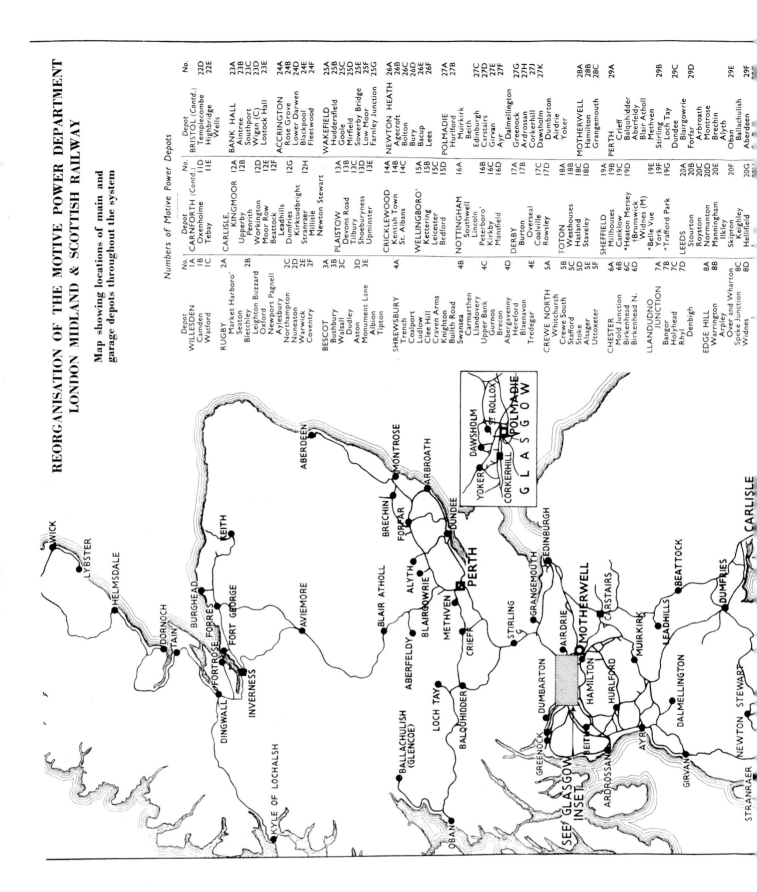

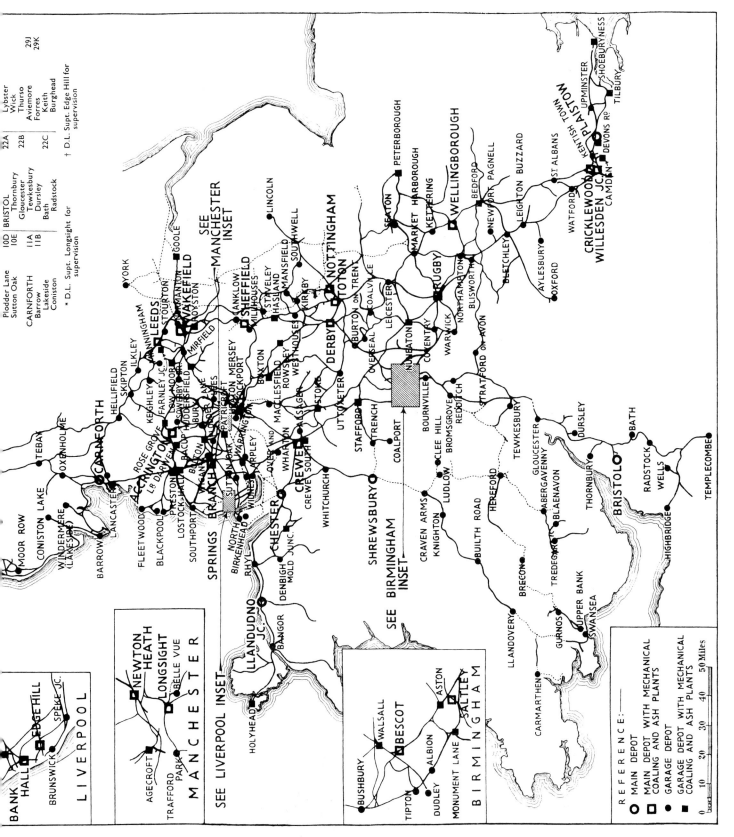

Map of LMS motive power depots in the late 1930s.

Boiler Mounting Shop

Once all the firebox work had been done, boilers were moved to an area where internal steam pipes and the main steam pipe and regulator head were fitted. This was apprentice work under supervision from outside and access to the boiler barrel was, of course, through the dome, the orifice of which was about 18in in diameter. No problem. In went the internal pipes, the regulator head was bolted in position in the dome and the main steam pipe coupled to it with a large conical joint. Now all the apprentice had to do was get out. Using a couple of 9in planks across the bottom of the barrel, with cord tied round them for retrieval, he wormed his way up through the remaining half of the dome, arms above head, past the regulator head (at least it did not have the valves in position at this stage!) and heaved a sigh of relief.

The general run of boilers – G7s and G8s – were comparatively easy. The G9s on the compounds were much more difficult, because the regulator head was bigger. But the Garratt and Lickey Banker boilers had bigger heads still. Only selected skinny apprentices were allowed into these, and even then it could be touch and go. At least one lad failed to make it from a Garratt boiler, perhaps due to a degree of panic induced by claustrophobia, and had to take out the main steam pipe and regulator head again to get his release.

The pace of change was snail-like during the 1920s. An order was placed in 1925 for a twin-bunker steel coaling plant with wagon hoist at Polmadie; no further orders were forthcoming for another six years. But under economic pressure, shed yard analysis committees were studying shed operations in depth; in 1929 each engine averaged only 11.4 hours a day *off* the shed, while coaling and fire cleaning times were very significant and augmented by engines queueing for attention. The outcome was a three-stage approach to modernisation, together with steady closure of sheds down to a figure of about 200.

Widespread modernisation started in 1931 with orders for a number of mechanical coal and ash handling plants at depots not needing major layout changes. They were a mixed bag, with both manufacturers and the railway outdoor machinery department feeling their way; both steel and concrete coaling plants were used, together with both wagon tippler and wagon hoist arrangements. At the same time an optimum yard layout was evolved to give fluidity and speed of throughput, particularly in the critical ashpit area. This formed the basis of an extensive modernisation programme launched in 1933 and which continued until World War II forced a halt. Even so, this activity left many depots largely unchanged, particularly the smaller freight depots in Lancashire and Yorkshire; a few small depots, such as Holyhead and Stranraer, were provided with small and simple coaling plants, however.

The third prong of the attack related to organisation. Certain larger sheds had always acted 'in loco parentis' for smaller ones, but heavier repairs and examinations were still widely scattered at depots ill-equipped to undertake them. The 1935 reorganisation divided the railway into 29 motive power districts (later increased to 32 by sub-division of over-large Scottish districts). One shed in each district (suffixed 'A') was designated the 'concentration depot', equipped with suitable machine tools and lifting equipment or wheel drop, and charged with carrying out major examinations (such as valves and pistons) and selected heavier repairs such as axlebox overhaul and boiler work. A curious result of this change was that 'garage' depots tended to be denuded of machinery and skilled staff, to the point where there were depots of 50 engines without even a powered grinding wheel for tools. Generally the system was successful: engine hours in traffic improved to 13.7 by 1936, and the availability of engines was consistently up to 84–85

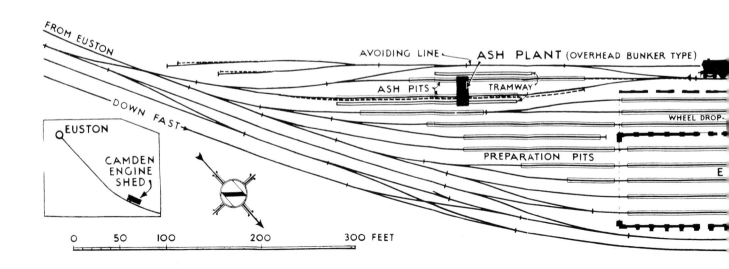

per cent, with 5 per cent in and awaiting works repair, 8–9 per cent stopped at sheds and 1–2 per cent awaiting material. The widespread adoption of water softening from 1931 also helped.

The war proved hard on shed buildings. Adolf Hitler removed considerable areas of roofing at places like Kentish Town and Saltley, much of which was never replaced. Many others, their roofs weary of a steady diet of smoke-induced acid rain on top of old age, succumbed and were removed for safety reasons. The LMS, in a post-war climate of steel shortage, turned to precast concrete sections to replace them; the result was a heavy, oppressive-looking structure which was also expensive. One or two sheds, having waited long under the stars for roof renewals, got it done only to be closed within two or three years; thereafter, the blessing of a new roof was regarded by staff with grave suspicion. Only one major shed renewal took place in LMS days, that at Carnforth being completed in 1944, though in the last year also two others were started, at Leicester and Carlisle Upperby. The latter were true roundhouses with concrete

Blackpool North shed in the late 1920s. On the left are L&Y 0-6-0s, centre is a Midland 4F 0-6-0, and on the right an LNW 19in Goods, L&Y Dreadnought 4-6-0 and a 'Crab' 2-6-0, mostly waiting to work return excursions.

Improvements to Camden loco depot layout as part of the modernisation of steam locomotive servicing.

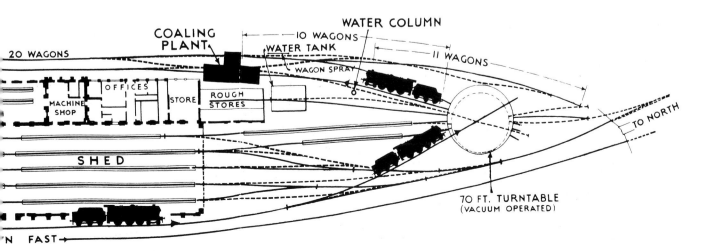

Midland Roundhouse. Burton shed in 1925 with a clutch of ex-Midland engines including 4F 0-6-0 No 4125, a saturated 2P class 4-4-0, probably 368 or 369, Class 3F 0-6-0 No 3205 and Kirtley double-framed 2-4-0 No 2. The latter still carried a large figure 2 on its tender and the LMS crest on the upper cabside.

roofs and window walls, and gave vastly improved working conditions.

The shed fitter, hardened to dirt, bleak winds and hot water dropping down his neck, was ever a versatile character, needing a wide spectrum of knowledge, an ability to improvise and to decide what was achievable against a demanding clock and what could bide for a more propitious occasion. They were inevitably looked down upon by the artisan staff in the company's main works where conditions were altogether better and there was the support of more and better equipment and specialist skills.

The main works taken over in 1923 were a mixed bag, ranging from very large units like Crewe locomotive and Derby carriage and wagon to small company shops like Bow and Lochgorm (Inverness). Some of them were cramped, inefficient, ill-equipped and geared to small locomotives. Barrow, for instance, was described by *The Railway Magazine* in 1913 as having an erecting shop which 'owing to its low roof, had at one time no overhead crane, the wheels taken from them and replaced by means of dropping pits. But one bay (out of three) has had the roof raised and an electric overhead crane erected.' Commonly 12–15 per cent of the locomotive fleet was in works at any one time, the duration of heavy repairs being dictated by the time to repair the boiler. The converse of this was that tenders could be overhauled faster than engines, and the LNWR had for long taken advantage of this by building fewer tenders than there were tender locomotives (this brought great fun in 1925 when the Midland practice of carrying the engine number on the tender side was standardised. While it lasted, there were such anomalies as engine and tender exhibiting different numbers or no number at all!

As has already been said, the LMS was quickly pitched into major schemes to rationalise the repair and new building capacity, to keep more rolling stock rolling and less stock still under overhaul. On the carriage side, thanks to work done by the Midland of Derby in the field of mechanising for mass production, which came to fruition in 1923, the way was clear to bring Wolverton and to a lesser extent Newton Heath (Manchester) into line. Between them they built most of the 700 or so carriages required each year. Some orders were put with outside builders, either to meet peak demands or to exploit new techniques: orders were placed with Leeds Forge, for instance, for vehicles with all-steel riveted body shells. Progressive development led the railway works to produce all-steel bodies from 1939, taking in on the way advanced monocoque construction of new stock for the Liverpool–Southport electric line. But with Derby and Wolverton able to build 350 coaches each a year, there was no role for Newton Heath, always a junior partner, and in the depression climate it ceased to build new coaches in 1932 and closed shortly after.

In the locomotive field the sorting-out process was much more fundamental. The keystone of the arch was Crewe: get that right, and the other stones could be fitted snugly round it. But major surgery was needed, for the works had grown like Topsy into a sprawl, difficult to manage, which included no less than *nine* separate erecting shops, four of which could only handle small engines. The LNWR had sanctioned a new erecting shop in 1920, but it was stopped in the climate of uncer-

Smell a . . .?

At a certain ex-LNWR main line shed just north of the West Midlands conurbation and during the early days of wartime rationing the staff found that there was a mini thief in their midst as packages of sandwiches were either interfered with or stolen from lockers. There was a pretty good attempt at identifying the culprit but no proof. So they set traps for the inevitable depot rats, caught a few, stewed and skinned them, made them into sandwiches and put them into an appropriate paper bag, leaving this in a suitable place. As the culprit was seen eating these there was an interesting but oblique conversation well within his hearing. He turned ghastly white and fled. There was no more trouble.

Opposite.
Midland Shed. Leeds Holbeck (two roundhouses) on 13 July 1939. This posed shot from the Derby archives shows a modernised shed with typical Midland Division locomotives for the period. These include Hughes 2-6-0 No 2850, Johnson 0-4-4T No 1428, Stanier 2-6-2T No 177, Stanier Jubilee (dirty and with cabside numbers specially cleaned) No 5621 Northern Rhodesia, Johnson 3F 0-6-0 No 3226, Stanier Class 5 No 5302 and Fowler 4F No 3944. The shed code was 20A and the allocation 111 engines.

Shed Modernisation. At their best, steam locomotive depots were of necessity smoky dirty places but most were also antediluvian, going back to the turn of the century and earlier with hand coaling, poor disposal facilities and primitive accommodation for staff and crews. This photograph shows the modernised Camden depot with its new depot buildings and coaling plant (a wagon was hoisted to the top of the tower and its contents tipped into a hopper above the tender), ash pit with hoppers and a standard water crane. Camden depot served Euston and was home to such express classes as the Duchesses and Scots along with driver heroes like Earl, Brooker and Bishop.

tainty leading up to amalgamation. The scheme was restarted, in modified and improved form, late in 1925; it comprised a large new erecting shop to undertake all locomotive overhaul and new construction, the switch of erecting shops 5–9 to other functions such as heavy machining and stores, and the conversion of erecting shops 1–4 into a new boiler building plant to provide all new boilers for the railway. The new erecting shop came on line in 1927, using a rigid system of moving engines under repair at pre-arranged time intervals, to the different functional gangs. The effect on repair times was dramatic, reducing the average time on the erecting shop pits from 29 days in 1926 to 13 days in 1928; the 'under and awaiting repair' figure came down to under 5 per cent of the Crewe-maintained fleet. From then on, all boiler building was carried out at Crewe – it proved a highly-skilled and successful operation – and Derby, Horwich and St Rollox were confined to repairs. There was considerable resentment.

Once Crewe's new capacity had played itself in, the slaughter of the lesser works began. Barrow had been an early victim and Stoke and Highbridge closed their doors in 1930. Only their geographic spread

Liverpool Shed. Edge Hill, Liverpool, c1947 with Duchess class 4-6-2 No 6254 City of Stoke-on-Trent *in 1946 livery and Class 5 4-6-0 No 5025. The Class 5 is now preserved and is normally to be found on the Strathspey Railway at Aviemore. The photograph clearly shows the dirt and grime of the steam depot in its later years.*

Joint Line Shops. Both the Somerset & Dorset and the M&GN owned their own locomotives and workshops. The photograph shows the S&DR shops at Highbridge (Somerset) with two 0-6-0s of typical Midland design undergoing repair. They are No 43, built by The Vulcan Foundry in 1880, and No 56, again by Vulcan in 1890.

saved other small works like Bow, Kilmarnock, Inverness and Rugby, and they were confined to the lighter repairs. But Crewe did not come through unscathed. In 1932 the steel works closed, a victim of pressure from outside steelmasters, the depression and a need for new investment.

The main works were always kept in the forefront of engineering development, notably under Stanier's direction. Two facets of this process may be mentioned: firstly, the emphasis on surface finish of machined surfaces as a deterrent to fatigue cracking (which went far to eliminate tyre fractures and enabled axleboxes to be fitted to journals without hand-scraping) and secondly the wide use of electric welding, both for fabrication and repair of work surfaces. At all the main works, but perhaps most notably at Crewe, welding was used in sophisticated fashion for repair of frame fractures; full depth sections of frame plate were cut out and replaced by insets welded in as a matter of routine, the distance between axle centres being maintained to a claimed accuracy of .003in.

Each works had its own individual character, which was slow to change. Crewe locomotive works was the largest, both in its rambling

size and in staff numbers, and from its opening in 1843 on a virgin site, the town had grown round it under the benevolence of the LNWR. Besides its locomotive activity it had various important sidelines: the manufacture of signalling equipment, oils and greases, firebricks and, until 1932, steel. Inevitably it developed an air of superiority over its rivals, augmented by its use for building the largest and most prestigious locomotives. At Derby the locomotive and carriage and wagon works, taken together, were even larger, but they had only limited common purpose. Having grown up in more orderly fashion, they were more content to get on with the job in unassuming fashion. The height of excitement in the locomotive works was when the Lickey Banker came in for repair, and the order to build ten Jubilees at the end of 1935 was a talking point for years. They sneered at Crewe's workmanship (which even Stanier had disparaged when the first Princess was built in 1933) and derived a perverse pleasure if called out to rectify some unsatisfactory fallout from the belt system.

St Rollox quickly realised that it was a long way from the new seats of power at Derby and Euston, and could quietly carry on as before and get away with ignoring instructions which did not commend themselves. At least it could assert its superiority over Scottish colleagues by putting Caledonian boilers on to Highland engines and getting rid of the engines of their old rivals, the G&SW, because St Rollox boilers would not fit. Horwich was rather inward-looking, its Lancashire stalwarts seeking a reputation from developing workshop techniques which would stand it in good stead in any future rivalry. Come 1948, and attitudes had changed but little.

Among the humdrum routine of building and repair, there was some small glitter. Wolverton, for example, took immense pride in the royal train, of which it was the custodian and provider of new vehicles. They were maintained and polished with loving care. One thinks of Derby Works' commitment to locomotive building for the Irish-gauge NCC. What fun they had when the time came to deliver 2-6-4 tanks after the war. The loading on to ships was done at Heysham, using the sheerlegs there since the weight of boiler and frame sections was beyond crane capacity, and to slew the frames through the legs left only a few inches of clearance. Derby carriage and wagon, too, was justly proud of its postwar all steel coach bodies (the ones with porthole windows) where the jig construction was so accurate that all the prefabricated components for the body, *including all the interior trim*, went into place without need for adjustment. And, of course, Crewe, preparing first the *Royal Scot* and later *Coronation* (or rather, two other engines disguised as the famous pair) with special finish and loving care for the delectation of the Americans and Canadians.

Oh, yes, the LMS might not be unduly proud of the image presented by its running sheds, but its tail went up for what its works achieved – and the nation could be proud, too, of the service they gave during World War II and well on into BR days.

Coal Tankies
Even in later LMS days the legacy of the LNWR's great CME Francis Webb was evident all over the system; in particular his excellent and simple 0-6-0s and tanks had considerable longevity. Thus a retired collier, asked what engines were used on the mountainous grades round Tredegar, with their 1 in 34 and 1 in 29, when he started at the pits replied: 'Coal Tankies same as that yonder even afore I went to school; they've changed their numbers now and again, but th' engines is just the same.' The Tredegar shed foreman felt strongly about this after trying the new standard engines just after the war: in spite of the new comfort for the crews they went back to using the old timers as being handier on the curved grades, double-manned and worked harder than ever. They were rostered to do 1,200 miles a week, all in very short trips too.

Crewe Works. A scene in the new erecting shop probably in the late 1920s. There is no date available but the assumption is made on the basis of the white LNWR type shedplate in the smokebox door of G2 class 0-8-0 No 9430 on the left of the photograph: this engine also carries a new type cast iron smokebox door number plate. The LNW plate would have originally been on the rear of the cab roof. The plate carried in the position shown is the LMS code immediately after the Grouping. Shed allocation 8 indicates Rugby (or one of its sub sheds, Warwick, Coventry, Market Harborough, Stamford or Seaton). Both leading engines have their piston valves removed. The line of locomotives to the right is headed by G2 class 0-8-0 No 9398 with two of its sisters. An Experiment class 4-6-0 No 5458 City of Edinburgh is sandwiched between them.

Carriage Works. Ex LNWR 0-6-0ST Earlestown, *one of the Wolverton works shunters, is on duty. These were the last engines of Ramsbottom parentage and remained as service stock for years after similar locomotives in capital stock had been withdrawn. The photograph was taken in early BR days. The LMS period III corridor brake third is in the first BR livery.*

LMS Workshops				
Railway	Loco	Carriage	Wagon	Closed by LMS
LNWR	Crewe	Wolverton	Earlestown	–
L&Y	Horwich	Newton Heath	Newton Heath	c 1932 (N. Hth only)
MIDLAND	Derby	Derby	Derby	–
NORTH STAFFORD	Stoke-on-Trent			1930
FURNESS	Barrow in Furness			1930
CALEDONIAN	St Rollox	St Rollox	St Rollox	–
GLASGOW & SOUTH WESTERN	Kilmarnock	Barassie	Barassie	–
HIGHLAND	Inverness	Inverness	Inverness	–
MARYPORT & CARLISLE	Maryport			c 1925
NORTH LONDON	Bow			–

Bangor Shed's Changing Allocation

In retirement, Bangor shedmaster J. M. Dunn compiled this study of the changing allocation. Apart from the fact that 2-4-0T engines 1000 and 1001 are known to have been stationed at Bangor in 1908 to work the Red Wharf Bay and Bethesda branches, the earliest references are for 1929.

The table below shows the locomotive allocation over a period of twenty years in the life of the LMS. Bangor serviced the ex-LNWR North Wales main line together with branches to Bethesda, Afonwen, Gaerwen and Red Wharf Bay. It illustrates the retention of LNWR locomotive classes during the 1920s with only very limited influx of LMS standard types. By the mid-1930s,

however, the larger LNWR engines had been almost totally withdrawn, the summer services to North Wales resorts being a last duty for the remaining superheated 4-4-0s which mostly spent the winter in store at Llandudno Junction. Only the Second World War enabled some of the smallest types to survive the LMS working the branch lines. The increased use of modern tank engines, often on work which would at one time have been done by tender engines, is also shown. This is emphasised by the Afonwen branch working which, in 1929 was LNWR 18in goods worked, then by LNWR 4-6-2 tanks lastly and to the end, by Stanier 2-6-4 tanks.

Passenger	Summer 1929	March 1933	Dec 1937	July 1938	March 1949
Class 6P 4-6-0 Royal Scot	–	1	–	2	–
*Class 5P 4-6-0 Claughton	3	2	–	–	–
*Class 3P 4-6-0 Experiment	2	1	–	–	–
*Class 3P 4-4-0 George V and superheated Precursor	3	5	–	2	–
*Class 2P 4-4-0 Renown	2	–	–	–	–
Class 4P 2-6-4T standard LMS	–	–	2	3	6
*Class 3P 4-6-2T	3	3	2	–	–
Class 3P 2-6-2T standard LMS	–	–	4	9	6
*Class 2P 0-6-2T 5ft 0in	–	–	–	–	2
*Class 1P 2-4-2T 5ft 6in	5	5	4	4	1
*Class 1P 2-4-2T 4ft 6in	2	–	–	–	–
Mixed Traffic					
Class 5 4-6-0 standard LMS	–	–	3	4	–
Class 5 2-6-0 standard LMS	–	–	–	–	3
Class 2 2-6-2T standard LMS	–	–	–	–	5
Freight					
2-8-0 ex-ROD	5	–	–	–	–
*Class 4F 4-6-0 19in goods	3	3	–	–	–
Class 4F 0-6-0 standard LMS	3	7	5	5	2
Class 3F 0-6-0 L&Y superheater	–	–	1	1	–
Class 2F 0-6-0 L&Y saturated	–	–	1	1	4
*Class 2F 0-6-0 18in goods	9	–	4	2	1
*Class 2F 0-6-0 17in coal	2	8	1	1	–
*Class 1F 0-6-2T side tank coal	12	12	8	9	1
Total	54	47	35	43	31
of which LNWR provided	46	39	19	18	5

*ex-LNWR types

Afon Wen Loco. Bowen Cooke 4-6-2 tank No 6994 outside Bangor MPD c1932/3; the station is in the background. These 4-6-2 tanks superseded the Webb 'Cauliflower' 0-6-0s over the Caernarvon and Afon Wen line and, in the late 1930s were themselves superseded by Stanier 2-6-4 tanks which remained on the roster until closure of the line on 7 December 1964.

14
BRANCH LINES AND CROSS-COUNTRY ROUTES

Though there was perhaps no such thing as an LMS branch line (certainly standardisation did not even begin to unify their characters), there were many thousands of miles of byways and cross-country routes of great fascination to the rising number of people interested in railways. It was indeed in the early Grouping years that, helped by cheap fare offerings and the growth in railway clubs, the exploration of byways and the hunting out of unusual layouts and practices first become something of an industry in its own right – though few followed in the footsteps of the late T. R. Perkins, a pharmacist of Henley-in-Arden and a notable railway writer, who succeeded in travelling over every mile open to passenger traffic and many that were not.

In 1937 the LMS claimed a route mileage of 'main and principal lines open for traffic' of 2,932, against a total route mileage of 6,700. So there must have been some 3,800 route miles of secondary and branch lines, some of which were of course freight only. Probably about half were double track (though whether two lines were always needed is a question that does not often seem to have been raised) and the remainder single.

The variety was enormous – in terms of geographical terrain, origin of company, business, kind of traffic, weather and other hazards. In the Railway Mania and even more the second passion for railway building, lines had been thrown out right and left, sometimes for the logical reason of serving additional populations, but often to penetrate an enemy's territory or to defend against enemy invasion. Thus in the seventy miles between Willesden Junction and Rugby, a dozen offshoot lines were added by the London & Birmingham and the LNWR, or by locally-promoted companies later taken over, ranging in length from the combined Oxford to Cambridge route of 77 miles down to Harrow–Stanmore (2 miles) and Watford–Rickmansworth LMS (4 miles), both the latter now closed.

In Lancashire and Yorkshire, railways proliferated not only in the great conurbations but also throughout industrial areas generally, with much competition and overlapping. Thus the LMS inherited three 'main' routes over or through the Pennines, with many a branch up a side valley to serve pit or mill. Including its share in the Cheshire Lines, the LMS also had three express routes between Liverpool and Manchester, each of course with its complicated offshoots. Nor did rural areas have a monopoly of romantic nomenclature: three adjacent stations on the Wigan–Chorley branch were Boar's Head, Red Rock and White Bear.

In the vernacular of the region, the LMS could book you between

Irlams o' th' Height and Besses o' th' Barn, a poetic tradition which British Rail seems to have inherited with the opening in the 1980s of Flowery Field – in suburban Manchester. A senior LNWR/LMS officer, recalled that on his very first day of training, in a Bolton booking-office at 6am, a bearded face thrust against the window and demanded 'Wkmntoopsarse'. The senior booking clerk gently advised: Give him a Workman's Return to Ramsbottom. Of course if he had been sent to begin training in the South Wales District, he might have had to book tickets between Gwys and Cwmllynfell.

Adding to the variety, some Scottish antecedents had availed themselves of the provisions of the Light Railways Act 1896, with its opportunities for government grants and certain relaxations in operation. Thus the Strathord & Bankfoot, acquired by the Caledonian to connect its main line north of Perth to the small town of Bankfoot, was opened in 1906 but closed to passengers in 1931, a short but characterful life –

Keswick Train. A Webb 'Cauliflower' or 18in goods 0-6-0 No 8499 of 12D shed (Workington) climbs up from the main line shortly after leaving Penrith station en route to Keswick and Workington via the CK&P. A look at the engine, coaches and signals and signalbox shows just how little some things had changed from the amalgamation of 1923 to the last year of the LMS (1947). Streamliners en route to Scotland may well have rushed past these ex-LNWR signals but the passengers en route to Keswick would have noticed little difference over 25 years.

173

LMS in South Wales. Ebbw Vale (LMS) station on 19 August 1950 with Webb 0-6-2 coal tank No 58916 on a train to Beaufort on the Heads of the Valleys line (Ebbw Vale High Level closed to passengers 5 February 1951, entirely 2 November 1959). No 58916 was one of two engines with extended side tanks adapted for use on the Wirral section, giving longer runs between water stops.

London Outer Suburban. A Watford Junction to St Albans push and pull set (rail motor unit No 39) at Watford on 27 August 1932. The engine is one of the then virtually standard class for this work – the ex-LNWR 5ft 6in 2-4-2 tank No 6729.

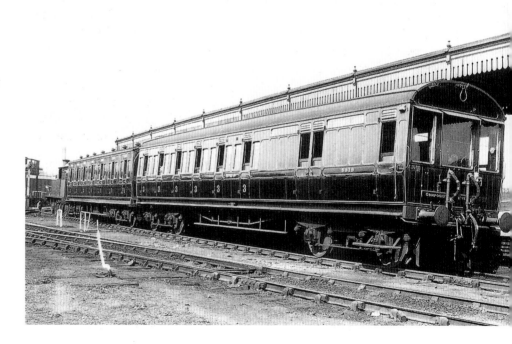

though for sheer individuality the lonely Leadhills line took some beating. Elsewhere in the Lowlands the Glasgow & South Western had two interesting light railways: the coastal Maidens & Dunure below Ayr, serving, en route, Turnberry with its railway-owned golf hotel. The other G&SW line was the Cairn Valley branch, between Dumfries and Moniaive, about 16 miles; its principal feature of interest the use on its single line of a variant of the lock-and-block principle without tokens achieved by interaction between the block instrument and track treadles actuated by passage of the train. All signals were of the banner type. On the Highland Railway, the Wick & Lybster was the most northerly light railway in Britain, while the Dornoch Light ran interestingly (and often with mixed trains) from the Mound on the HR Far North line to Dornoch, where the Highland built a resort hotel.

The other Highland Railway hotel was the Strathpeffer Spa, at the little town of that name (population still only 1,250 or so) five miles west of Dingwall, junction for Kyle of Lochalsh. The Strathpeffer branch was not a light but an ordinary branch considered sufficiently important to be served by the Strathpeffer Spa Express from the south, and even by a sleeping car from London which must have overshadowed the train engine, a small 4-4-0 tank of a design originally intended for South America.

Among other branches in Scotland was that extending for best part of a mile from Gleneagles station on the main Glasgow–Perth route to the

Motor Train. An inheritance from the L&Y 0-4-0 tank No 10614 and railcar waits at Stainland and Holywell Green the terminus of the Calder Valley branch from Greetland c1927. There was one intermediate station at West Vale; the branch closed on 23 September 1929.

175

back of the Caledonian's (and later the LMS's and British Transport Hotel's) flagship hotel, opened in 1924 though of course started well before Grouping. The route, which included a reversal half way, was used by two or three weekly trips bringing in the fuel, linen and comestibles. It was worked by a small tank engine, whose crew seemed to enjoy a somewhat privileged and not wholly arduous position. One can only guess what happened during the generous stop at the terminus, though once a fireman, having eaten a redundant but not life-expired smoked-salmon sandwich was alleged to have commented on the 'fine wee bit o' haddie'.

Except where they served heavy industry and large centres of population, minor lines quickly suffered from road competition – the first losses being among suburban services as trams became popular well before LMS days, of course. Infrequent and irregular services from badly-sited stations did not help against bus competition over journeys of up to about fifteen miles. Many branches suffered a break of service, often in the middle of the day, to allow the pick-up goods to make its slow passage or for shunting blocking the running track at some quarry, colliery or works. Though by modern terms there was a prodigious use of manpower on lesser lines, economy was made by mixed grades including (first on the Midland) the hybrid porter-signalman-clerk. The signalman part would usually only involve opening up the box for the arrival, shunting and despatch of the daily pick-up, the remaining time being devoted to more humdrum tasks such as sweeping the office and waiting rooms, checking the toilet paper, changing the posters, white-washing the platform edges, making up the accounts, checking the signal

Train from Windermere. Lakeside station of the former Furness Railway with FR 4-4-2T as LMS No 11080 on a local train to Ulverston. This comprises a vintage collection of Furness six-wheel and bogie stock while the locomotive is painted in the handsome LMS crimson lake which was used for all passenger classes until 1928. Behind the locomotive can be seen a Furness signal and the top of the sheerlegs used for servicing the railway-owned vessels on the lake. A section of this branch from Lakeside to Haverthwaite is now run as a preserved railway.

lamps and filling the oil reservoirs – and in the lengthening intervals between the final trains on spring evenings tending the nearby allotment and brewing tea.

If labour was used on the grand scale, it was not paid for generously. The hours were long, often lonely, and though there was always a sense of loyalty to the railway service (if only because in country areas alternative employment was harder to find), the mere coming into being of the LMS was more resented in rural conservatism. 'The company', as all railwaymen referred to their employer even after nationalisation, had become remote – and the new engines and carriages naturally took longer to reach byways than smarten up services on principal routes. Life was especially lonely in railway settlements serving isolated junctions and locomotive sheds (such as Hawes Junction, later Garsdale), and at crossing loops and other remote locations without full shopping facilities. On Glasgow & South Western lines there were weekly specials for 'surfacemen's wives' to go on getting their provisions from the nearest town. Hundreds of lonely signalboxes and crossing keepers' houses had to have special fuel and even water deliveries arranged: 'No 4 calls at Broughton Crossing between Marston Gate and Aylesbury to put out water for Crossing Keeper'.

Mixed trains had a lore of their own. In former days *Bradshaw* had identified them to warn susceptible passengers; in LMS times you had to read the schedules more carefully to note when there was a lull in proceedings. Indeed, this held true well into BR days, as on the Aberfeldy branch even when the motive power had become a powerful diesel and freight had become so rare that intermediate shunting seldom actually took place. Especially on former LNWR lines and on shorter Scottish branches, mixed trains ran on many routes even where there was a proper daily goods; in particular they delivered urgent traffic early in the morning and lifted outward wagons not ready until after the pickup had departed. Livestock was often carried this way, and again well into BR days. Well after local trains had been dieselised, a summer Saturday steam-hauled express from Manchester regularly conveyed livestock for Cockermouth's market early the next week, of course unloaded for the weekend.

Well into LMS, but certainly not BR days, stations in more prosperous and hunting country kept a horse box in a dock ready to be loaded by a rider eager to get home (only 24 hours notice was needed for a special train), and some motorists similarly used the railway to spare their cars or the fatigue of driving at the then maximum of 20mph. Mainly because of delays caused at junctions and the determination to quicken the pace of expresses, 'tail traffic' business was less encouraged in later years, and despite its general drive for traffic the LMS ended with a reputation for paying more attention to profitable traffic and less to gross receipts. You were then more likely to find a horsebox at the end of a GW branch train for the GW turned little away.

Looking back at LMS routes that were 'cross country' because, unlike the general pattern of main lines, they ran from east to west, the prime example was the former L&Y from Liverpool (Exchange) to York or

A Body(?) on the Buffers
Making a final trip over the Somerset & Dorset Joint in the last months of the LMS regime, an observer noticed, as the Pines rolled into Bath, that the leading vehicle, an open third, was reserved for a party of schoolboys returning to an establishment in Dorset. Black Five No 4945 came on the other end of eight, for 243/260 tons, and they were off over the Mendips, with the open third now on the rear.

First booked stop should have been Evercreech Junction, but it was not to be. Breasting Masbury Summit at 22mph – slower than usual because of a pw slack lower down the ascent – acceleration was cut short by furious whistling and a fierce brake application; Shepton Mallet distant and home had been reversed against the train for 'Stop and Examine'. As it ground to a halt in the platform, the signalman (complete with red flag) was standing outside his box well up the embankment on the down side, shouting 'They say there's a body on the buffers!'

True, as was discovered when they cautiously inspected the front end of 4945, there were lots of bodies on the smokebox door, but merely those of flying insects. Meanwhile, the signalman was explaining that he had never said 'body', it had been 'boy', a member of the school party, whom the bobby at the box in rear had seen climbing out of the door on one side of the open third, across the buffers, and back through the door on the other side! The guard (who one might have expected to refer to 'them there young varmints' but didn't) nipped smartly into the open third: 'Roll yer trews up to yer knees, hands on the table, palms up!' (Somewhere an echo of parade grounds) Dirt revealed. Culprits discovered, names taken. District manager writes, more in sorrow than in anger, 'Dear Headmaster . . .'

H&C

In the official shorthand of the LMS operating Department, these initials stood, not for 'Hot & Cold' but for 'Horse & Carriage', a remarkable breed of train which seemed largely peculiar to the main lines of the former LNWR; its historical origin possibly derived from the earliest days when extra trains were run to accommodate those horses and carriages of the nobility and gentry for which room could not be found on passenger trains. In modern times, their principal function was to convey vacuum-braked passenger train traffic vehicles which could not conveniently be worked by booked passenger services: vehicles for repair, horse-boxes, odd empty passenger or parcels vehicles, milk vans, pigeon vans, hound vans, proprietary sausage vans, and (in the 1930s) mobile cinema-theatre coaches. At the outbreak of war in 1939, there were still three horse & carriage trains booked out of Euston or Willesden Junction on weekdays, and oddly, one from Oxford to Cambridge and back.

Of necessity these H&C trains made a good many intermediate stops, some only 'if required', and were thus probably the slowest coaching trains in the country; apart from necessary shunting, a path had to be found for numerous expresses to overtake, and possibly for several changes of engine. Thus, the 7.30am H&C Euston to Carlisle was booked to arrive Carlisle at 8.25pm, its overall journey time of 12hr 55min including nine scheduled intermediate stops of an aggregate duration of 5hr 23min.

Not surprisingly, the Crewe divisional control periodically felt the urge to tackle a spell of erratic punctuality on the part of H&C trains. Keen and eager LNWR cadets or LMS traffic apprentices were despatched on a week's ride on the offenders.

Hull, 75 and 98 miles respectively, though on North Eastern metals from Normanton and serving or affording connections with Goole where the LMS took over the L&Y's major maritime interests.

But as railway enthusiasts understand the term 'cross country', one is tempted to recall routes formed by the linking up of long-forgotten local companies which existed ever precariously and never came near fulfilling the high hopes of their promoters. The 'Oxbridge Line', the Stratford-upon-Avon & Midland Junction Railway, and the lesser LNWR Joint Lines from Market Harborough, towards Nottingham and Newark, for example.

Though the Oxford–Cambridge line appeared on the official map as a continuous route, 77 miles, with a connecting branch of 21¼m from Verney Junction to Banbury, prospective travellers soon discovered the real position: even the timetables showed Oxford–Bletchley and Bletchley–Cambridge as separate operations, on different pages. Despite the obvious demand for through trains between the two university towns, they were disliked by the operators because of track arrangements at busy Bletchley. Terminating trains from either Oxford or Cambridge could slip quietly into a bay, while through ones had to traverse the whole of the passenger trackwork fouling the heavily-occupied fast tracks of the West Coast main line. Even less popular were the excursions developed by the salesmen of the 1930s to Oxford for tours of the city and perhaps Blenheim Palace or in connection with river steamers. Worked through by locomotives from as far afield as Colne in Lancashire, they stopped on the up fast line at Bletchley for remanning or a conductor with local knowledge.

This Oxford–Cambridge branch mirrored almost all the varied traffic patterns of the old rural railways. The stations were spaced specifically with the radius of horse-and-cartwork in mind; domestic and gasworks fuels, fertilisers and feeds, raw materials for the local factories and mills . . . it was all there along with an almost continuous orchestra of milk churns. But modernisation also showed its face, the LMS glass-lined milk tanks from the Carlisle district being routed off the West Coast main line and worked as a special to Verney Junction for transfer to the Metropolitan & Great Central Joint en route to the bottling plant at Rossmore Road, Marylebone.

Consider how many lines this cross-country route connected with! Though the LMS had its own all-over-roof terminus (not a charming place) at Oxford, it connected with the GWR both there and at Yarnton. A connection with the section of the GC/LNER near Claydon only came later on and then as part of the war effort. Next Bletchley, already discussed, though the fly-over of later days should be noted. Never used by booked passenger services, it was part of a BR scheme for a freight ring outside London, a kind of M25 precursor not pursued when the future for rail freight became less promising. The mightily heavy second World War traffic routed this way of course had to cross the West Coast main line on the level.

On eastward, through a continuing forest of brickwork chimneys of the 1930s, the cross-country route had its own St John's station at

Far North Branch. Ex-Highland Railway 4-4-0 'Yankee' tank No 15013 waits at Lybster with a rake of three six-wheeled vehicles for Wick on 19 May 1929. The engine is carrying large Midland style numbers on its side tanks as well as a cast iron smokebox door plate, it would most likely have been painted in LMS red.

Road/Railer. An experimental (but unsuccessful) venture was this bus which was conceived with the idea of linking the prestigious Welcombe Hotel at Stratford with the LMS tracks at Stratford (Old Town) station and then on to Blisworth to connect with the up Perth–Euston express. It is shown on trial on the Hemel Hempsted branch in 1931.

SMJ Junction. Woodford Halse station (formerly Woodford & Hinton, renamed 1 November 1948) on the old Great Central main line. This was the junction for the SMJ route, that company's trains normally using the platform on the far left. This is a post war photograph showing a Birmingham Locomotive Club special train, which traversed the whole of the former Stratford-on-Avon & Midland Junction Railway on 14 July 1951

Bedford, ignoring the Midland main line's until Bletchley–Bedford remained the only section of the whole route to retain passengers. Then the trains were diverted over a new connection to the Midland station.

Next the East Coast main line at Sandy, hopped over by the LMS but to the east a connection made with the GN station. Sandy station was picturesquely situated against a wooded hillside on the up side; it had a distinctly old-fashioned aura on the occasion of Sandy Flower Show, when a train of vintage GN non-corridor stock, having emptied its load, would back into the sand siding behind a small Ivatt 4-4-0, which would simmer away waiting its return to Finsbury Park via the Hertford Loop. The LMS representation was challengingly modern: a rake of elegant non-corridor coaches in absolutely pristine condition, ex Wolverton carriage works on its final running-in trip.

Into this placid scene entered an LMS goods from Cambridge, headed by *Sisyphus*, a George Whale Experiment 4-6-0, built Crewe 1909. Its name excited suspicious comment, largely unfavourable, when the driver was informed (courtesy of Hampstead public library) that *Sisyphus* was a mythological king of Corinth who, having offended the gods in Hades, was made to roll a huge stone up a steep incline to the summit, whence it rolled back again, the fireman chipped in: 'Silly B . . ., he should have whistled for a banker'.

Beyond Sandy the Oxbridge line became small beer; passenger trains which had been semi-fast Oxford–Bletchley, then next stop Bedford, changed category from 'Express' to 'Passenger' and were now all stations. The only express run enjoyed by the writer was with the three-car articulated train set built at Derby in 1938, powered by six 125hp

180

Leyland oil engines with hydraulic transmission, and carrying 24 first and 138 third class passengers for a tare weight of 73 tons. The two end (driving) vehicles had air-smoothed noses, rather in the German style of the period. The Oxbridge line was regarded as a suitable venue for experimental units of this kind, on the principle of making sure they could and would operate track circuits before worse might befall. On this trip the 16¼ miles from Sandy start to passing Lord's Bridge, was run in 17½min, with repeated slacks below 70mph. Incidentally, the complete run of 77 miles involved some thirty stations and halts; no wonder the younger members of the universities preferred their sports cars.

Another central England local company system, independent until absorbed into the LMS as a subsidiary company on 1 January 1923 (when it was reported from Derby that somebody from Stratford-upon-Avon had rung up to ask for an engine or two to help them out!) was the Stratford-upon-Avon & Midland Junction Railway, made up in 1908 of four small local companies, the imposing titles of which were almost as long as their respective mileages. The earliest, the Northampton & Banbury Junction, opened in 1872 to serve deposits of ironstone near the LNWR main line at Blisworth and elsewhere; from Cockley Brake Junction west of Towcester it enjoyed running powers over the LNWR branch to Banbury. Banbury thus witnessed at separate but adjacent stations, the locomotives of four different companies: GWR, LNWR, GCR and SMJ.

As eventually completed the SMJ system of 67½ miles comprised the original Banbury branch plus an east-west main line between Blisworth and Broom Junction, where it made a junction with the Midland's Evesham–Redditch branch, and an eastward extension from Towcester to Ravenstone Wood Junction, on the Midland's Bedford–Northampton branch. The latter crossed over the LNWR main line just south of Roade station, to which a little-used spur was provided. The writer recalls the consternation on the faces of a Western Division footplate crew on a summer Saturday about 1937 as they braked a portion of the Sunny South Express to take the Northampton line at Roade: a passenger train, about ten MR non-corridors behind a Fowler 0-6-0 (express headlamps and all!) crossed the impressive girder bridge. Investigation of the Midland Division special train programme revealed that this was a 'Halfex' (half day excursion), Evesham–Bedford, for Bedford regatta. There used also to be a race special, St Pancras–Towcester, also 0-6-0 hauled, on Easter Mondays.

The SMJ offered a useful through route between London and Stratford, enjoying the shortest mileage. There were through coaches between Marylebone and Stratford-upon-Avon taking 2¼ hours – until the operation of slips was discontinued by the LNER in the 1930s – via Woodford & Hinton (whence a short spur connected with the SMJ at Byfield).

In 1932 the LMS invented the 'Ro-Railer' – a bus with road and rail wheels – which performed an experimental service between the company's Welcombe Hotel and Stratford and then on to the tracks at Stratford SMJ station for Blisworth to connect with the up Perth–

Sectional Appendix
There were always special rules in rural areas, and study of the LMS *Sectional Appendix, Northern Division* covering Oban to Dunblane and branches in 1937 does not disappoint. Between Taynuilt and Loch Awe. 'Drivers must occupy not less than 9 minutes in running the distance between the 52 and 55 mileposts through The Pass of Brander during the day and 15 minutes at night, as stones (sic) are liable to become detached.' Even in the detailed instructions on the automatic signals on this section, they were always referred to as 'stone signals' and still *are* in the Scottish Region Appendix.

The down night mail was worked while signalboxes were closed to save wages. So 'The guard in charge of train will exchange tokens at each token station and leave the token received from the driver in the place where the one to be handed to the driver is taken from. Passenger guards and freight guards must pay particular attention to the closing of carriage and van doors before leaving stations, and also see that the loads of wagons which are liable to shift on the journey and come in contact with the token exchanging apparatus are properly secured. Should there be a possibility of a load coming into contact with an apparatus, the guard in charge must instruct the driver to stop the train short of the apparatus and arrange for the apparatus being reversed clear of the train.'

Busy Achnasheen

When the LMS extended the use of restaurant cars in Scotland in the thirties (after the sparse Pullman service north of the border was bought out), Achnasheen's lunch time rush became even busier. Already up and down passengers on the Skye Road crossed here, each often overtaking a lengthy goods. Only one of these could normally be accommodated in the yard, so the other had set back on the running line toward Kyle after the up passenger arrived. The down passenger then pulled into its platform. Now the locomotive of the up passenger plucked the restaurant car from the rear of the west-bound train whose passengers had had to take an early lunch. Only when the restaurant car was attached to the up train (some of whose passengers could not wait for their meal) and the up passenger set off on its way, and the freight then followed into the up platform, could the Kyle train proceed on its way. The whole operation, restaurant car switch included, was resumed in the early 1950s and at the time seemed a perfectly normal piece of railway operation.

GW/LNW Junction. An ex-LNWR Bowen Cooke Class G2 0-8-0 No 9345 shunts the yard at Abergavenny Junction on the ex-LNWR/GWR North to West line from Shrewsbury. This was the junction for Abergavenny and the Heads of the Valleys line into the South Wales coal areas taking in Nantybwch with its connection down to Newport via Tredegar, Brynmawr and on to Merthyr. Abergavenny shed was the home of the huge Bowen Cooke designed LMS built 0-8-4 tanks which worked the freights over the steep grades to Brynmawr.

Euston express. The day the writer sought to ride it, the Ro-Railer was out of commission, so he reached Blisworth as the only passenger in a vintage Midland brake composite, the single vehicle handled by a small Johnson 0-6-0.

The real value of the SMJ route was the short cut it provided to the West of England via Broom and Ashchurch, and to the St Pancras main line north of Bedford. Competing for the London–Bristol traffic, a daily fitted freight came this way, and there were four or five 'Q' paths (run when required) for express banana trains from Avonmouth Docks to Somers Town, St Pancras. Some of the wayside stations were as quiet as they were lonely. Father of the SMJ's manager and engineer was a notable railwayman, Harry Willmott, formerly general manager of the Lancashire, Derbyshire & East Coast Railway. The story went the rounds that one day he alighted at Salcey Forest or Stoke Bruern from the inspection saloon (did they have one?), absorbed the distinctly rural scene and asked the station master if he played the violin. 'No, sir,' came the astonished reply. 'A pity; it looks as if this would be a good place to learn.'

The Barnt Green–Evesham–Ashchurch route on which Broom Junction was situated was perhaps typical of many secondary routes in LMS days. Eighteen Monday to Friday trains provided a not particularly good outer Birmingham suburban service so far as Redditch; interestingly BR cut it back to a single daily commuter service, but now it enjoys possibly the best service in its history. One afternoon train terminated at Alcester; another seven, some one-class only, trundled on to Evesham where the Midland station looked across a joint yard to a far busier GW establishment. Several trains made Stratford connections at Broom.

Though some of the route was single track, the southern end with the lightest passenger and local freight business was double, in a typical timetable again seven trains running on Mondays to Fridays. Several missed some stations, but more because there was no business than that they sought to be expresses. Each station had its own master, fully occupied only during the fruit season, and indeed did so well into BR days when the monotony of life with fewer passenger trains carrying virtually no passengers at the southern end was still broken by the clanking of the occasional freight joining the system at Broom Junction or using it as an alternative to the main line down the Lickey incline.

And at Ashchurch, passengers had a choice between the West of England line, always main line as opposed to London in Midland parlance, or joining another non-corridor coach for views of the Severn on to Tewkesbury (about eight weekday only services) or Great Malvern (about four). By the late thirties, most kinds of passengers had found better alternatives to such services, though if daily passenger receipts were disappointing, the staff still handled large quantities of parcels and general freight – and everywhere there were occasional excursions to tax platform capacities.

Equally rural but more important were the 45 miles of the Great Northern and LNWR joint lines which in 1879 opened up a large tract of pleasant countryside, well-endowed in foxhunting, in the South and East

Midland by the Marches. An ex-MR Johnson open cab 0-6-0 No 1720 of shed 22B (Gloucester Barnwood) waits at Dursley station on 5 July 1947, the last year for the LMS. This was the terminus of the short branch from Coaley Junction on the main line from Gloucester to Bristol. There was one intermediate station (Cam); the line closed to all traffic on 1 November 1966.

Midlands between Northampton, Market Harborough, Newark and Nottingham. The LNWR had reached Market Harborough from Rugby in 1850 and from Northampton in 1859 – two years after the Midland came Londonwards from Leicester – having previously reached Melton Mowbray via Syston in 1848, its link-up with the St Pancras main line north of Kettering, to complete a new through route from Nottingham. To an enthusiast making the 46½ mile journey from Market Harborough to Nottingham (London Road Low Level) in a two-coach train hauled by an LMS 2-6-2T, there seemed an awful lot of junctions.

First you started off on the Rugby–Peterborough line (a Prince of Wales or Superheated Precursor on the 4pm from Birmingham often did 76mph coming down past Theddingworth); then 'Market Harborough Midland Junction' as the points to and from the adjacent St Pancras line were officially designated; and in three more miles another fascinating cross-country connection for the collector, 'the Joint' at Welham Junction. Entering Hallaton, the first stop, were the remains of a 3¼ mile east to north curve from Drayton on the Peterborough line; in the middle of this curve was a solitary station, Medbourne, served only by a sparse Great Northern service between Peterborough and the terminus of the GN's Grantham–Leicester branch at Leicester's Belgrave Road. Nine miles and two more stations further on at Marefield South Junction was a south/west curve also used by this GN service, while at the north end of Marefield Junction the triangle between North and West Junctions was completed for the benefit of the GN's Grantham–Leicester service.

A mile beyond this junction was the romantically named John O'Gaunt station, and in a further seven miles, Melton Mowbray; the only place of any size actually on Joint Line metals; not surprisingly, perhaps, the Joint Line sailed across both Midland lines without connection. At Scalford beyond Melton a short branch went off eastward to Waltham-on-the-Wold and two other small spurs for ironstone traffic; the Midland's freight branch from Holwell Junction on the Nottingham–Kettering main line hopped over the Joint Line to join the Waltham Branch at Wycombe Junction. The Joint Line split into two at Harby & Stathern, the Nottingham route keeping left to join the GN Grantham–Nottingham line at Saxondale Junction, thence to London Road Low Level, while the Bottesford branch went straight under the Grantham–Nottingham (junctions in two directions) and along the GN branch to Newark. The Joint Line services terminated in Nottingham, while the rather exiguous services between the Joint Line and Grantham or Newark were maintained by the GN.

On and off the GNR/LNER sought to develop through traffic, scarcely competitive, between Joint Line stations by means of semi-fast trains to both Harborough and Northampton, with onward connections to St Pancras or Euston. There was also a good seasonal business in weekend trains and excursions to Skegness and other East Coast resorts. Freight traffic was substantial; the LNWR/LMS had its own freight depot at Manvers Street, Nottingham, while six or more daily coal trains ran from Colwick Yard via Market Harborough and Northampton to Willesden.

One feature which railways had in common with one another in the hunting shires of the South and East Midlands was a love-hate relationship with the masters, huntsmen and followers of the local packs of foxhounds. In the formative period of railways, when many big landowners had their own packs of hounds, they vigorously objected to proposals for new lines which might interfere with hunting, or worse still, cause casualties among the hounds. Later they were only too pleased to use the railways' facilities, many bringing their horses and hounds to larger meets by train.

With so many railways running through hunting country, from time to time the LMS re-issued to all motive power depots a large poster headed 'Notice to Enginemen: Hounds on the Railway Line', adjuring drivers and firemen to take every care to avoid running into packs of hounds likely to cross the line: 'In cases where there is not enough time to stop the train, steam blown through the cylinder cocks will probably have the effect of frightening the hounds off the line,' it added.

So, there was veteran driver Old Sam, all 17 stone of careful experience, wheeling along when he descried ahead hounds milling at the foot of an embankment with the field waiting expectantly for the terrier-man; clearly Reynard was in a culvert or drain. So Old Sam goes through the routine of blower, regulator, brake, drain-cocks and creeps by at a walk. He leans from his cab and touches the visor of his cap, the master responding by raising his riding crop to the brim of his black topper. As they got away under full regulator and 30 per cent just to start with, the fireman in contemplation of a lot more shovelling being required, ventured to protest. 'Remember, mate', says Sam, 'the gent in the red coat and black 'at is likely a lord but more likely he's a director of the company!'

> **Double Headed by Horse**
> BR London Midland Region as successor to the LMS and LNWR owned and operated a 3ft 6in gauge tramway, the Nantlle. This section (all that remained after the completion of the LNW main line from Pen-y-Groes to Caernarvon and the Nantlle branch itself) began with the Stephensons as early as 1825–8, served a number of slate quarries and was horse worked to the end. The tracks extended eastwards from Nantlle standard gauge terminus through to Nantlle Pool: it was in daily use with 'engine sheds' found at Pen-yr-Orsedd incline foot and behind the houses at Nantlle. Up to four horses worked the service, the heavy trains being 'double headed'.
> J. I. C. Boyd, *Railway World*.

Joint Lines

The LMS inherited four joint railways, two working alongside the LNER, the third the Southern. Each was the result of earlier arrangements entered into by the Midland Railway.

Midland & Great Northern Joint Railway. This was an amalgam of Norfolk, Lincolnshire and Cambridgeshire lines forming the Eastern & Midlands Railway acquired by the Midland and GNR companies on 1 July 1893. Among other attributes this joint ownership gave the Midland, and later the LMS, access to Norwich and the eastern seaboard towns of Yarmouth, Cromer and Sheringham. The M&GN was perhaps best described as 'benevolently independent' until it was handed over to the LNER in 1936: its headquarters were at South Lynn with extensive workshops at Melton Constable. M&GN locomotives were originally painted in a form of yellow ochre but by grouping this had become a drab brown; coaching stock was in varnished teak. It was a system put together piecemeal and built on the cheap with pretensions to be a major traffic route though this in practice only applied to summer Saturdays. In its later years the LMS transferred a number of ageing Midland and LNW coaches to Joint ownership, some of which survived longer – even into BR days – than similar types on the LMS itself.

Somerset & Dorset Joint Railway. Also an amalgamation (acquired under the nose of the GWR), taken over by the Midland, this time in conjunction with the LSWR, vesting day was 1 November 1878. Known previously for its sloth and mismanagement this cross-country route from Bath to Bournemouth gave Midland trains access to the south coast from as far away as Manchester – the route of the LMS Pines Express. Until transfer of responsibilities direct to the LMS (operating and locomotives) and the Southern (civil engineering and coaching stock), the S&DJR had its own headquarters at Bath with a works at Highbridge; locomotives and stock were painted a smart dark blue. Even in early days Derby took care of locomotive construction – mainly 4-4-0s of Class 2P and 0-6-0s, though there was a fine batch of 2-8-0 freight engines designed specially for the steep gradients including the toils out of Bath and up to Masbury summit. After nationalisation the S&D eventually came under the Western Region which closed it down as from March 1966.

Cheshire Lines Committee. To the uninitiated observer this section of railway appeared to be an extension of the Great Central. In early British Railways (LMR) days most of its steam motive power was ex-GCR including some of the last regular turns of the handsome 4-4-0 Directors. Serving Chester, Manchester and Liverpool the CLC was made up of a series of local lines acquired by the GNR and MS&L in 1865 with the Midland taking a third share in 1866. Through coaches from St Pancras to Liverpool Central used the route via Chinley thus giving the Midland access to Merseyside. The LNER constituents worked the CLC from the beginning; the only locomotives, if one can use the term, belonging to the Committee, were some Sentinel railcars from 1929 to 1944.

County Donegal Railways Joint Committee. The greatest of Ireland's 3ft gauge systems, extended from Strabane to Killybegs and Ballyshannon on the wild Atlantic coastline with branches to Letterkenny and down the Finn Valley. By 1 May 1906 the Midland Railway of England was spreading its tentacles widely across the Six Counties and this alarmed the Great Northern Railway (Ireland); the result was that it purchased the Donegal line jointly.

Midland & Great Northern Joint. An M&GN train in its independent days. Class A 4-4-0 No 24 leaves West Runton with a train consisting of mainly ex-Great Northern coaches: one has a roofboard and may be through from King's Cross. The engine was built by Beyer Peacock & Co in 1882 for the Lynn & Fakenham Railway. The frames of this locomotive and the boiler from No 25 were combined in 1936; the amalgamation known as LNER No 025 was withdrawn in May 1941.

186

Joint Line Livery. Somerset & Dorset Joint Railway 4-4-0 No 70 in blue livery on what appears to be a specially posed train (probably near Glastonbury) of three bogie coaches and a six-wheel van on 10 September 1924. The locomotive carries the standard headlamp code for express passenger trains rather than the S&D code of one lamp at the chimney and one over the left hand buffer. It was built at Derby in May 1914 and withdrawn in March 1953 as BR No 40323.

S&D Miscellany. Radstock shed Somerset & Dorset Joint Railway on 21 May 1929 showing four different types of S&D locomotives. The 0-4-0ST No 26A was built at Highbridge in October 1895 and scrapped in December 1930 without receiving an LMS number, 0-6-0T No 21 was a standard LMS design built by W. G. Bagnall of Stafford in 1929 which was finally withdrawn as BR No 47312 in March 1961. Sentinel No 101 was built by the Sentinel Waggon Works Ltd of Shrewsbury in 1929 and became BR No 47190, also withdrawn in March 1961. The final locomotive on the far right was No 9, an 0-6-0ST built by Fox Walker & Co in 1876 and scrapped in December 1930.

Both No 26A and 101 were built to a restricted loading gauge to enable them to work under Tyning Bridge at Radstock and reach the Great Western exchange sidings.

A section from Londonderry to Strabane remained pure Midland and LMS. The Donegal suffered along with other cross-border lines by partition, its only real salvation being the introduction of railbuses by general manager Forbes (pronounced by the locals 'Forbess') in the late 1920s and the elimination of expensive steam hauled passenger trains. Some of the great days of the post-war years were the bank holiday excursions run from Strabane and Stranorlar to Ballyshannon using all the available rolling stock and hard pressing the ageing 2-6-4 tanks, still wearing their geranium red livery and carrying cast brass nameplates. The end came on 31 December 1959; it was still half BR owned though operating very independently and deep into the Republic. It was a fine railway and it will be long remembered.

15
EUSTON'S GHOST: NATIONALISATION AND AFTER

WTT Taxis

During the electrification and resignalling work on the West Coast main line in the 1960s train services were often rearranged and suspended, particularly at weekends, and road services substituted to maintain connections. Normally these were provided by buses but not always. During the weekend of 13–15 February 1965, for example, the LMR issued a traffic notice for the resignalling at Northampton with taxi connection schedules (to run if required) for several services between Long Buckby and Northampton during Saturday and another in the early hours of the Monday morning at 02.02 from Rugby arriving Northampton at 02.57 (if required to convey passengers for Northampton off the 00.40 Birmingham–Rugby).

The working notice did not say whether tickets were checked as passengers boarded and alighted or whether station staff had to hail any passing taxi or whether they were pre-booked. If the latter, were the drivers paid even if the journey was not required and if it was made, did the taxi switch on its notice to ply for hire on the return?

At midnight on 31 December 1947 many engine drivers of the night trains, and on depot, sounded their whistles; as good trade unionists they had nearly all supported nationalisation, and though the LMS had achieved much after its unpromising start, it was not the same as killing off the legend of the Great Western. The LMS company became a ghost undertaking, its assets gone, but its final annual general meeting a few weeks later had none of the dramatic sorrow of the GW's or the drama of the LNER's where shareholders demanded more dividend instead of compensation for the directors' loss of office. Those of the LMS sought no compensation.

But again it was an unpromising start. Lord Stamp was dead, senior officers Ashton Davies and Stanier had retired, and three outstanding LMS men went elsewhere, Sir William Wood to the Transport Commission, Robin Riddles to the Railway Executive and F. A. Pope to become chairman of the Ulster Transport Authority. The names of the new bodies were as forbidding as the changes. In Britain, under the British Transport Commission came the Railway Executive and under that the six Regions. The London Midland always sounded (as it still does) the most awkward title in terms of railway geography. The far-flung system of the LMS had originally developed through history and competition and emerged as a shot-gun-wedding in 1923. It made even less sense after nationalisation but the Region perpetuated it.

The London Midland Region began by inheriting the LMS minus the Scottish lines which were amalgamated with those of the LNER. Joint lines were also allocated, the London Midland taking over the Cheshire Lines and the Eastern Region the Midland & Great Northern Joint (this had often been proposed by the LMS and always firmly rejected by the LNER.) The Mersey Railway was also swallowed up at this stage together with a string of minor joint lines. Derby's involvement in providing motive power for the Somerset & Dorset (responsibility for the infrastructure had long passed to the Southern) continued awhile. Canals, docks (other than 'packet ports'), hotels and other interests were hived off to other Executives, as were the extensive road transport investments.

The first adjustment after the initial move was to transfer the South and Central Wales penetrating lines away to the Western, and on 20 February 1949 the London, Tilbury & Southend was transferred to the Eastern. But that still left many penetrating routes, and stations of two regions in many cities and towns. It took much more than an act of nationalisation to prevent rivalries continuing. In the 1960s Great

188

Northern line and ex-LNER men delighted in the fact that their trains were sometimes reaching northern and Scottish destinations faster than could be done from Euston or St Pancras. At that time, said Gerry Fiennes, 'it was fun to emulate the Great Northern's attitude to the Euston Confederacy. Edmond Denison to Mark Huish: "You may leave when you like and arrive when you choose. We will leave later and arrive before you".'

From April 1950 the London Midland, beginning to lose much of its LMS identity while the Western and Southern had rolled themselves up in tight balls, lost many former Midland routes to the Eastern and North Eastern while much of the former Great Central came in. For some years, however, the operating and motive power departments continued working on 'system' lines, which involved a certain amount of continued 'penetration'; not until February 1958 were universally-geographical

A Euston Ghost. In the twilight of its years, LMS-built Compound No 41162 takes the 3.5pm semi-fast service to Northampton on 13 July 1957. Surely one of the last turns for one of these classic 4-4-0s carrying class A headlamps on the main line.

189

A New Era Dawns. Euston station about 1967 with the rebuilding almost complete and a full service running. The train on the extreme left, 1H44, is the 5.20pm Euston to Manchester via Stoke, 1G70 the 5.15pm Euston to Wolverhampton and 1P79 the 5.05pm Euston to Carlisle.

boundaries enforced. Ultimately there came the Beeching axe not merely on branch and secondary lines but also on duplicate main ones. No longer does St Pancras serve Leeds and Bradford, or Paddington have real expresses to Birmingham. Duplicate goods and marshalling facilities were removed, sadly including some of the new yards conceived under the 1955 Modernisation Plan, and of course collieries and steelworks which had enjoyed formerly competitive rail links now had only one.

As we shall see later, in an all-Scotland Scottish Region the first five chiefs came from the LNER, and eventually the London Midland was also to come substantially under LNER officers, though to begin with LMS influence was strong at the Railway Executive (R. A. Riddles was in charge of mechanical and electrical engineering and research, and S. E. Parkhouse, who had been assistant chief operating manager at Euston, took up the national operating role) and it was widely assumed that because of its greater strides toward standardisation and mechanisation LMS thinking would predominate. And after the abandonment of the first Railway Executive blood-and-custard livery, LMS red was applied to most locomotive-hauled passenger stock for some years.

The first shake-up was when John Elliot was moved from the Southern at the start of 1950. Though he only headed the London Midland for thirteen months before becoming chairman of the Railway Executive, he imported various Southern ideas, especially about station appearances. Horrified about the dilapidations on the London Midland's electrified North London line, he rapidly put inexpensive face-lifting and redecoration in hand. He opened up the management team. S. G. Hearn came from the Western as operating supremo, though his assistant, S. A. Fitch, was from the Southern. However motive power and train services showed little immediate change. The two LMS pioneer diesel-electric main line locomotives, Nos 10000 and 10001 (the latter entering service after nationalisation), continued to be employed. After trials on the St Pancras–Manchester service, they ran coupled together between Euston and Glasgow, where they could cover twice the daily mileage of the Stanier Pacifics. But they had no successors other than three contemporary prototype diesels from the SR until the modernisation plan of 1955.

Robin Riddles at Railway Executive headquarters was not interested

Intruder. In 1963 the London Midland Region took on all the Great Western's lines from Shrewsbury down to and along the Cambrian Coast soon displacing clean Manor class 4-6-0s with filthy BR Standard Class 4s of the same wheel arrangement, and closing the section from Ruabon to Barmouth Junction. One of the classes to intrude was the LMS 2MT 2-6-0 as can be seen by No 46519 with a two-coach train making its smoky way out of Barmouth with a Dolgelly train in September 1963.

The Older Order Changes. Birmingham New Street station during the early stages of rebuilding c1964. Construction of the present concourse level has just begun on the Station Street side while No 4 signalbox (bottom left) is closed and ready for demolition. The old cross station footbridge is clearly seen together with the Midland style station awnings adjacent to the central Queen's Drive and the remnants of the huge overall roof. A dmu is entering old platform 6 while an 8F class 2-8-0 trundles a van train through platform 4 – a rare occurrence. It is virtually the end for the old station and for steam. The post-war rebuilding of the LNWR side can be seen in its stark reality to the left of the picture. During the demolition of the refreshment room on platform 6 the contractors uncovered an unopened crate containing genuine MR cups and saucers – it was sold to an enthusiast for half a crown.

End of an Era. The last days of steam. Attacking Shap bank are BR Class 4 4-6-0 No 75032 and a grimy LMS Class 5 4-6-0. They head the 8.45am Morecambe–Glasgow on 15 January 1962.

in main line diesels. His attitude was not unique. One evening at Euston, two VIPs arrived to catch the night sleeper train and walked to the end of the platform to observe the locomotive. An inspector deferentially suggested that the gentlemen should join the train as it was about to depart. 'But we have no engine yet, only a couple of parcels vans in front' said one of the pair, peering into the dusk at No 10000 and No 10001.

Elliot was followed at Euston by James Watkins, an ex-Midland Railway operating man who was unlikely to start a revolution. Meanwhile there had come the upheaval of the 1953 Transport Act and the uprating of Regions, in accordance with the Conservative Party's desire to see something like a touch of renaissance of the old railway company pride. Area Boards were formed to whom the regional chiefs – renamed first Chief Regional Managers, and then Regional General Managers – now owed allegiance as well as to the Transport Commission itself. Policy directives now came from the Commission through the Boards and general managers, who were no longer by-passed. Watkins, known as 'the Colonel' on the LMS because of his impressive World War I service, was called to the Commission in 1955 by General Sir Brian Robertson.

His place at Euston was taken by David Blee, from the GW via the Executive and the Commission – the term musical chairs was beginning to be mentioned – who was intimately involved in the first modernisation plan and has sometimes been said to have been responsible for its weak commercial justification. As Sir William Wood had once commented, the LMS was too large for effective management and even the Region was always seen as unwieldy, though a scheme for a separate North Western Region based on Manchester, parallelling the North Eastern, died (like many others) for want of financial attractiveness.

By 1960 Sir Reginald Wilson had moved from the Eastern chair (where he had devised an organisation to break up that Region into 'Lines' which were good operating and business units). He felt the same recipe could invigorate the London Midland, initially calling for a North Western and a Midland line organisation. His boast that he had at last broken up the over-centralised Euston establishment was premature. David Blee had begun reorganisation in 1957, but keeping the big Regional office at Euston and establishing a number of Divisions for primarily commercial functions, retaining the operating headquarters at Crewe, Derby and Manchester. Not enough for Sir Reginald, who then had H. C. ('Bill') Johnson brought in as general manager; they had established an excellent working relationship on the Eastern. Johnson stayed through a critical period before going to the Board, first as vice-chairman and then chairman. He was followed at Euston by no less than three ex-LNER protégés with his own background – W. G. Thorpe, R. L. E. Lawrence and J. Bonham-Carter. There were other LNER imports, too, though some of the upset among former LMS men was reduced by the fact that the Region was no longer recognisable as a clear successor to the LMS – and ex LMS men held key positions elsewhere.

The first seven or so years from 1948 were an attempt to return to pre-war standards. New steam locomotives came from H. G. Ivatt's drawing

Forerunner of the InterCity 125. St Pancras on 6 July 1960. While the electrification of the ex-LNWR main line was progressing, train services were diverted to alternative London termini. Here the Midland Pullman is leaving St Pancras on the 12.45pm trip to Nottingham and back. This diesel-electric set ran between Manchester and St Pancras and vice versa morning and evening to give Manchester businessmen a high speed luxury service. Between times and to avoid standing idle in London it also ran to Leicester or Nottingham

board, some being modifications of Stanier designs; then came the first BR standard locomotives produced by R. A. Riddles's team mainly of LMS descent. The Class 5 mixed traffic locomotive was almost pure Stanier. Familiar named trains reappeared together with some new titles, even if the streamlined Coronation Scot never returned as such in its blue and silver glory. There was though the Caledonian, a fast lightweight Euston–Glasgow service providing a late afternoon link.

The 1955 modernisation plan brought the first major changes, though, with hindsight, curious priorities. Investment was poured into freight facilities: even if the Carlisle marshalling yard and the Bletchley flyover seemed well justified at the date of their inception, they quickly became white elephants. Electrification was held back for some years while the

Track Modernisation. The LMS pioneered track relaying with cranes but a more sophisticated system was adopted by BR – using 60ft sections on concrete sleepers. A length has just been laid and the cranes will shortly move along to lift the next section into the gap. This work was a preliminary to the electrification of the West Coast Main Line. The location is Hest Bank at the only point where West Coast passengers can see the sea – just!

pros and cons of investing in the East and West Coast main lines were debated. When finally London to Birmingham, Liverpool and Manchester emerged as the obvious prime candidate, there was further delay because the Commission and Ministry of Transport were dissatisfied with the Region's presentation (done hastily, to beat the rival King's Cross to Leeds and York scheme).

Eventually electrification came in by the back door: instalment one was the Styal Loop near Manchester, ostensibly to test the 25kV 50Hz system. The, predictably, favourable reports enabled the wires to be strung up over the Crewe–Manchester and Crewe–Liverpool sections. The extension southward to London and then northward to Glasgow became irresistible, though causing massive inconvenience and temporary traffic losses. Most of the small goods yards at wayside stations were retained in the associated resignalling.

Completion of Britain's first true main line electrification including continuous welded track, and the reconstruction of Euston, were crowned in 1968 when HM The Queen opened the rebuilt terminus. It matched the stark reconstruction of New Street, Birmingham. And 100mph running revolutionised the timings: Manchester in just over 2½ hours and Birmingham in just over 1½ hours fought off that growing threat from internal air services. Electrification to Glasgow was completed in 1974 but air services could still outpace the 5–5¼hr rail times.

The Midland's St Pancras–Manchester and the Great Western's Paddington–Birmingham routes enjoyed an Indian Summer with their Blue Pullmans during the disruption caused by the electrification. Then many things changed. Sheffield became the effective end of the line from

Interim Development. Hampton-in-Arden in 1967 just after the completion of electrification. A Class 310 EMU enters on a Coventry to Wolverhampton working. Hampton-in-Arden station was rebuilt for the electric service and the platforms were roughly doubled in length to accommodate 12-coach trains, as main line expresses were scheduled to stop there covering this important dormitory area. With the construction of the nearby Birmingham International station (completed 1979) serving the enlarged airport and with access to the M6 motorway, Hampton reverted to a suburban station with no expresses stopping.

195

West Coast Electric. A modern scene on the ex Caledonian main line at Hartsope (Beattock) showing the 14.10 Glasgow to Euston express on 24 July 1982 – a named class 87 electric locomotive No 87 029 takes a standard ten coach train over flat bottom track under 25kV wires. The coaching stock is varied – Mark I brake, three Mark III, Mark I catering vehicle, four Mark III and a Mark II.

St Pancras; the Paddington service to Birmingham was relegated mainly to semi-fasts via Oxford; South West and South Wales services to Liverpool and Manchester were diverted via Birmingham. New Street became an Inter-City provincial cross-roads with through services or cross-platform connections to and from all parts of the country; in LMS days things centred more on Crewe, whose great station has recently been rationalised.

Electrification was successful in transforming the quality of service, passenger traffic eventually – though not at first – increasing far more rapidly than forecast. With local government backing, New Street also now handles dramatically increased suburban, especially cross-city, business. As though finally to lay the ghost, the new Regional offices (with Cyril Bleasdale, former Inter-City director, as general manager) are nearby, administering a more compact railway with ever fewer point ends – and an especial reduction in St Pancras's former empire, the former main line to Manchester now terminating as a single-line branch at Matlock, while the Settle & Carlisle hangs on a thread.

196

In hindsight, not only were resources constantly being wasted on changing the basic political structure, the Railway Executive and then the Commission eventually disappearing until there was just the Railways Board or British Railways (later British Rail), but a prompter sort out of regional boundaries would have been far less demoralising to staff than what seemed constant tinkering.

Changing political demands and patterns of trade and competition would of course have ensured problems enough, and with the need to reduce staff numbers dramatically it is hard to see how morale could have been kept high almost whatever detailed decisions had been taken. But the constant meddling, moving key people around and changing their responsibilities, opening and closing administrative offices, changing the basic emphasis meant that customers, the public, and even MPs were bewildered. Large amounts of hard work and goodwill were wasted. It perhaps all went back to government policy. In the 1840s, the French had observed the logic of regional systems. The British insisted on competition, and then after nationalisation, over a century later, tried to forget history and pretend that a geographical solution was easy. Few politicians, and even some staff at headquarters, realised the pain and grief they were giving the men who kept the wheels moving.

The Scottish framework was at least more understandable. HQ was established in Glasgow, rather to the disgust of those LNER staff who had to move from Edinburgh, though the head man was from the LNER, T. F. Cameron, who excited comment by continuing to reside in a flat in the North British Hotel in Edinburgh and commuting to Glasgow in an official *car*. Though seeming rather lugubrious and outspoken, he was an able railway manager, and set about the task of unification with skill and energy. By his retirement in 1956, Cameron had completed his main task. The next four also came from the LNER. No wonder the LMS contingent sometimes growled.

National Pride?
Shortly after nationalisation the chairman of the new British Transport Commission, former civil servant Sir Cyril Hurcomb, went out on an official visit. A procession of bigwigs paused in front of a 2-6-4 tank engine at Derby, and the driver was accorded a few words of greeting and a handshake. As the party moved on, an assistant was ordered to 'get that man's name and address and tell him the chairman will send him a signed photograph.'

'I've been for nationalisation all my life, but I'm sorry to say goodbye to the chairman of my old company,' came the reply.

Modernisation on the G&SW. Dumfries station in July 1984 showing the 13.40 Glasgow (Central) to Carlisle headed by Class 27 diesel-electric locomotive No 27 041 complete with snowplough and BR Mark I coaching stock. The station is still very much in original condition.

The first fruits of the 1955 plan were dieselisation; steam was completely banished north of Perth by the end of 1961. Electrification of the Glasgow suburban lines at last got under way. Rationalisation of routes involved leaving only the end of the Oban line, linked to the West Highland at Crianlarich by a spur previously mainly used for freight. The Sou'West 'Port Road' from Dumfries to Stranraer went, so that the London boat trains later made an absurd detour via Kilmarnock. The LMS Princes Street station in Edinburgh also went and express Glasgow–Edinburgh traffic was concentrated on the former LNER route, while Aberdeen lost its former LMS racing ground from Perth to Kinnaber. There were dour years here, too, but the railway has again identified itself closely with the needs of Scotland. 'Scotrail' has given the Scots greater charge of their own affairs, obviously a sensible move.

Finally a note on Ireland. After nationalisation in Britain, the Government of Northern Ireland arranged with the British Transport Commission for the Northern Counties Committee lines to be transferred to the Northern Ireland Road Board, set up before the war. The NCC fetched £2.6 million, paid to the BTC of course not to the LM Region. The Road Board was then merged into the new Ulster Transport Authority. Frank Pope was at first delighted to move from being an LMS vice president to take over as chairman of the UTA; but Ulster politics proved their predictable minefield and he was glad to come back to the BTC before the break up of the UTA. The story of railways in Northern Ireland since the war does not make pretty reading, though there has been a new management spirit in recent years.

The Dundalk, Newry & Greenore Railway closed at the end of 1951 and the BTC sold off the assets at more or less scrap value.

Midland Modernisation. Class 45 diesel-electric No 45 110 takes a Manchester to St Pancras express, possibly the 18.55 (Sundays) Manchester Piccadilly via Sheffield, through Chinley North Junction in September 1976. The wagons to the left of the photograph are 32 ton air brake hoppers with canopies, maybe with coal ex the East Midlands for Garston shipment.

16
PRESERVATION

The 07.45 from Derby is the first of the day's Inter-City 125 HST trains to Birmingham and the South West for the hours of darkness are given over to the comings and goings of the many interlinking TPO services using the station as a connecting centre. It is a dull and damp January morning but even so a chill wind blows across the platform as Cliff Pegg and Bernard Bartram come down the steps from the footbridge looking forward to the warmth of the solitary first class coach in the 125's make-up; they are on their way to Birmingham to look at the Railway Museum's Stanier-designed Jubilee class 4-6-0 No 5593 *Kolhapur* currently into its third year of BR main line certification. Cliff Pegg is LMS born and bred and the London Midland's chief boiler inspector. Bernard Bartram, later to the railway, is his companion from the mechanical side.

As they settle down for the forty minute journey they reflect on their jobs as guardians of the standards set for any privately-owned locomotive allowed to run over BR tracks, with safety their watchword. Unless the engine is passed out by them it simply does not run. First comes the five year (extended under certain circumstances to seven) heavy examination with the boiler out of the frames, tubes removed permitting detailed examination inside plus corresponding checks on the mechanical side; on completion of that job, costing well over five figures, the treasured certificate becomes available. But this is only the entrance fee to the club, for biennial inspections are also called for (with charges to the owner accordingly) and a constant watch is kept on the engine with the co-operation of members of the museum's workshop staff – all to be sure that the sight and sound of what is, after all, a museum piece today, can give joy and satisfaction to thousands as it once more takes to the rails to haul a trainload of passengers.

Today, they muse, it is Tyseley. Last week was Carnforth and Hereford; next it will be Bridgnorth, all homes for preserved ex-LMS engines covering main-line duties. Nearer to Derby is Butterley, the Midland Railway Centre concentrating on things Midland as is proper for a museum operation so close by to the still extant railway town. *Kolhapur* has a number of trips to make, all away from home, during the next few months; Derby, Manchester, Southport, York and over the Long Drag via Settle and Appleby to Carlisle. Cliff Pegg is to meet Dave Tobin, Tyseley's LMS-trained boilersmith to check that the new firebox stays are tight while Bartram's job will be to look at the bogie wheels (one pair off an LNWR Claughton) which have been returned to the correct BR profile on the one time Bescot shed lathe. Tyseley, like Carnforth (once an LMS shed) and Bridgnorth on the Severn Valley Railway, is well equipped to undertake heavy locomotive repairs.

The LMS is very adequately represented in today's preservation field though sadly no Patriot was kept and no Royal Scot is currently available for main line running. But there is much to see and enthusiasts (many with railway skills) have made sure that most of the classes in latter day use are alive and in working order. Major examples include No 46229 *Duchess of Hamilton* (originally an exhibit along with several other classes at a Butlin's Holiday Camp and back in 1939 masquerading as No 6220 *Coronation* in streamlined red and gold livery for the North American tour of the Coronation Scot), No 6201 – the record-breaking *Princess Elizabeth*, Jubilee class 4-6-0s 5593, 5596 and 5690, several Class 5 4-6-0s and somewhat remarkably an ex-Somerset & Dorset Derby-built 2-8-0. Running routes vary; the Duchess, for example, is particularly well travelled, being at home on the BR Shakespeare Limited running on Sundays from Marylebone to Stratford-upon-Avon or over the hills to Carlisle. One popular and well-used steam route is that of the old LMS/GW Joint line from Shrewsbury to Hereford.

But high standards also apply to museum and tourist railways, those with an LMS content highlighted by the Keighley & Worth Valley Railway in Yorkshire, the Midland Railway Trust in Derbyshire, the Lakeside & Haverthwaite adjacent to Windermere, Dinting Railway Centre near Glossop, and the Strathspey Railway out of Boat of Garten in Scotland. Add to these the popular and well-run Severn Valley Railway in Worcestershire, an old Great Western line but with a strong LMS flavour today, it is a fascinating variety. Here are Class 5s, Fowler 0-6-0s, Jinty 0-6-0 tanks, Fairburn 2-6-4 tanks and the later 2-6-0s all alive and very much kicking due to one thing only, the inordinate strength and determination of Britain's railway enthusiasts. Facilities are also available at the National Railway Museum, York, which not only cares for *Duchess of Hamilton* but has also steamed and run on the main line Midland Compound No 1000 and the LNWR 2-4-0 Precedent class *Hardwicke*.

The LMS can take credit for some initiative in the preservation field, setting aside a number of locomotives on withdrawal from service, but generally speaking the company's attitude was patchy. True the LNWR had kept the high flying *Cornwall* and the Crewe-type *Columbine* while

Sad Omissions. The last three London & North Western Railway express passenger locomotives specially posed for a photograph before being scrapped, 20 June 1949. They are superheated Precursor class 4-4-0 No 25297 Sirocco, rebuilt Claughton 4-6-0 No 6004 and Prince of Wales class 4-6-0 No 25752. None carried its BR number and none was preserved, thus leaving Hardwicke *as the only typical LNW express locomotive.*

Doomed Engines. Kirtley 2-4-0 No 156A stands in Derby paintshop with Johnson 0-4-0T No 1226, Kirtley 0-6-0 goods No 2388, 4-2-2 No 118 and North London 4-4-0T No 6445. Originally kept by the Derby authorities for preservation, the plan was thwarted by W. A. Stanier who ordered them to be scrapped. Only a great deal of begging reprieved the single wheeler – the others had to go.

Caley Veteran. The last single driver locomotive in regular service, LMS No 14010, formerly Caledonian No 123/1123. It was built by Neilson & Co in 1886 for display at the Edinburgh Exhibition and was later purchased by the CR. For many years No 123 was used as Royal Train pilot engine and to haul officers' inspection saloons. This photograph was taken about 1935 at St Rollox works in Glasgow alongside Royal Scot No 6107 Argyll & Sutherland Highlander, probably just before No 14010 was withdrawn pending preservation.

the Furness bar-framed 0-4-0 *Coppernob* stood on a plinth at Barrow station but preservation was not a matter which found general favour. To start with, there was little room to store relics except perhaps in the paint shops at the various works. Crewe kept *Columbine* and *Cornwall* and on withdrawal in 1932, a champion of the 1895 Races to Scotland, the 2-4-0 Precedent class *Hardwicke*.

In the earlier years Derby showed less interest although there were at one time the 7ft 9½in driving wheels from 4-2-2 *Princess of Wales* under the clock tower at the foot of the 'Clerks Bridge'. Otherwise there was something of a tradition that once the last of a locomotive class had been withdrawn no-one was expected to have any further interest in it.

Irish Survivor. Ex-NCC 2-6-4 tank No 4 (built Derby 1947) was one of the last steam engines to work over the Northern Ireland Railways system, being kept for work on a series of civil engineering specials. Purchased for preservation it is now cared for by the Railway Preservation Society of Ireland and is shown here leaving Belfast York Road station with a public excursion in 1976. Other ex-NCC locomotives are preserved along with County Donegal Railway's Joint Committee stock in the Belfast Transport Museum.

This precept possibly led to the scrapping of all the Kirtley general arrangement drawings. Nevertheless in the late 1920s there seems to have been the beginning of a change of heart with the retention of two Kirtley double framed engines, No 2385, a Kitson 0-6-0 of 1856 (one of a class of 560) and 2-4-0 No 1, formerly No 156 built at Derby in 1866. There followed Johnson 4-2-2 No 673 of 1897 (restored as No 118) and 0-4-4 tank No 1226 which was repainted Midland Red with its old number 6 on the bunker and MR on the tanks. Last and for Derby the most unusual was the survivor of the North London Railway 4-4-0 tank LMS No 6445: even more surprising the engine was repainted in LNWR black livery and fully lined out. All were kept in the paint shop. But in 1932, disaster struck.

In January W. A. Stanier became CME with a remit to 'get things done'. It appears that within a short time of his arrival he was being taken round the works and while in the paint shop, a comment was dropped on the lack of space to paint engines with the preserved locomotives taking up so much room. 'Preserved engines?' said the great man, 'I haven't authorised any engines to be preserved. Scrap them.' It took a lot of begging to get a reprieve for the single No 118 but the others had to go. Probably nobody at Crewe was prepared to mention keeping a George 4-4-0 – the biggest gap on the present day list – after that.

The Scots did a little better – possibly because they were far enough away not to be noticed. In 1935 two engines were put on one side, representing the Caledonian and Highland Railways, single wheeler No 123 which, like *Hardwicke*, had played a part in the 1895 Races and No 103, a Jones Goods as an example of the first British 4-6-0. The Glasgow & South Western was unable to be represented as its stock had been decimated in the early years of the LMS. Both locomotives were kept in store at St Rollox works.

Another ancient to survive, by good fortune rather than design, was an example of the first constituent company of the LMS; the Liverpool & Manchester Railway's 0-4-2 *Lion* built by Todd, Kitson & Laird of Leeds in 1838. On withdrawal by the LNWR in 1859 this had been sold to the Mersey Docks & Harbour Board and the frames, cylinders and motion used as a pumping engine. In 1928 it became redundant but was fortunately recognised as an early locomotive and presented to the Liverpool Engineering Society. To everyone's credit it was restored, using a slightly different boiler and ran in the cavalcade celebrating the centenary of the Liverpool & Manchester Railway in 1930. The other

historic engine from the same company, *Rocket* was already in the Science Museum, London.

Fortunately, the historic engines were unaffected by World War II, surviving the various drives for scrap, though post war management was more concerned with survival than preservation. At the eleventh hour in 1947, H. G. Ivatt gave permission for LMS No 20002, formally MR No 2 to be retained, replacing old No 1 cruelly sent for scrap by his predecessor.

The new British Railways era had little time for the past and let the last LNWR superheated Precursor class No 25297 *Sirocco* go for breaking up but not before Crewe works had tried to hide her away. Sadly authority once again followed Stanier's example and she went for scrap with 'farewell Good and Faithful Servant' chalked on her smokebox door. The nameplates were preserved.

With some pressure from the premier amateur organisations, particularly the Stephenson Locomotive Society and the Railway Correspondence & Travel Society, the British Transport Commission was persuaded to form a collecting policy and set up a Museum at Clapham, fortunately taking ex-LMS locomotives into consideration exampled by the Midland compound No 1000 and LT&SR 4-4-2 tank *Thundersley* and an L&Y 2-4-2T. Later with the formation of the National Railway Museum at York all these exhibits have been properly housed and cared for – some including *Hardwicke* and No 1000 have been steamed on BR tracks, as has an LNWR 0-6-2T now owned by the National Trust.

But the accolade goes to private preservation, for without the determination of hundreds of individuals, Cliff Pegg and Bernard Bartram would have not been on the 07.45 from Derby on that January day.

The Long Drag. The sun shines through a hole in the clouds on a bitterly cold and windy 21 March 1987, pinpointing the stark bleakness of the Settle–Carlisle line, once the Midland's route to Scotland. The photograph shows preserved Jubilee class 4-6-0 No 5593 Kolhapur *with a ten coach train of 360 tons tare leaving Garsdale. The train, which has come from St Pancras, is a Birmingham Railway Museum charter to Carlisle with steam haulage Leeds to Carlisle. No 5593 was shedded at Leeds (Holbeck) shed in its last years of BR service, working parcels trains to Manchester during the week with Saturday express turns to Carlisle; the engine was withdrawn in 1967 and this was the first visit over its old stamping ground for twenty years.*

203

CHRONOLOGY

LMS Chronology

1923	1 Jan	LMS formed under provision of Railways Act 1921; eight constituent and 27 subsidiary companies.
	1 Jan	Passenger fares reduced from 75 per cent to 50 per cent over 1914 rates.
	Dec	Royal Academicians commissioned to paint posters.
1924	23 Apr–1 Nov	British Empire Exhibition Wembley.
	Mar	Sir Arthur Watson retired as general manager.
	Mar	Rt Hon H. G. Burgess appointed general manager.
1925	9 May–31 Oct	British Empire Exhibition Wembley.
	Aug	George Hughes retired as chief mechanical engineer and Sir Henry Fowler appointed.
1926	4 Jan	Sir Josiah Stamp appointed president of the executive and from Jan 1927 chairman
	1 May–early Dec	Coal miners strike.
	4–12 May	General Strike.
1927	19 Feb	Burton & Ashby Light Railway closed.
	31 Mar	Rt Hon H. G. Burgess retires.
	6 Apr	Introduction of Garratt locomotives for working Toton–Brent coal trains.
	15 May	Introduction of Tilbury–Dunkerque steamship service in conjunction with Alsace Lorraine–Angleterre Steamship Company and Northern Railway of France.
	14 Aug	Introduction of Royal Scot class of locomotives.
	26 Sept	Non stop runs Euston–Carlisle (Kingmoor)
1928	1 Jan	Schedule of Standard Charges fixed by Railway Rates Tribunal under 1921 Act now operative.
	30 Apr	Special non-stop runs of Royal Scot London Euston to Glasgow (locomotive No 6113) and London Euston to Edinburgh (locomotive No 1054), setting records for the distance.
	30 Apr	Steamship services between North West England and Northern Ireland concentrated at Heysham. Fleetwood services discontinued.
	3 Aug	Road Transport Act passed empowering the company to operate its own passenger and goods vehicles or to enter into agreement with local authorities or companies running omnibuses.
	24 Sep	Introduction of third class sleeping cars.
	13 Oct	Charfield accident.
1929	Jan	Early trials with ultra high pressure 4-6-0 compound No 6399 *Fury*. Inspector killed when tube burst (10 Jan).
	16 Apr	The longest railway platform in Europe, between the LMS stations of Victoria and Exchange, Manchester, was opened by Miss Ena Best, the 'Railway Queen'. 2,238ft long, it took three years to complete.
	9 Aug	The Royal Highlander from Euston to the north of Scotland ran in six portions, each train serving a different locality. One went to Inverness and north, one to Oban, one to Aberdeen, another terminated at Perth and the fifth and sixth portions served Aviemore and Boat of Garten.
1930	Sep	Liverpool & Manchester Railway centenary celebrations.
	–	Closure of approximately 22 branch lines to passenger traffic.
	–	As result of Road Traffic Act the LMS buys substantial minority bus interests but ceases as its own bus operator.
1931	1 Jan	Sir Henry Fowler appointed assistant to vice president.
	–	Karrier Ro-railer bus trials on Hemel Hempstead–Harpenden branch.
	22 Mar	Leighton Buzzard accident.
	11 May	MSJ&A line electrified at 1,500V dc.
	1 Jul	Historic mansion near Stratford upon Avon opened as the Welcombe Hotel. Part of the estate once belonged to William Shakespeare.
1932	1 Jan	W. A. Stanier appointed chief mechanical engineer.
	Apr–Jul	Ro-railer in service (intermittently) between Blisworth, Stratford upon Avon and Welcombe Hotel.
1933	1 Jan	Pooling of receipts over competitive routes between LMS, GWR and LNER.
	Jan	Sir Henry Fowler retires.
	27 Jun	First 4-6-2 type locomotive on LMS introduced No 6200 *Princess Royal* and first Stanier express design.
	3 Jul	New station at South Kenton opened (Euston–Watford dc line).
	1 May–11 Nov	Visit of *Royal Scot* locomotive and train to USA and Canada.
1934	20 Aug	Railway Air Services Glasgow–Belfast–Manchester–Castle Bromwich (Birmingham)–Croydon route opened.
1935	1 Jan	Monthly return ticket, 1d per mile introduced experimentally during summer from 1 May 1933, made permanent and available all year.

Jan	Reorganisation of motive power depots into 29 districts.	3 Sep	Outbreak of Second World War.
13 Mar	Kings Langley accident.	11 Sep	General speed restrictions of 45mph introduced.
Sep	Sir Josiah Stamp elected president for 1936 of the British Association for the Advancement of Science.	Oct	Relaxed to 60mph maximum.

Jan — Reorganisation of motive power depots into 29 districts.

13 Mar — Kings Langley accident.

Sep — Sir Josiah Stamp elected president for 1936 of the British Association for the Advancement of Science.

1936 Spring — Rudyard Lake near Leek, Staffordshire was restocked with some 10,000 roach, perch and carp. It was a favourite haunt of anglers and a reservoir for the Trent & Mersey Canal owned by the LMS.

6 Jul — The Royal Scot, 10.00am Euston–Glasgow accelerated to cover the 401½ miles in 7½ hours with one stop at Kingmoor to change crews.

16/17 Nov — High speed runs between Euston and Glasgow and return with locomotive No 6201 (preliminary trials before introduction of Coronation Scot).

1937 29 Jun — Locomotive No 6220 *Coronation* reaches 114mph between Whitmore and Crewe.

5 Jul — Introduction of Coronation Scot high speed service Euston–Glasgow in 6½ hours.

27 Sept — Accelerated train service on Midland Division. 34 runs at over 60mph.

1938 14 Mar — Wirral Railway (Birkenhead–New Brighton and West Kirby) electrified and trains run over Mersey Railway to Liverpool Central Low Level.

Jun — Sir Josiah Charles Stamp created 1st Baron Stamp of Shortlands.

22 Jul — School of Transport, Derby, opened.

Sep — Centenary of London & Birmingham Railway, special exhibitions at Euston and New Street.

– — Hudd ATC trial introduced on LTS section (not fully operational until 1949; predecessor of BR AWS).

1939 21 Mar-
14 Apr — Locomotive No 6229 disguised as 6220 *Coronation* and train visited USA on tour. Exhibited at New York World Fair after tour but meanwhile war started in Europe. (Locomotive returned in 1942, coaches in 1946.)

3 Sep — Outbreak of Second World War.

11 Sep — General speed restrictions of 45mph introduced.

Oct — Relaxed to 60mph maximum.

1940 – — Construction of one hundred 350hp diesel shunting locomotives authorised.

27 May-
4 Jun — Evacuation of British Expeditionary Force from Dunkerque. SS *Scotia* sunk.

24 Aug-
10 May
1941 — 170 air attacks on LMS (97 heavy).

1941 11 Feb — Authorised maximum speed increased to 75mph.

16/17 Apr — Lord Stamp, his wife and eldest son killed by German bomb.

Jun — Sir William Wood appointed president.

1943 — W. A. Stanier awarded a knighthood in New Year honours, presentation from King George VI at Buckingham Palace 9 February.

Apr — First rebuild of Royal Scot class locomotive with taper boiler.

1944 Apr — Sir William Stanier retires; C. E. Fairburn appointed acting chief mechanical engineer.

1945 8 May — VE Day. (End of the war in Europe). All freight traffic cancelled this being a public holiday. Two days' notice given.

15 Aug — VJ Day. (End of the war with Japan). All traffic cancelled, notice only being given of public holiday BBC news 11pm the evening before.

30 Sep — Bourne End accident.

1 Oct — Restaurant cars reinstated.

1 Oct — Exchange of mail bags by TPOs reinstated.

12 Oct — Death of C. E. Fairburn.

1946 Jan — H. G. Ivatt appointed chief mechanical engineer.

1947 18 Dec — First main line diesel locomotive No 10000 runs trials.

1948 1 Jan — BR formed under powers of Transport Act 1947.

ACKNOWLEDGEMENTS

Any authors attempting to put together a work of this kind without the constant help of railwaymen who knew and worked for the LMS would have been out of their minds. So it is with uninhibited thanks that we record the very great assistance that has been given from the conception through to proof reading by D. S. M. Barrie, A. J. Powell and John Edgington who have formed what has proved to be an editorial and writing panel. Derek Barrie (who ended his career as General Manager BR Eastern Region) worked in the LMS Press Office at the same time being an enthusiast and observer of the highest order supplementing his meagre income (as will be seen) with honest cash raised from snippets and articles in the railway press. John Powell was a Derby apprentice rising through the ranks of the locomotive department to Traction and Train Crew Manager BRB. John Edgington worked in LMS control and later the PR department at Euston before joining the National Railway Museum in 1975. They have been a tower of strength. Other railwaymen who have made their solid contributions include Michael Bonavia who from retirement has been able to reflect (with a BRB hat) on Euston's ghosts whilst Gerald Aston (LMS operating) has been able to check facts with an eagle eye, R. G. Jarvis (another Derby man who also designed the rebuilt Bulleid Pacifics) tells of LMS preservation and the 8Fs in Turkey. Don Rowland has kindly provided information on freight, Geoffrey Kichenside on coaches, and Cyril Bleasdale from his perch as General Manager LM Region has written the foreword. So it has been a great team.

Others too have dug into their memories and notebooks, Basil Cooper, R. T. Coxon, Nelson Twells, Peter Tatlow, Roy Anderson, Ron Whateley and Colin Judge in particular. This book would have been poorer without their help and support. We have also been able to use material from other sources which has given the work life and character, excerpts from the Night Mail and Auden's wonderful poem reproduced by permission of The Post Office, the piece from *Punch* on Crewe, excerpts from LMS publications and from the learned journals of the Stephenson's Locomotive Society and the Railway Correspondence and Travel Society. The editors of *Railway Gazette International* and *Railway Magazine* have kindly allowed the reproduction of diagrams, maps and snippets, in particular we must mention the valuable contributions from the LMS Centenary issue of the *Railway Gazette*. Other pieces have come from the columns of that magnificent magazine for boys of all ages, the *Meccano Magazine* – many from Derek Barrie's pen. We have also taken information from the three volumes on LMS sheds (LNWR, MR, L&YR) by Chris Hawkins and George Reeves along with *Branch Lines in North Wales* by W. G. Rear all published by Wild Swan Publications Ltd.

Nor must the photographs be forgotten for no authors can fill a book with pictures of their own taking or even from their own collections. Where the photographer is known then full credit is given below, where we have been unable to discover the photographer the credit is to the author's collection but thanks is given here to the holder of that camera. We would also like to pay tribute to all those who have unknowingly made this book possible, the Rev David Bulman who as a small boy was one of the author's constant companions on railway (especially LMS) expeditions, railwaymen of all grades, fellow enthusiasts, and compilers of books and journals.

One of the pleasures of compiling this book has been looking back over the years, remembering the LMS as boys and in early adulthood, at school and on holiday, of parents who if not actually encouraging us, cast a kindly eye on our hobby, allowing us to spend happy days just looking, taking numbers and laying the foundation stones for a fascinating and lasting hobby, absorbing the atmosphere of the railway.

David St John Thomas is responsible for the Introduction. Most of the other chapters are the work of more than one contributor, the leading characters being B. K. Cooper and A. J. Powell for chapter 2; D. S. M. Barrie for Chapters 3, 6, 7, 11 and 14 plus 8 with D. Rowland; G. M. Kichenside for chapter 12 and A. J. Powell for chapters 4, 10 and 13; Patrick Whitehouse for chapters 5 and 9, plus 16 with R. G. Jarvis; M. R. Bonavia chapter 15. The Chronology was compiled by John Edgington. Original material for the shorter items came from the two authors and from M. R. Bonavia, D. S. M. Barrie, B. K. Cooper, R. T. Coxon, R. G. Jarvis, G. M. Kichenside and A. J. Powell as well as the aforementioned magazines.

The authors would also like to make acknowledgment to the following photographers or collections for the use of their illustrations: P. M. Alexander 11 (upper), 55, 183 (lower); V. R. Anderson collection 71 (upper right), 74, 81 (upper), 110; H. G. Ashman 52; D. S. M. Barrie collection 50, 73 (lower), 85 (upper), 91, 99 (lower), 101, 103 (upper), 124, 136, 179 (lower); DP Battery Co 112; L. Billingham/Millbrook House collection 109; British Railways 16; H. C. Casserley 19, 122 (upper), 179 (upper), 183 (upper), 187 (lower); C. R. L. Coles 30, 105 (upper left); Colour Rail 44; B. K. Cooper 10, 105 (upper right); K. Cooper/Millbrook House collection 80 (lower); A. W. Croughton/Millbrook House collection 126; M. W. Earley/NRM 100, 102 (lower); Alan Fearnley 150/1; J. C. Flemons/Millbrook House collection 131; A. W. Flowers 58, 69, 81 (lower), 163, 164 (upper); W. L. Good/Millbrook House collection 48 (upper and lower), 51 (upper and lower), 53, 87 (upper), 99 (upper), 168, 176; John Goss 193 (lower); G. F. Heiron 41; J. M. Jarvis 80 (upper); R. G. Jarvis 59, 61 (upper), 123, 125, 201 (upper); G. M. Kichenside 82, 95 (lower left), 144, 145 (all), 146, 153, 156, 189; L&GRP/David & Charles 54 (upper); Millbrook House collection 6, 9 (upper), 31, 46, 92, 95 (upper and middle), 108, 113, 116, 128, 133, 140, 142, 157, 158, 171, 175, 187 (upper), 193 (upper), 194 (lower), 195, 201 (lower), 202; National Railway Museum 71 (upper left); P. Robinson 196, 197, 198; E. S. Russell 73 (upper), 184; J. Shuttleworth 203; Roger Siviter 152; P. Tatlow collection 93; Eric Treacy/Millbrook House collection 13, 14, 56, 86, 129, 166, 167 (upper), 173, 190; H. N. T. Wells 139; P. B. Whitehouse 11 (lower), 66, 75, 77, 80, 85 (lower), 88, 115, 149, 170, 174 (upper), 180, 191; Courtesy of the National Railway Museum, York 12, 22, 25, 61, 65, 68, 70 (top left and right), 74, 95 (lower right), 119, 137, 164 (lower), 167 (lower), 187 (upper), 200; Ransome-Wallis collection/NRM York 102 (upper), 107 (lower), 186; Cowan collection/NRM York 133 (upper).

INDEX